PENGUIN BOOKS

AMERICA OBSERVED

Alistair Cooke was born in Manchester in 1908 and educated at the universities of Cambridge, Yale and Harvard. He was the BBC's film critic from 1934 to 1937. Returning to the United States, he was Special Correspondent on American Affairs for *The Times* (1938–41), American feature writer for the *Daily Herald* (1941–4), UN Correspondent for the *Manchester Guardian* (1945–8), and Chief Correspondent for the *Guardian* (1948–72). His history of America, a BBC television production seen in thirty countries, was expanded into his highly successful book *Alistair Cooke's America*. For this work, and for his outstanding contribution over many years to Anglo-American mutual understanding, he was made an honorary KBE in 1973. He is, however, best known at home and abroad for his weekly BBC broadcast *Letter from America*, which is heard in fifty-two countries and is far and away the longest-running radio series in broadcasting history. Penguin have published three collections of the letters, *Letters from America*, *The Americans* and *Talk About America*, as well as *Six Men* and *The Patient has the Floor*. His other books include *Above London* (with Robert Cameron) and *Masterpieces*. He lives in New York City and on Long Island and is married to Jane White, the painter. Reviewing *America Observed*, *The New York Times* wrote: 'Mr Cooke has an uncanny knack for singling out the hidden, the topical and the peripheral as a stand-in for the cosmic, the universal and the eternal.'

Ronald Wells has lived and worked on both sides of the Atlantic. Born in Boston, Massachusetts, he studied at Boston University and has repeatedly been a research associate at the Institute of United States Studies, University of London. His several books connecting British and American history and current affairs include a collaborative work with Brian Mawhinney, MP. Described by Alistair Cook as his Boswell, Wells lives with his wife and two sons in Grand Rapids, Michigan, where he is Professor of History at Calvin College.

ALISTAIR COOKE

America Observed

**The Newspaper Years of
ALISTAIR COOKE
Selected and Introduced by
Ronald A. Wells**

PENGUIN BOOKS
in association with Reinhardt Books

PENGUIN BOOKS

Published by the Penguin Group
27 Wrights Lane, London w8 5TZ, England
Viking Penguin Inc., 40 West 23rd Street, New York, New York 10010, USA
Penguin Books Australia Ltd, Ringwood, Victoria, Australia
Penguin Books Canada Ltd, 2801 John Street, Markham, Ontario, Canada L3R 1B4
Penguin Books (NZ) Ltd, 182–190 Wairau Road, Auckland 10, New Zealand

Penguin Books Ltd, Registered Offices: Harmondsworth, Middlesex, England

First published in Great Britain by Reinhardt Books 1988
First published in the USA by Alfred A. Knopf, New York 1988
Published in Penguin Books 1989
1 3 5 7 9 10 8 6 4 2

Made and printed in Great Britain by
Richard Clay Ltd, Bungay, Suffolk
Filmset in Linotron Sabon

CONTENTS

Acknowledgments, ix
Author's Note, xi
Introduction, 1

Other People's Christmas, *December 24, 1946,* 21
The Colonel and the *Tribune, June 10, 1947,* 23
Harry S. Truman: A Study of a Failure, *November 1, 1948,* 27
Mr. Laski's Democracy, *March 29, 1949,* 30
The Fourth of July, *July 5, 1949,* 34
A Lesson for Yale, *May 21, 1951,* 38
An Epic of Courage, *September 14, 1951,* 43
Harold Ross's *New Yorker, December 11, 1951,* 47
Soviet Light on Baseball, *September 25, 1952,* 51
The U.S. Negro and the Constitution, *January 1, 1953,* 53
Traubel Quits *The Ring, June 12, 1953,* 57
High Fashion Comes to Texas – and Stays There, *July 30,*
    1953, 60
Revulsion Against McCarthy, *June 12, 1954,* 64
Billy Graham Comes to Babylon, *March 10 and 17, 1955,* 68
Change in the Deep South, *April 28, 1955,* 76
Mr. Lippmann's First Quarter Century, *May 8, 1956,* 79
Segregation Above the Line, *May 10, 1956,* 82
The Untravelled Road, *June 7, 1956,* 87
The Roman Road, *June 14, 1956,* 91
Look Away, Dixie Land, *June 21, 1956,* 94
Making a President, *August 12, 1956,* 98

Senator Kennedy Looks Ahead, *July 11, 1957*,   102

America Discovers Mr. Muggeridge, *October 24, 1957*,   105

The End of Reticence, *June 15, 1958*,   110

Frank Lloyd Wright, *April 16, 1959*,   114

New Ways in English Life, *July 16, 1959*,   119

The Unexplained Mr. Nixon, *July 21, 1960*,   123

The Man Who Defeated McCarthy, *October 13, 1960*,   126

Mr. Kennedy Takes Over, *January 26, 1961*,   128

The Legend of Gary Cooper, *May 18, 1961*,   131

A Woman of Integrity: Marilyn Monroe, *August 9, 1962*,   135

The U.S. Science Pavilion, *October 18, 1962*,   137

Maker of a President: Eleanor Roosevelt, *November 13, 1962*,   142

Scourge of the Book-burners, *April 25, 1963*,   144

The Thirty-sixth President, *November 28, 1963*,   147

Rally in the Valley, *May 17, 1964*,   151

How It Happened in Watts, *August 19, 1965*,   156

Hasty Marriage Better Part of Valour, *September 2, 1965*,   160

The Coronation of Miss Oklahoma, *September 15, 1966*,   162

The Rise and Fall of J. Robert Oppenheimer, *February 27, 1967*,   165

Henry Luce: His Time, Life, and Fortune, *March 2, 1967*,   168

Mary McCarthy in Vietnam, *September 26, 1967*,   170

The Permissive Society, *October 26, 1967*,   175

Reagan's Reasons, *December 28, 1967*,   178

Harvesting the Grapes of Wrath, *January 4, 1968*,   181

A Mule Cortège for the Apostle of the Poor, *April 9, 1968*,   185

Out of the Boudoir, into the Laboratory, *April 21, 1968*,   188

Bedlam in Chicago, *September 5, 1968*,   190

Where Now Is the New World?, *October 24, 1968*,   195

The Most Beautiful Woman I Know . . . , *February 27,*
      1969,   197
Eisenhower, *April 3, 1969,*   200
The Lost Hours of Edward Kennedy, *July 24, 1969,*   205
The Ghastly Sixties, *January 3, 1970,*   207
'Put Not Your Trust in Princes . . .', *November 6, 1971,*   210
J. Edgar Hoover, *May 11, 1972,*   213
M*A*S*H: One of a Kind, *February 12, 1983,*   216
The Best of His Kind, *September 6, 1984,*   219
Golf: The American Conquest, *March 31, 1985,*   223

Notes, 232

ACKNOWLEDGMENTS

This book was several years in preparation. During that time I incurred many debts, some of which require public acknowledgment. First among these, of course, is to Alistair Cooke, whose helpful conduct toward me has been characterized by an unfailing grace. His numerous interventions on my behalf, both public and private, made the book possible. Moreover, in the context of that support, I have always understood that whatever skills I brought to the preparation of this book, its interest to readers would lie in his writing, not mine.

As an academic historian I am also conscious of many debts to colleagues who made it possible to have released time from teaching at Calvin College and who encouraged my work: Peter DeVos, Gordon Van Harn, Bert DeVries, Robert Bolt, and George Marsden. My research assistant, William Vander Meulen, and our departmental secretary, Cindy Boender, worked hard to meet my deadlines. A travel grant from the National Endowment for the Humanities was very helpful. I thank the Nelson Bennett family for vital support at a critical time. Finally, thanks seem scarcely enough to my wife, Kathleen, and to my sons, Jonathan and Christopher, who encouraged me throughout this work.

Grand Rapids, February, 1988   R.A.W.

Author's Note

All but five of the pieces in this book were filed as daily dispatches to what was then known as the *Manchester Guardian*, between 1946 and 1972, when I retired as the paper's chief American correspondent. Throughout that time, as for the eighty years or so before it, the *Guardian* was the editorial voice of the Liberal Party in Great Britain, and so regarded in Europe. This is not quite the same as saying it was an unflinchingly liberal paper in the more ideological sense. Of course, it attracted mainly liberal writers, but it had a colourful quota of other believers, especially among the writers on the arts, music, sports, and even among its foreign correspondents. In my day, most notably under the editorship of Alfred P. Wadsworth, it held pretty firmly to the injunction of the man who edited the paper for fifty-seven years and raised it from a provincial to a national newspaper: the formidable C. P. Scott, who laid down the much quoted and lately derided passage:

'A newspaper is of necessity something of a monopoly, and its first duty is to shun the temptations of a monopoly. Its primary office is the gathering of news. At the peril of its soul it must see that the supply is not tainted. Neither in what it gives, nor in what it does not give, nor in the mode of presentation, must the unclouded face of truth suffer wrong. Comment is free but facts are sacred.'

That was written over sixty years ago, and no doubt to a modern newspaper publisher it has a quaint Victorian ring. The face of truth, even though it has emerged from behind the masks of diplomatic cables and privileged Establishment friendships, and been exposed to the glare of television and the flashlight of investigative reporting, is often seen still to be very clouded indeed. All the more reason why a reporter should not add to the confusion by taking on the 'taint' of the paper's editorial prejudices. I must say that the exercise of this restraint is much easier for a reporter who is 3,000 miles away from his boss. Not only does he not have time to keep up with his paper's bias, but he is too close to the heaving and pulling, the ebb and flow, of the political and social life of the country he is reporting from to guess at his editor's long-distance view of what used to be called 'the tide of affairs.'

Of course, this is the situation of all foreign correspondents, but I ought not to leave the impression that all newspapers accept, let alone insist on, the correspondent's independence. From much association, in my time, with Washington correspondents of other European newspapers, I came to see myself as a lucky beneficiary of another of Scott's rules: in choosing a foreign correspondent, 'pick your man carefully and then give him his head.' I ought to add that, on most serious American newspapers, the tradition is still maintained of having the reporters put down the facts as they find them, however contradictory or uncomfortable they may seem to the editorial writers. But in Britain in the past decade or so it appears to me that too often the foreign reporter is turning into a missionary.

At any rate, Wadsworth and his successor, Alastair Hetherington, never hinted at a line to take and hardly ever offered instruction in the topics to be covered. I was on my own to pick and choose and sometimes – no doubt to the editor's distress – delivered a report on, say, the Miss America finals when he had been expecting a definitive piece on a foreign affairs debate, which every other paper (and, in the event, ours!) took from the news agencies.

When Ronald Wells began his safari through the jungle of the *Guardian*'s files, he had no preconceived idea about the specimens he was going to collect. But early on, during his heroic trudge through several million words, he found that the principle of selection – or, rather, of rejection – pretty much announced itself, if only by the proliferation of hundreds of pieces of 'straight' reportage that, however apt or informative they might have seemed at the time, now read as elaborate glosses on the sort of event, great and small, you look up in an almanac. Many of the burning issues of a given period (the debate over the Marshall Plan and the Soviet blockade of Berlin are good examples) eventually turn to ashes, through which only a mole of an historian would want to rake, at least for the purposes of this book. There were stories too about several dramatic events that I was present at (e.g., the 1946 mutiny at Alcatraz, the assassination of Bobby Kennedy) which have been published in one or other volume of my broadcast talks. Dr. Wells has left in one or two bald pieces that give an outline of events that still affect contemporary politics (the report on Chappaquiddick the day after the drowning seemed a useful thing to put in). Otherwise his selection has the broad aim, I take it, of being representative of a running commentary on American society throughout the quarter century that I was writing about it to a daily deadline. Pieces that carry no dateline were usually written in New York City.

I am grateful to the present editor of the *Guardian*, Peter Preston, for giving Ronald Wells such ready access to the files and, of course, for his permission to reprint these pieces. Only one of my broadcast talks (in the weekly B.B.C. series, 'Letter from America') is included here. Though they have taken up many other big and little American themes – which are consequently omitted here – they are written in a looser, conversational idiom for a worldwide audience considerably more varied than the readership of any newspaper. I also thank the editor of the Chicago *Sun-Times* for permission to reproduce the piece on Mary McCarthy in Vietnam.

As a kind of coda or tailpiece, three pieces from other sources have been added that Ronald Wells charitably thought would show me, since the early 1970s, to have avoided declining into 'the brooding silence of senility.' I should like to thank the editors of *The New York Times* and *TV Guide* for allowing two of them to reappear here. The third ('The Best of His Kind') was originally written as a talk and rewritten for publication in the *Listener*, to whose editor I offer similar thanks. I should have hated, in the cause of verbal symmetry, to see this talk excluded. It sums up my admiration for my only American publisher, Alfred A. Knopf, the man who, in 1950, told me he would publish anything I cared to write, and who, for the following thirty-four years, was as good as his word.

A.C.

Introduction

'Have you ever been to England?' asks Martin Chuzzlewit in Dickens's novel. The American being questioned replies, 'In print I have, sir, but not otherwise.' Many modern British men and women, if asked if they had been to America, might reply that they had, because they had read and listened to Alistair Cooke for years.

Travelling in the mind's eye, through reading and, recently, through electronic media, is a European habit of long standing. Ever since the 'age of discoveries' in the Renaissance, Europeans have been interested in reports of life in faraway places. Of all the places in which Europeans were interested, America has received more attention than others for a variety of reasons, the most important of which is that many Europeans themselves emigrated there. The report about America from the person who has been there is a literary genre that Europeans have devoured. The most widely read and listened-to European on America has been Alistair Cooke.

As Europeans watched the United States grow from a British colony to one of the dominant nations of the world, a pattern of conversation developed among them about the meaning of this emerging Colossus of the New World. There emerged a question, aptly stated by Richard Rose: Is America inevitable or inimitable? The question is easier to ask than to answer, and both sides of the question are amply represented in American and European writing about America. The one stresses the uniqueness of America, that no nation or people can be compared with the experience of Americans. The other stresses that America is the forerunner of what European, even world, society will be tomorrow.

There is a subsidiary question to the main one asked: Given the obvious fact that the history of any nation is unique, how is it that the United States came to be viewed as the forerunner of world change? To be seen as the laboratory for mankind's future possibilities is a great burden. J. Martin Evans has noted that no other modern nation has had to bear as great a weight of idealism as this.

The one view – America as model for world development – is a creation of European wishful thinking. 'In the beginning,' John Locke once remarked, 'everything was America.' In Thomas More's *Utopia* we see the first mature reflection on the New World in the literature of the Old World. The genius of More's work was that, by 1516, there was no longer any need to speculate about an imagined Atlantis southwest of Europe: America was there and could be travelled to and settled in.

When Alexis de Tocqueville visited America in the 1830s, he put theories behind him and offered Europe a real glimpse of a working democracy, the only one in the world at the time. Everything was available for world scrutiny, from government to economics to the attitudes of the people. Americans welcomed this scrutiny because they wanted to show the world that their beloved nation offered a workable model of the thing Europeans wanted – a society equal and free. Tocqueville believed that democracy (in all the affective meanings of the word) *was* the wave of the future, and that the United States was worthy of examination because it was experiencing first what Europe *must* experience later on. While, as some commentators suggest, Tocqueville may have personally disliked the advent of mass democracy, he accepted it as the prevailing tendency of world development, hence the reason for studying the lead society in that process. He came to America believing that its social experiment was a success, and while he may have feared mass rule, he nevertheless thought that America demonstrated that a democratic people could remain free.

Tocqueville's *Democracy in America* is, by common consent, in Harold Laski's words, 'perhaps the greatest work ever written on any country by the citizen of another.' For Tocqueville, democracy as a political system would replace the 'old order,' based on aristocracy, because the driving spirit behind the process was social equality. In the most famous section of *Democracy*, he wrote:

'It is not then merely to satisfy a legitimate curiosity that I have examined America; my wish has been to find there instruction by which we may ourselves profit ... I confess that, in America, I saw more than America; I sought there the image of democracy itself, with its inclinations, its character, its prejudices, and its passions, in order to learn what we have to fear or to hope from its progress.'

He saw America as a 'type' of the coming order. Tocqueville held as given the malleability of human institutions, so there was great relevance for Europe in studying America, not because Europe had to experience the coming of democracy in just the same way as America, but because the American experiment 'proved' that democracy as a system was both feasible and tolerable.

The reason for the long-lived acclaim for Tocqueville's *Democracy* is that he spoke less about the United States than about the idea of democracy. It is a timeless work because it speaks of timeless issues. In this sense, no European commentator is likely to surpass Tocqueville as *the* European commentator on America. At the same time, I believe William Safire was correct in asserting that 'Alistair Cooke interprets America better than any foreign correspondent since Tocqueville.' This view was reinforced by Kingman Brewster, then president of Yale University, who, in bestowing the Howland medal on Cooke, called him (for Europeans) 'the most authoritative interpreter of the American scene and American mores.'

Cooke may deal only from time to time with the grand themes of Tocqueville, but he deals very carefully with what

Roland Gelatt calls 'the threads and textures' of life in the United States. He is the prototype of the 'mid-Atlantic man,' equally at home and equally strange in both the United States and Britain. To Britons he is almost an American in manner, accent, as he is in citizenship. To Americans he typifies the English gentleman in manner, accent, and ideology. Both perceptions are correct. He retains enough European understanding to render America explicable on European terms. He is Americanized enough to have, as Gelatt puts it, 'an astonishingly acute fix on the lay of our land.'

Alfred Alistair Cooke was born in Salford (then a part of Greater Manchester) on November 20, 1908. His mother, Mary Elizabeth Byrne, came from one of those Protestant Irish families that, two generations before, had chosen to leave Roman Catholic Ireland and start a new life in Lancashire. Cooke's father, Samuel, of a Cheshire family, was an artist in metalwork by trade and, by vocation, a Methodist lay preacher who founded the Manchester Wood Street Mission, a shelter for runaways, drunks, and battered wives. After the First World War, he went into the insurance business and became the national secretary of an insurance agents' union.

Cooke's introduction to Americans came during the First World War. His father, then in his fortieth year, was too old for combat, and was drafted into service in an airplane factory in Manchester. Blackpool, the great Northern seaside resort for the cotton workers of inland Lancashire, had many hundreds of boardinghouses and miles of sandy seashore. It was ideal for the sudden accommodation of American troops when, in the autumn of 1917, they poured into England. Cooke's mother was required to house seven American servicemen for the last stage of their training before they embarked for France. Cooke has spoken warmly of the way they treated the nine-year-old as a kind of regimental pet: He wrote, 'No doubt my inclination to take to Americans was incorrigibly determined then.'

Cooke was educated at what then was the Blackpool Secondary (later Grammar) School. In his last year there, he sat for, and won, a scholarship to Jesus College, Cambridge. (He chose Jesus because of a warm schoolboy admiration for the writings of Sir Arthur Quiller-Couch who, as King Edward VII Professor of English Literature at Cambridge, had his rooms in Jesus College.) After taking first-class honours in the first part of the Tripos, founding the Cambridge University Mummers (the first university dramatic society that recruited members of the women's colleges to play women's parts), and – in his last year – editing the *Granta*, the undergraduate university weekly, Cooke was rewarded with a Commonwealth Fund Fellowship from an American foundation that annually subsidized twenty-five graduate students from British and Commonwealth universities for further study in America.

By that time, 1932, Cooke had directed several plays at Cambridge and spent most of the summer of 1931 teaching school, and studying the German *Volksbühne* (folk theatre), in Silesia. He had decided to become a theatre director.

To his surprise, the Commonwealth sponsors, who invariably rewarded purely academic research, approved his request to attend the Yale Drama School. Its student body was then drawn mainly from young graduates of junior colleges and its curriculum, mainly in the history of drama, was elementary – too elementary for a twenty-four-year-old English graduate who, during his fourth and fifth years at Cambridge had, apart from his theatre experience, tutored advanced students in tragedy and the history of criticism. At any rate, Cooke discovered that there was no prospect of his directing a play until the last term of his two-year fellowship. He accordingly spent the Yale year on private research in dramatic criticism. When he heard that Harvard offered a graduate course, under the eminent linguistic scholar Professor Miles L. Hanley, in 'the history of the English language in America,' Cooke at once requested a transfer to Harvard for his second year, and the Commonwealth Fund readily agreed. So Cooke worked there under Hanley; did a little field work for the *American Linguis-*

tic Atlas (which was then in the making) and exercised his theatrical ambitions by directing the Harvard Dramatic Society in a play by Lennox Robinson; formed a student company of his own, which put on a reading of W. H. Auden's *Paid on Both Sides* and staged productions of a Japanese Nō play and of *Cymbeline* in modern dress; and directed the Hasty Pudding's annual musical.

Cooke has since remarked on the indelible effect of Hanley's course in American English in 'opening up the view of America as a new found land.' But, there was another experience, quite outside the realms of Yale and Harvard, which Cooke has called the turning point in his life and work. It was an actual requirement of a Commonwealth Fellowship that the recipients should, in the summer break between their first and second years, buy a car and travel through as many of the States as possible. Accordingly, in the summer of 1933, Cooke travelled the length and breadth of the country.

'The trip was an absolute eye-opener for me. First, of course, there was the discovery of a land and a people infinitely more varied than anything I had imagined or been taught by the British newspaper stereotypes. But, 1933 was also the first year that the American people were beginning to crawl out of the pit of the Great Depression. To see what the depression had done to them, and how Roosevelt was rousing them very slowly but positively to assert their old vitality: all this was far more dramatic, and moving, and – to be cold-blooded about it – more sheerly interesting than anything that was happening on Broadway. I did not realize for another year or two that that trip, and the undimmed memory of it, were to mark the twilight of my life in the theatre and the dawn of the idea that a foreign correspondent's was a better trade for me.'

As he indicates, he did not at once forsake the theatrical world. Walking up Washington Street in Boston one day in early spring of 1934, when his Fellowship was coming to an end, he was attracted by a front-page headline on a news-stand: 'B.B.C. Fires P.M.'s Son.' Oliver Baldwin, son of the then Prime Minister and film critic for the British Broadcasting Corporation, had quarrelled with B.B.C. officials and they had let him go. The newspaper piece ended with the suggestive sentence 'So now, the B.B.C. is looking for a new film critic.' Cooke decided at once that 'that would be a very agreeable method of entry to the ranks of the gainfully employed.' He telephoned the director of the Fellowships in New York and asked if they would honour, in his case, their regular promise to send any retiring Fellow over to England for an interview if he might be considered 'on the short list' for an advertised post. Cooke then cabled the B.B.C. (The previous autumn, he had published in the London *Observer* a six-part series on Holly-wood, garnered from a long stay there during his summer trip.) His name clicked with Desmond MacCarthy, the distinguished literary critic who was the regular book reviewer for the B.B.C. Cooke received a responsive cable saying that although there were two hundred applicants for the job, they would be pleased to interview him ('without obligation on our part'). The Fund thereupon sent Cooke home again on the *Aquitania*. ('Only Lindbergh,' said Cooke, 'flew the Atlantic.') Having arrived at Broadcasting House for an interview, he requested a typewriter, immediately tapped out a five-minute review of the last film he had seen, went into a studio, and broadcast it over closed circuit to the Director of Talks, who promptly gave him the post.

Cooke's main job remained that of B.B.C. film critic until, in the spring of 1937, he resigned and sailed back to the United States on an immigrant visa. In the meantime, he had broadcast many B.B.C. programmes about America and begun work as a correspondent for N.B.C. with weekly talks from London. The latter duty culminated in an exhausting ten-day stint – the broadcasting, he later calculated, of some 400,000 words – that ended in the abdication of King Edward VIII. In 1941, he became an American citizen.

It was after the Second World War that Cooke's career as a writer and broadcaster took its final shape. In 1945, he was assigned to cover the founding conference of the United Nations in San Francisco for the B.B.C. On the strength of a sudden cable from the editor of the *Manchester Guardian*, he covered the same story for that newspaper. For the next two years, he was United Nations correspondent, and in 1948 he became the paper's chief American correspondent, a post he held until he retired in 1972. But his broadcasting was not forgotten. In 1946, the B.B.C. asked him to experiment for thirteen weeks (the length of a usual contract) with a series of fifteen-minute weekly talks on America that would replace the purely political 'American Commentary' he had done during the last three years of the war. Alistair Cooke's 'Letter from America' has been going ever since, and, after forty-two years, is the longest-running programme in the history of world broadcasting.

On three occasions Cooke has made a selection of his broadcast talks, slightly reshaped them as literary essays, and published them. Taken together, *One Man's America* (1952), *Talk About America* (1968), and *The Americans* (1979), offer readers the keenest collection of insights extant on America in the postwar period. A significant lacuna, however, is Cooke's writings for the *Guardian*, and other periodicals, which have not been published in a similarly permanent form. Having read the transcripts of all of Cooke's broadcast talks and all of his *Guardian* essays, I am struck by the fact that there is so little duplication between the two. One marvels at Cooke's ability to speak and to write, during any given week, about so many different things. And, even regarding great events, his B.B.C. talk and his *Guardian* story would emphasize different aspects of the topic. In presenting Cooke's best from the *Guardian*, and elsewhere, we thus present a Cooke whom readers of his previous books have not read.

As all but four of the pieces in this book first appeared in the *Guardian*, it might be well to mention a few points about

Cooke's relationship to that great newspaper. Under the editorship of A. P. Wadsworth, Cooke was given great freedom to roam America and report on what caught his fancy. Once, when the U.S. Senate was debating the Marshall Plan – surely a prime subject for the newspaper's American correspondent – Cooke asked Wadsworth if he instead might go to California to cover the 100th anniversary of the Gold Rush. Wadsworth cabled Cooke to go ahead to California, adding, 'Why do we employ Reuters?' There was one occasion, however, when the redoubtable Wadsworth recalled Cooke to New York. Cooke was in California in 1951 to write on the opening of the Central Valley hydroelectric project. With the title fight between Britain's Randy Turpin and 'Sugar Ray' Robinson in the offing, Wadsworth cabled, 'Go New York soonest. Blood thicker than water in this country.'

The *Guardian* is, along with *The Times*, one of the important 'quality' newspapers in Britain. Their relative merits used to invoke hot dispute from partisans. But, as T. S. Matthews wrote, thirty years ago, *The Times* is often thought to be the servant of the Establishment while the *Guardian* is thought to serve the national conscience. This is what Matthews meant by the 'Roundhead' tradition of the *Guardian*. Among these sometimes-too-earnest 'Roundheads' Matthews sees Cooke as a 'laughing Cavalier,' and wonders if founder C. P. Scott would have approved of him. While Matthews saw Cooke as 'something of an anomaly, a significant oddity,' he also correctly noted that Alistair Cooke was 'the fair-haired boy of the *Guardian*, with editors and readers alike.' The plain fact was that Cooke just does not sound like a *Guardian* man:

'Sprightliness . . . the feather touch are his specialty. The heavy weights he has to lift (reports of U.N. meetings, for example) sometimes slow him to the tempo of an adagio dancer, but even then he will kid the act when he gets a chance, and whenever he can, which is nearly always, he turns the job into a light-hearted juggling act.'

In any case, readers liked him; as Matthews observes, Cooke's dispatches from America were, for a quarter century, 'the most generally popular feature in the *Guardian*.'

In congratulating Cooke on his 1,000th B.B.C. 'Letter from America' broadcast in 1968, the editor of the *Guardian* remarked on his style ('his pieces will often contain a sentence or phrase which will crystallize a torrent of facts or a cascade of opinion') and on his impact. But, at the same time, the editor insisted:

'Cooke is a nuisance. There is no pretending that he is not. He telephones his copy at the last moment, so that everything else has to be dropped to get it into the paper. He says that he will be in Chicago and he turns up in Los Angeles. He discards the agreed subject ("pick that up from the tapes") to write about something which has taken his fancy, news of the moment or not. If all his colleagues were like him, production of the paper would cease. But, we think he's worth it and we love him just the same.'

If Alistair Cooke indeed was an 'anomaly,' an 'oddity,' and a 'nuisance' on the *Guardian*, no one, least of all his readers, seemed to have been much bothered by it!

Does America, then, represent the wave of the future for the rest of the world, or is it unique? Europeans, as we noted at the outset, have continually asked this question over the years; we ask it today. And while Alistair Cooke typically eschews the grand theme in favour of the particular event or person, he too has much to say, in his own way, about the 'meaning' of America. America's experiment in mass democracy should be of interest to Europeans, he argues, if only because American experience may help them to interpret both their own encounter with democracy and the democratic aspirations of developing nations. Cooke, it should be stressed, does not view the United States as qualitatively better than any other nation, nor as possessing any moral warrant to lead the world. In his view, the best lessons it teaches are the smaller, more pungent, more memorable ones. It is no accident that the bulk of Cooke's writing and speaking has delighted in those characteristics of America which are unique to it. And even though these characteristics may well be impossible to reproduce elsewhere, they reflect universal human traits. Cooke's aim is 'to run up and down the human scale that unites a Lancashireman to a Texan and a German to a Siamese.'

Tocqueville spoke memorably about what Europeans have 'to fear or to hope' from the practice of democracy in America. While Cooke is not unaware of the untoward aspects of American culture, he generally sees more hope than fear in it, both for America itself and for the world. Still, it is a hope tempered by realism. Cooke does not join in that tradition of European thinking which sees America as the hopeful 'sign society' of world progress. For Cooke, it is more than enough of a sign of hope that one nation has proven, over two centuries, that a democratic people can remain free. His hope is not one of pious idealism but of tough-minded realism – a realistic hope for the future based on a realistic assessment of the past.

No better example of Cooke's realistic hope can be found than the address that he delivered before the House of Representatives on September 25, 1974. In being chosen as keynote speaker on this occasion, he received a singular honor: that of initiating the Bicentennial celebrations in Philadelphia on the anniversary of the first Continental Congress, which began meeting there on September 25, 1774. In this address, presented less than two months after Richard Nixon's resignation – a time at which America's confidence about its political institutions was at a low ebb – Cooke reversed Lincoln Steffens's remark about the Soviet Union, 'I have seen the future – and it works.' He looked over the 200-year history of America and, noting the decisive role of the House Judiciary Committee in voting articles of impeachment, remarked that Americans could well say, 'with legitimate pride, I have seen the past – and it works.'

We who have in this century seen the rise of many forms of tyranny, from both right and left, know that to have survived at all with some semblance of a free and democratic society is no mean achievement. The American 'experiment,' begun more than two centuries ago, can be declared moderately successful. Nevertheless, as Alistair Cooke said in concluding his television history of America, 'In this country – a land of the most persistent idealism and the blandest cynicism – the race is on between its decadence and its vitality.'

That sentence of sixteen years ago has been widely quoted since. The reader is bound to wonder how, in Cooke's opinion, the race is going after all that time. In late February 1988, he agreed to sit down and make the following comments in a taped conversation, prefaced – as always – by a reminder of his temperamental reluctance ever to write a piece called 'Whither America?':

'Well, to begin with, let me say my reluctance to predict the future of this country, or any country, is based on more things than my own poor record as even a short-range prophet, which you've demonstrated with that early piece on the coming demise of Harry Truman's presidency. It has to do also with sharp recollections of the long-range predictions of some very eminent prophets, among them Shaw, Wells, Count Keyserling, Ortega y Gasset, Spengler. I especially recall a small book, published in the early thirties, by J. B. S. Haldane, on the future of science. He was a daring pioneer in biochemical experiments, one of those brave men who used themselves as guinea pigs in experiments that could, and sometimes did, lead to death. You read his book today and it's dead wrong from beginning to end. The simplest advances not anticipated, and revolutionary changes cheerfully predicted for the nineteen-fifties which may not happen in another fifty years.

'But beyond – or before I'd read – these cautionary tales, I think I picked up from my father a distrust of dogma. Not by precept, but by the example of his behaviour. He was a religious man and lived, quietly, privately – with absolutely no evangelical fife and drum – by the Ten Commandments as much as anyone I've ever known. But if someone broke any of 'em, and the church elders began to fish out the statutory punishment, he'd admonish them by nervously noting the way Christ treated sinners. Forgiveness was all. It was something in those days, in a strict Methodist chapel, to go on acting as if there were just as many good people outside the church as in it. He felt the same way about politics. He was a staunch Manchester Liberal (to the constant grief of my mother – she always voted Conservative) but even there you never knew who, from any party, he'd decide was a good man. I think – I hope – this habit of mind passed over to me. So dogmatic opinions were always shadowed by what I later learned was called "the cloud of unknowing." This may be a character flaw, though religious people say it's the steady companion – or, guardian, perhaps – of Faith. However, I now think it may have moved me early in life, before I ever guessed it, to become a reporter – to leap to a seat on the fence and develop the habit of swivelling from one view of things to another, a habit fatal to the care and feeding of an ideology.

'During an evening I once spent with Pandit Nehru, I mentioned to him one of the problems of reporting to a country – and from a country – whose people have been brought up to believe that "there's much to be said on both sides." I found so often that going after a story on, say, racial discrimination, hospital care, the arms race, the drug problem, women's rights, – any really serious matter – as often as not there were not two sides to the story but five! "Ah," he said, "you have discovered the Hindu view of truth." Very flattering. But if you're going to govern a country, instead of simply reporting it, that view can lead to at least five different parties and, I suppose in the end, to proportional representation. Which, on paper, is wonderfully fair, but can produce what my old headmaster called (*à propos* of the many parties in the French government in those days, and the constant reshuffling of power) the sort of chaos produced by a streetcar that has to run on six or seven different levels of track.

'Well, enough of reluctance. You want me to say what I see as signs of decadence or vitality in the life of America today – it would be better to say in the life of the West – because most of these symptoms are at least as lively in Western Europe as in the United States. Let's put them down and call them trends, which I can't help seeing as other than characteristic or decisive one way or the other. (You remember Justice Holmes's definition of the truth as "what a man can't help believing must be so.")

'I have several times sat down to check what I take to be present symptoms of decadence on the model of Gibbon's remarkable and penetrating diagnosis of the decline of Imperial Rome. Let's mention first some of the nagging constants, in our social life. First, no doubt about it, money mania, that is, money sought as power. Our business schools are graduating fewer and fewer people who are going into manufacturing and more and more who are going into investment banking. Fewer people making things, more making money.

'Of course, the money mania is nothing new. It comes at us in waves, riding on a tide of unusual prosperity. It partly explains Jefferson's distrust of inherited wealth, and Andrew Jackson's detestation of banks. And in the 1870s, Mark Twain saw the hog-wild gallivanting of the money men as the main symptom of "an era of incredible rottenness." But I do think it's as bad now as at any time since then.

'The collapse of public education, due, I think to the constant setting of – you might say, revisionist – standards that are easy and dithering. The gross over-commercializing of all sports. Child actors in television commercials. The arts – in theatre, music, painting, especially – going the way Gibbon astutely described: "freakishness pretending to originality, enthusiasm masquerading as vitality." The widespread persistence of a phoney counterculture: the replacement of thrift, work, minimum social duties, by what Philip Larkin called the new hippie syllabus: sex, not working, drugs. I suppose, not to beat around the bush, that much of what I take to be the social sickness of the time – beginning in the Sixties and exacerbated in the Eighties – could be attributed by a moralist to a clutch of certain deadly sins: namely, greed, envy, lust, covetousness. Not to leave anyone with the pious feeling that he/she is out of "the mainstream," I'd say that the conservative sin is secret greed (holding on to what you've got); whereas the liberal sin is self-righteousness: "Why aren't you more like me?"). I guess lust is no respecter of class, gender, colour, or party – just epidemic.

'Now, for government, and disturbing trends which may or may not have a moral root. Once a year, the self-defeating, elephantine Congressional budget process: the stuffing of a five-thousand-page budget – which nobody has time to read – with every pet pork barrel project of every Congressman who has a bridge to repair, a defense plant to build, a soybean subsidy to maintain, and so on. Maybe it's an inevitable concomitant of the two-year Congressional term: the only budget a Congressman has any say in is the one to be spent in his reelection year.

'Then, there's the apparently unavoidable need, in a much advertised democracy, for political candidates to solicit millions of dollars in order to run any campaign at all. There is the shameful fact of a bare fifty per cent turnout of eligible voters in national elections – much the lowest of any democracy.

'In foreign policy, there's the attempt to extend American influence beyond the reach of American power. It could be argued, I think, that this is, on an international scale, the same urge as that of corporations, big and small: the urge to live beyond one's means. I'm taken with Paul Kennedy's thesis, which he supports by tracing the rise and fall of the great empires, that they all in the end are the victims of what he calls "imperial overstretch," of the Romans' effort to maintain their power far beyond the borders they were able to discipline or contain. I think America falls into line with this thesis in three stages. First — and you could call it the first fatal declaration of intent — was President Kennedy's inaugural, which was wonderful as rhetoric and hair-raising as policy. To give a guarantee to forty-three nations. What was it? We shall "pay any price, bear any burden, meet any hardship," et cetera, "to support any friend, oppose any foe." Wonderful! The fact was that few Americans were ever going to give up their automobiles or dishwashers to help Zambia or Angola or a whole raft of countries whose names they could barely pronounce and which — it now comes out — about sixty per cent of their high school and college students couldn't place on a map.

'The second stage was Vietnam, when we *acted* on the promise — against the warnings of Generals Eisenhower and MacArthur. Not only did we not — at home — bear much of a hardship, but it was the only war Americans didn't have to pay for — there were no extra taxes. The payment was to come later, in the form of a whacking national deficit. Which, to maintain the social services already established, and a defence programme each succeeding president has felt bound to increase, leads us to Ronald Reagan and the compounding of the deficit. In his first five years, Reagan added 950 billions to the budget, Congress about seventy. Of course, it's true that while all Presidents are blamed for their budgets, it's Congress that approves the final figure, so it must share the blame. And I'm afraid that given the unpaid debt of Vietnam, the guaranteed growth of Social Security, and our enormous loans to Third World countries, it was probably impossible to lower the ceiling drastically. I doubt that a Democratic President would have managed it, without a stiff tax increase that the country was not ready for. As for knowing any feasible way out of the deficit, that is something that certainly boggles *my* mind, and which I have to leave to the Volckers, Greenspans, Rohatyns, Galbraiths, and other competing wizards.

'Well, that's quite a lot of decadence, or, say, decadence and decline. Now, against this jeremiad, we have to set the vital signs, and they are easier to define because, whereas sickness has a series of symptoms, health can usually be summed up in a word: vivacity, humour, courage, serenity.

'In general, then, there doesn't seem to be any decline in curiosity, inquisitiveness, enlisted in the dogged belief that things can be made better, that tomorrow ought to be better than today. The stoic and fatalist are not yet familiar American types.

'There is now more concern for the poor, even when there are proportionately fewer of them than ever this century. Most people believe that whatever else the government should or shouldn't do, it has the primary responsibility for children, for the poor and the old, the sick and the disabled. And, government or no government, I'm constantly impressed by the restless experimenting that's being done all over the country, and the self-sacrifice of ordinary men and women, with disabled and sick people once given up as hopeless wards of the community.

'Most of all, three things: First, the unflagging energy of the media in digging out and facing all the nastiest problems of the country, not shunning the worst that's happening, by way of crookedness or incompetence or injustice or default, both in the nation and in the local neck of the woods. Second, very many rich Americans, far more than the rich of any other country, do go on making great fortunes in order to give a good deal of them away to worthy causes of every kind. Europe may have its dozens of philanthropists, but America has its many thousands. And, third, among the people at large, an unsleeping passion for liberty, even when it slops over into forms of licence absurdly defended by the First Amendment.

'Well, the odds may seem to be on the side of decadence. I suppose I'd have felt much the same way, about most of our sins, if I'd been writing in 1929, never anticipating the crash or the arrival of a Roosevelt to summon up reserves of stamina and work and courage we didn't know were there, which showed, dramatically, that the President, whoever he is, sets the moral tone of the country. I have written elsewhere that, in many matters, which should require an administration to avoid even the appearance of wrongdoing, the Reagan Administration has been too often notable for moral numbness, even though its genial leader – like a bearable Pecksniff – has appeared "a most exemplary man: fuller of virtuous precept than a copybook." Perhaps, in every period of affluence and self-indulgence, America needs a national crisis – a depression, a collapse of the money market – to throw up a benevolent leader (he had better be benevolent if the system is to hold) who mobilizes the best of America instead of the worst. At the moment, I do not see one. As it is, if I were filing daily pieces today, instead of in the Forties, Fifties, Sixties and Seventies, I don't think I could be – shall we say? – so sprightly without guilt.'

America
Observed

Other People's Christmas

December 24, 1946

Anything you care to write, or to imagine, about an American Christmas is bound to be true about some part of the country. Up from Florida comes a postcard containing the gentle sneer of a friend, naked under a coconut palm. Down from Vermont, the apologies of an invited guest, buried in his farm under thirty inches of snow. From Hollywood we hear the alarmingly modest confession that it would be nice once in a while to see some of God's own snow, as distinct from the usual studio product of sand and limestone with a coating of cornflakes. Only New York, suspended precariously between the American Arctic and the American tropics at about the latitude of Madrid, can keep up its chronic conceit that everything about it, including the climate, is typical of the best and brightest in American life. This, on Christmas Eve, means a temperature in the low forties, 'considerable cloudiness and shifting winds.'

However, New York has at times a flair for civic showmanship. Christmas is one of those times. The plot of green that runs down Park Avenue, dividing northbound from southbound cars, was planted last week with thirty fine firs at two-block intervals. On Sunday their oyster-white bulbs were switched on for the first time and a city sound-truck visited each tree in turn and stopped as long as it takes to broadcast a single carol, sung as it seemed by choirs of invisible angels wired for sound. Outside the churches that touch on Park Avenue, services were held dedicating the trees to the memory of men and women who died in the war.

Half a mile down from my window, skaters bright as beetles are performing in an ice pageant (New York has less trouble manufacturing its own ice than Hollywood making its snow). The 18,000 patients and residents of the city's municipal hospitals were promised a turkey dinner on Christmas Day by the Commission of Hospitals and this morning the New York police began the first of forty-five parties they will give at their stations for the children of Harlem. The Red Cross this year reaches out into Mid-Atlantic with its promise of special presents for the 100 war brides headed here on the Cunard liner *John Ericson*. To-morrow night the radio networks will perform their annual good deed of rounding up all the leading comedians and calling a closed season on their undying – because very profitable – feuds.

Once again Christmas morn will be heralded four times by frantic studio announcers, as time marches on across the time zones of the country. The time-zone business is mostly a nuisance, but at Christmas and New Year it gives revellers, by the magic of radio, the chance to get drunk four times over.

In Washington, President Truman could look out of his windows and see a line of pickets dressed in convicts' uniforms demanding the release from jail of 300 imprisoned conscientious objectors. The President was reported ready to-day to sign pardons to get the men out of jail and the pickets out of uniforms. Down in the Carolinas, Federal agents were still hunting the hills for moonshiners, one of whom this week, caught working an illicit still on a mountainside, was reported not to have heard that the Prohibition Act had been repealed. 'Wait till President Harding hears about this' is the unconfirmed report of what his brother said.

In Baltimore, where the air is heavy to-night with the harmonies of the traditional German carols, the ageing but incorrigible H. L. Mencken, the bad boy of the Twenties, was preening himself on a Christmas duty well done: he had managed to get out a new book in time to have it banned in Canada and Boston. It is a short tale about a bunch of old-time Baltimore tramps who held a Christmas Eve party on the understanding that no hymns should be sung. However, as Christmas came in, the strong drink was too much for them and they wound up tearful in each other's arms bellowing the whole repertory of Ancient and Modern.

To Americans with friendships in England there was a further last-minute cause for rejoicing, for *The New York Times* reports that 'Britain rejoiced to-day when a thaw set in after the coldest night of the year.' Sympathetic readers who imagined a temperature matching Minnesota's twenty below zero, or even New York's fourteen above ten days ago, were puzzled by the news that the thermometer was only in the twenties. However, *The New York Times* charitably explains that 'Britain is always ill-equipped for cold spells because of the lack of steam heating and the faulty construction of windows in most houses.' A murrain on you, British builders, a chattering New Year to you, members of the National Glaziers and Plasterers' Union!

The Colonel and the *Tribune*

June 10, 1947

To-morrow night Chicago's sky will be redder than at any time since Mrs. O'Leary's cow kicked over the lamp that burned up the town. The imperial edict has gone out from the Gothic tower of the Chicago Tribune Building that Colonel McCormick summons all the faithful to what his city editor calls 'the damnedest fireworks show anybody ever saw anyplace.' For to-morrow is the hundredth anniversary of the *Tribune*'s birth, and the night will be filled with all the accumulated sound and flaming fury of a century's editorials against the British, the Democrats, the labour unions, the Roosevelts, and the Wall Street agents of the decadent East.

The paper was only eight years old when a young man with a jutting Irish chin bought a third interest in it and became its managing editor. In itself this is a minor historical event, but his name was Joseph Medill. And Joseph begat Katherine and Elinor, who begat Robert Rutherford and Joseph, who begat the Patterson–McCormick axis, which begat America First, Last, and All the Time.

Only a few months after Mr. Medill was settled at his desk a gawky Illinois politician walked into the office, announced his admiration for the paper, and took out a subscription. Six years later Joseph Medill was in on the founding of the Republican party, wangled its convention at Chicago, and had contrived the nomination of the *Tribune*'s same subscriber. The subscriber became President Lincoln. After a hundred years it is the *Tribune*'s most unalloyed deposit on the altar of fame.

Medill was the progenitor of all the *Tribune*'s most tenacious traditions. Starting on the smallest paper in Chicago, he never doubted its coming pre-eminence. 'The Almighty,' he wrote, 'has ordained it.' He denounced an early enemy, Stephen Douglas, as 'anti-American.' He demonstrated from the start that no idol was too hallowed to turn on, and attacked Lincoln for countermanding an order that would have freed some slaves. Similarly his grandson, who once praised Henry Ford for 'giving the world the day's lesson,' was so maddened by Ford's pacifism as to invite a 10-million-dollar libel suit. 'Get the British out of Canada,' Medill roared in 1863, eighty years before the Colonel confessed his part in helping the United States General Staff to arrange to resist a British invasion from Canada. For forty years Medill's tremendous energy and irreverence battered out the *Tribune*'s mould: anti-slaver, anti-graft, anti-British, anti-big business, anti-labour. His detestation of strikes and the eight-hour day drew from him the advice: 'The simplest plan is to put arsenic in the supplies of food furnished to the unemployed.'

Like any other great city paper that has lasted through a century, it has had its historic scoops, its doldrums, its ecstasies of team spirit. Once, long ago, it nearly went bankrupt. While the windows of its buildings cracked from encroaching flames, its printing crew sweated against time to run off the latest news of the ruinous fire and to rouse Chicago with the slogan 'Cheer up!' The paper was handsomely rehoused, but if the building was fireproof there was no corresponding guarantee about its future owners. For in a single year, between 1879 and 1880, Medill's daughters presented him with two inflammable grandsons: Joseph Patterson and Robert Rutherford McCormick.

Between Medill's decline and the grandsons' rise to omnipotence, the paper only once threatened to slip from the family's hands. By one of the ironies that embarrass the *Tribune*'s fame, Joseph Patterson in his youth was too reckless a Socialist to trust with the paper's fortunes. It was turned over to a solemn, inexhaustible Englishman named James Keeley. Under him the paper kicked a United States senator out of office and deliberately sacrificed $200,000 a year fighting patent medicines. Says one biographer, 'He made the property, if only for a few years, a newspaper.' By another typical irony, Keeley once sat nursing a sick daughter on the Fourth of July, while the rockets zoomed and banged outside. He started a *Tribune* campaign to have fireworks banned on the Fourth. The restraining laws that stand on many a state statute-book are to his credit. So to-morrow's fireworks display will not only redress this shameful British infringement of the most American of festivals but will symbolise, in a way, the Colonel's crackling repudiation of the best editor the paper ever had.

When the cousins came to power in 1914, the paper had already registered in Washington its patented trademark, 'The World's Greatest Newspaper.' To make it so, Patterson introduced 'Little Orphan Annie' and other comic strips. And Colonel McCormick brought a business acumen to leasing Canadian forest lands against the day when the *Tribune* would need more paper. In seven years it was the dominant Chicago paper. Its history since then has been a triumph of political scalp-hunts, circulation wars, hordes of features, much mechanical ingenuity, and resounding profits. The British, of course, have a hand in this. For to-day it is Canadian virgins, of spruce and balsa, reared in the 500 square miles of Quebec the

Colonel owns, that invade Chicago and turn, every morning, into a million lusty *Tribune*s, going out to do battle like an army with banner headlines.

Most great newspapers come to fame through the force of a single great character whose descendants signal with diminishing voltage the original impulse that eludes them. Not so with the Medill–Patterson–McCormick dynasty. It has provided the finest demonstration in the history of prejudice of the triumph of the Mendelian theory. 'The offspring,' wrote the learned priest, 'of two hybrid parents, which carry a dominant Medill and recessive McCormick, characteristically exhibit outwardly the dominant character in the ratio of three to one.'

To-day the editorial attitudes that Medill struck in the eighteen-sixties are intensified in the thoroughbred stance of the Colonel, standing now over Chicago like the finest strain of pointer, watching with pen poised for the migrations of all the queer birds – the Easterners, the C.I.O., the British – who might sully the pure Midwestern sky. Only the British is he powerless to keep out. From nowhere is he more hounded and sabotaged by them than in his own instinct. For whenever he relaxes from this patriotic vigilance he finds himself still talking with a trace of British accent, taking afternoon tea, wearing a wrist watch on each hand, and being forever to his friends known as Bertie. Freud, thou shouldst be living at this hour! Robert Rutherford hath need of thee! Yet it ill behooves any Briton on this great day to point and snicker over this dilemma of character. Better to turn the other cheek and hail the Colonel as a true son of the bulldog breed. Arise, then, ye crooked sons of Albion, and raise your bloodstained glass to your cousin from Chicago, in whom the blood of Blimp flows so strong and free. A toast, gentlemen, to the Chicago *Tribune*, born 1847, still going crazy.

Harry S. Truman
A Study of a Failure*
November 1, 1948

There is often a heartless contradiction between American ideals and the general willingness to accept them in action. Mr. Truman's biography is the stuff of which all Presidents are supposed to be made. It is the character and the career that party campaign handbooks attribute to their chosen leader. It is on file in every Hollywood studio, heading the category of thoroughly reliable 'characters,' whom not even the House Un-American Activities Committee would question. It is described in the schools as the very root and flower of what is best about the American way of life. Yet it appears uneasily in the White House and is remembered as the object of characteristic jokes. Coolidge's memory is green in the popular recollection for his cracker-barrel cynicism and his opposition to sin. And now we are ready to recall 'To err is Truman' and 'Don't shoot the piano-player, he's doing his best.'

Yet the fame of the Truman Investigating Committee was justly earned: it wrote the most searching and sympathetic record of a war Administration's blunders and successes. Mr. Truman's history in the Senate was that of an alert debater, a practical humanitarian, a courageous New Dealer from a state festering with political corruption which has never tainted his personal history. Many a more pretentious statesman would have quietly forgotten his machine connections when that machine was exposed and punished in the law courts. But to Harry Truman it was a simple courtesy to leave Washington, and his new glory as Vice-President, and go home to Missouri to attend the funeral of the squalid Boss Pendergast, who came

---

* This piece was published in the *Guardian* the day before the presidential election, in which Truman defeated Thomas E. Dewey by 303 electoral votes to 189.

out of jail to die. Pendergast had picked Truman as his man for the Senate. And Mr. Truman came from the sort of people who despise a man who forgets favours. Truman had come up the 'folksy,' traditional way of the machine politician – a road overseer, farm-tax collector, a bridge-mender, a drainer of dirt roads after heavy rains; then a postmaster, a club organiser; then tedious nights learning enough law to justify his election as a county court judge. But he knows as well as most that it is also the hard way. At various times he had gone into debt and worked at all sorts of jobs because the convention of going bankrupt was odious to him. 'He ploughed the straightest row of corn in Jackson County,' his mother kept on telling reporters. To Harry Truman the moral implications of that compliment are as binding as the words of a Methodist hymnal. Being present at Pendergast's funeral was an obvious duty.

It is, I think, the acting out of such straightforward maxims in a great office that requires tact, timing, and a goodly gloss of two-facedness which has bewildered Mr. Truman and made his administration in the end admittedly inept. When the late Secretary of the Navy, Frank Knox, made a speech in Boston and, with Roosevelt's private approval, came out for Atlantic convoys for British shipping, the grateful cries of Englishmen were as loud as the screams of protest over here. Questioned at a press conference, Mr. Roosevelt said surely Mr. Knox had a right to speak for himself. Truman would have told all, as he did over the misbegotten plan to woo Stalin with Chief Justice Fred Vinson. When he was a haberdasher, he bought at boom prices and sold at depression prices. His shop failed, but he is not a despondent man and one can admire the sigh and the plucky grin with which he has, throughout his life, tried to learn by his mistakes. Unfortunately it is too late to learn in the White House, and Americans who admire the hard-luck story in their neighbour will not tolerate it when that neighbour is raised to 'the elective kingship.'

The failure of President Truman cannot be called a failure of principle or even a betrayal of the programme he inherited. The things he is genuinely noted to have done have been every bit as New Deal as Roosevelt. In one proposal, the uncompromising demand for a Federal Fair Employment code, he went headily beyond even Roosevelt's boldness. And of all the campaigners, he has made the most sense of the politics of survival. While Governor Thomas Dewey has promised 'a firm hand on the tiller' and 'a rudder to our ship,' Truman has been talking about the need for veterans' housing, about drastic enlargements of the social security and sickness insurance programmes, about federal ownership of transmission lines, about the Taft-Hartley Act, about inflation, about longer terms for the Atomic Energy Commission.

But there are over sixty million Americans at work. In this time of deceptive prosperity, Mr. Truman's voice sounded somewhat hollow as he went on asking for things that the country was ready to accept in a depression. The recoil against the New Deal is too easily interpreted abroad as a positive reaction against liberal reform. There is enough evidence in the fight for Senate seats, and in the good showing of unrepentant New Dealers, even in states where Dewey will be chosen, to show that if an impressive man is spouting New Deal doctrine he will be heeded. But Mr. Truman is by now worse than unimpressive. He has committed the unwritten un-American crime of being out-smarted. When he took the oath of office, he was helped along by the legendary assumption that, when all is said and done, homespun men are the shrewdest. His early press conferences gave pause to this comfortable notion. He gave impulsive answers that had to be corrected later. The episode of Henry Wallace's dismissal, demanded by the Secretary of State, was only the first of the rude disillusions.

It will not do to say that greatness is lacking. Very few Presidents have had any claim on it. But mediocre Presidents must depend on careful advice and preserve in public the appearance of authority. Mr. Truman surrounded himself partly with sincere political hacks and made impressive military men substitute for the grand façade he lacked. This latter has been the most interesting and could be the most serious fault in his conception of the President's office. It has puzzled many who would expect so humble a man to be uncomfortable in the presence of so much big brass. It seems to be, however, a true character trait. As a small boy he was 'mercifully ridiculed' in school for reading books from choice and, what is worse, taking piano lessons. He made up for the ridicule by boning up, in stealth, on military history. He amazed the town by applying for, and winning, a place at West Point. Then he was turned down on account of bad eyesight. It must have been a shocking blow. He has revealed throughout his administration a fearful respect for the judgment of military men. And, by the same mechanism of wistful envy, the Truman doctrine was conceived the day he sat at Fulton, Missouri, in the immense shadow of Churchill.

Mr. Laski's Democracy

March 29, 1949

Mr. Harold Laski has written what, in the nature of mortality, must be his definitive work on the United States [*The American Democracy*]. It is nearly 800 pages long and contains full-dress studies of American government, Federal, State, and local; religion in America; education and the professions; the history of American labour; the American role as a world power; and a debatable and less than definitive chapter on the press, the movies, and the radio. Lurking derisively in the wings is the Mephisto to whom, in Mr. Laski's view, the American has all but sold his soul – the American business man.

It is a shattering work: immensely and nobly learned, dogmatic, never less than generous in intention. Yet behind its confident learning, its most splenetic lamentations, its monumental tributes, and the intense ambivalence of Mr. Laski's feeling about big business, there is a modesty and an uncomfortable awareness that his indignation is directed at the humanness of human nature. For once, we must believe implicitly an author's humble preface: 'No one, I venture to believe, knows its defects more fully than I do ... I have realized more and more how disproportionate is the fulfilment to the task I had set myself. There is so much more in America than any one man can know.' There is indeed. And though Mr. Laski would seem to have about as limitless a knowledge as any man alive, penetrating and profound as he is in every field that can be explored by the mind rather than the legs and eyes, his limitations can be gathered from his list of acknowledgments. Ninety per cent of them are to venerable historians both quick and dead, professors of law, and sociologists. There are none to ranchers, realtors, lumbermen, labour organisers, movie producers, district leaders, or newspapermen. You will find here, then, most of America that can be apprehended as ideas embodied in institutions, beliefs that split into political parties, the life of the spirit as it has flowered in documents, religions, universities. You will find a great concern for freedom of speech on the radio as it is restricted deliberately by sponsors, indirectly by the Catholic Church.

But you will not find anything about the satirical onslaughts on sponsors, on Main Street, and on American institutionalism by Fred Allen or Henry Morgan. Much erudite assertion of the 'revolutionary tradition' of American life but little about the revolutionary reflexes of oilmen, cattlemen, Pennsylvania Dutch farmers, in revolting against the government or their competitors who would monopolise water-terminals, set high minimum prices in a fat year, or insist on any other form of crop-insurance than neighbourly self-help. Mark Twain, we are told, was 'broken' when the 'free and easy comradeship of the small town' was transformed by great financiers into 'a restless and dissatisfied society in which wealth and corruption had stifled the dynamic optimism of youth.' But there is no explanation for the continuing optimism of so many 'broken' Americans, or for their stupidity in remaining optimistic, or for their restless absorption with what money can buy. You will read here an appalling and true tract about the conservative blight of the 'alumni' on college faculties, but you will not learn what are the ambitions of the students at a junior college.

A thousand times Mr. Laski makes an acute generalisation that ought to be his conclusion drawn from the evidence he has examined. But he starts with the idea and his supporting historical examples sometimes prove other things than the idea. Thus he notes that 'it is part of the deep-rooted social egalitarianism of America that the idea of a profession is far more inclusive than it is in Europe'; but he does not then begin with the campaign of Jonathan Turner a century ago for industrial universities, or with the Land Grant Colleges Act of 1862. Having noticed an important difference, he hews to what is different about a similarity and launches into exhaustive studies of the professions of law and medicine, and rounds them out with an apology for not examining the professions of the engineer, the realtor, the advertising man, the insurance salesman, which have a unique and universal prestige that is just what the reader ought to be told about in order to learn what is so American about America. His historical analogies are, of course, famous, but they often seem to be plucked out of their context, in which they illustrate something less than the particular 'principle' that Mr. Laski is so cogently revealing.

Most historians assume that the long view is governed by perspective. But perspective is itself an idea. And Mr. Laski's picture of America is more like one of those Diego Rivera primitives in which cows, farmers, university presidents, chuckling financiers, railroads, trees, and Lincoln and Roosevelt are taken out of their time and their function and arranged in the imperious two-dimensional pattern of the painter's theory of composition. Bestriding this allusive world, and shaping its human energies into essentially impotent gestures, is the Machiavellian business man.

Mr. Laski proceeds in this winning way. The American tradition is not an enormous train of oddly coupled Pullman cars, ox-carts, covered wagons, and Diesel engines. It is the linking of certain great ideas and the story of their corruption by monopoly capitalism. For always at the back of Mr. Laski's mind is an ideal United States, a Platonic image of what America might have been if the great men of the Constitutional Convention had gone on reproducing their kind and managed to exert their fascination over the popular mind instead of succumbing first to the pioneer and then to the business man. In time they could have become non-resident members, charmingly 'different,' of the British Labour party, able by their incredible energy to guarantee the abundant life that a completely planned State alone can do.

I am sorry to see that all this reads so ungratefully. It is a dedicated book, greatly learned, and even its prejudices (about the movies and the press especially) are enforced by a driving wit. But it is humourless. And Mr. Laski's urge to clean up the rich and profound untidiness of American life with one great swab of economic planning amounts almost to an obsessive cleansing ritual, and is in that sense a repudiation of the raw materials of life itself. Bridgeport, Connecticut, has had a succession of Socialist regimes, but life there is very American; yet all of Mr. Laski's learning would not explain how this is so. It would be enough to say 'Hallelujah' and not probe the infinite ways in which the citizens of Bridgeport would share hardly anything but a voting preference with the pillars of the British Labour party.

It is not, I hope, left-handed at this stage to say that no admirer of Mr. Laski will want to come to this conclusion, but that it seems to be inescapable. Against it must be set the evidence on every page of a selfless teacher, a brave man, and a passionate idealist who believes with his heart and soul as well as his mind in an America where the immigrant can find 'the right to fulfil dreams he could hardly have dared even to imagine in the Old World,' in an America whose true glory ought to be, and sometimes is not, 'the glory of ordinary people.'

The Fourth of July

Cutchogue, New York, July 5, 1949

Of all American festivals, the Fourth is the truly rural one. It is right that it should be so, if only because Jefferson, its patron saint, hoped there never would be cities in America, cities being foul and noisome, inviting class distinctions, and tending to establish the typical European corruptions of manufacture, adultery, and public statues, from which an agrarian democracy was to be wholly free. For one day, then, the Jeffersonian dream is realised again with permissible variations, like 'Grand Prize Drawing for 1949 De Luxe two-door Pontiac Sedan,' concerning which the heirs of Jefferson are not consulted.

The slickers desert the cities for the lakes and beaches and the countryman gives himself and his family over to the statutory orgies of wiener roasts, Legionnaire parades, the firemen's ball, and a firework show when the sun goes down. May Day was the favourite colonial holiday, but the Puritan Fathers abolished it on Long Island when the maypole became a mere preliminary to the hellish antics of the young, who, says one diarist, 'did madly light on horseback, each youth with his own handmaiden, and gallop off into the neighbouring brakes with an abundance of strawberries, never appearing again until the sun was in the east.' The automobile has replaced the horse, among the humblest of the Long Island farmers, and the national mores have changed enough to make the youth and his handmaiden back from a midnight ride on the Fourth of July greet the fretting parents with 'Wanna make something of it?' In theory then it is a day when anything goes, a day of unbuttoned inhibitions, provided that in the end you strip down to the all-embracing sanctity of 'Old Glory.' The farmers can be tolerant enough for one more night, for they bide their time knowing that the trucks are already pounding through the night from New York, and to-morrow the potato harvest begins.

But this year in most farming regions of the east coast the usual mood will be hard to bear. This morning a golden sun came up on the forty-first day of the drought, the longest in New York's recorded history. It is just as well this village is so used to the 'ogue' endings of the Indian place-names hereabouts that it has probably forgotten the suffix stands for 'water.' There is a lot of water around here, glistening with a Mediterranean blueness, but it is all salt water, the inlets and creeks and main body of the Great Peconic Bay which, at Riverhead, divides the 120-mile fish of the island into two flukes, enclosing the bay for the last sixty miles of the south shore, the last thirty miles of which is called the North Fork.

It is in the middle of this north fork that you come on, or flash through, Cutchogue, which is two blocks of shops and a traffic light, and a wide fringe of farms. It is the heart of the potato country, run mostly by Poles who gravitated here at the turn of the century, as they did also to 'the sand country' in the middle of Wisconsin, in search of a sandy soil that looked like home. They surpassed in patience, hard work, and thrift, especially thrift, the Yankees who have been here since 1640. Germans moved in too, and in the last two decades the huge duck farms, for which Long Island is also famous, have passed out of the hands of people with names like Young and Corwin into the hands of people with names like Lukert and Pfifferling. Down the road from a small colonial church with a Wren spire, battered by the 1938 hurricane, is another church whose steeple has a heavy square overhang of shingles and would look very much at home anywhere east of Breslau. The gramophone shop on Cutchogue's main street is lucky if it has more than a hundred records. Thirty of the best sellers at any time are polkas recorded by Polish bands in New Jersey, or in Bridgeport, on the Connecticut shore across the sound.

But there is no sense of a colony of Poles. They mix in freely with the surrounding families of Harrises and Hortons and Tuthills and Hands, families who are living on the same sites they did three hundred years ago and who to-day do much the same things they did the first winter when they had friendly Indians to help: they plant vines, raise chickens, mend leaky roofs, build houses, and do the paint and plumbing jobs. Most of the heavy work and the big farming is done by the Poles. The limping trucks and the smashed motor-cars are straightened out by the brothers Doroski. The potato farms are the pride of the Stepnowskis, the Novatkas, the Anaskys. Or used to be. This year the fields were dying when they were in flower two weeks ago. The fruit vines have withered, with the raspberries only just starting. The plantbeds are rotted. And the fields of grass look tawny and inflammable as Nebraska in August, and good for nothing but starting a flash fire, which everybody is sufficiently scared about to keep the civil air patrol on a twenty-four-hour alert.

There is a chance, they say, of rescuing about forty per cent of the potato crop, which is one of the two main sources of supply for New York City. The yield will be a little more in proportion for those farmers who luckily heeded the Government's advice last year and put in a third of their acres to rye. These are the only farmers who have anything to crow about. The Government last year started an acreage control plan, meant to reduce the excessive acreage of potatoes by twenty-four per cent. Only those who joined in are eligible for the Government's price support, which this year is sixty per cent of parity, against ninety per cent last year. Another week of drought and they figure a lot of cautious Poles, who have a habit of living in frugal, not to say squalid, homes while keeping $20,000 in the bank, will be back where their grandfathers started. There is a young ex-Service man near here who had done odd jobs before the war and ached to become a farmer. What with bonuses and veterans' benefits and help from the bank and one thing and another, he bought a 200-acre farm last winter and planted it all in potatoes. In his mid-twenties, he is learning early about proceedings in bankruptcy. So the parades, the distant oompah of the local band, the firemen's ball will be heartless exercises this Fourth. And the usual civic phobia about fireworks will spread to-night to every farmer with a field like tinder.

For deeper comfort, the editorials of this morning's big-city papers, with their heady talk of 'our glorious heritage' and 'teeming resources,' are no help at all. The people here are slow, dour folk, unimaginative maybe, yet they can give off surprising sense and pride at the roots. Not many metropolitan newspapers in the cities across America will hit off a better leading article than the one that appeared this week-end in the lowly *Long Island Traveller and Mattituck Watchman*. Into seven paragraphs it tucks these thoughts:

'July Fourth is not the anniversary of American independence. It is the anniversary of America's Declaration of Independence. Our observance is the celebration of a hope . . . for . . . the ambitions of colonial Americans were not absolutely pure. They were alloyed with much that was selfish, unjust, ignoble, and worldly. But the spiritual element persisted and asserted itself increasingly in admirable institutions and policies . . . It is a fact that in democratic civilizations the greatest steps forward have been those signalized by Declarations. The Magna Carta was not a treaty but an agreement upon rights . . . The Habeas Corpus Act . . . the charter granted in the Plymouth Company . . . It has been the English people who have wrested from their governing classes the essentials of freedom, and from whom all the peoples now aspiring to independence derive both practical criteria and spiritual example and encouragement.

'The Fourth of July is a good day upon which to declare ourselves independent of the invisible but powerful tyrannies of suspicion and fear, superstition and prejudice, race hatred, and class bigotry. But our patriotism is noblest when it refuses to boast of the excellence of our institutions and achievements and turns to a serious inquiry into the ways and means of remedying defects in American life. The highest patriotism is to feel oneself a citizen of the world, with a special duty to one's native land, and with the constant responsibility of having to give by an upright private life, and an honourable public life one's services for the welfare of the human race.'

In spite of the draw for the deluxe two-door sedan, it sounds as if Jefferson would be still quite at home in these parts.

A Lesson for Yale

Cambridge, Massachusetts, May 21, 1951

The rivalry of Yale and Harvard is going into its third century and has been bloodied down the years by many a student riot and pitched battle on each other's campus, to say nothing of the more routine muscle-matching of football games.

By the end of the last century the typical Yale man had evolved into a human type as recognisable as a Cossack or the Piltdown skull, and there was a tense period in the late twenties and early thirties when Harvard could no longer bear close proximity with these well-developed anthropoids and primly refused to play them at anything. The football and chess fixtures were summarily cancelled. But by now even a Harvard man has heard of 'one world,' though he recognises no obligation to belong to it. So to-day, in a wild lunge of global goodwill, Harvard recalled the sons of Elihu Yale to their common heritage by suggesting a revival of the ancient joust known as cricket.

Not for forty-four years have Yale and Harvard together

attempted anything so whimsical. But a far-sighted alumnus lately gave $100 to revive the match and encouraged Harvard men to learn how the other half lives. Accordingly, with this bequest, pads and bats were fetched from Bermuda and Canada, and a roll of coconut matting was bought wholesale in Philadelphia. These props were assembled to-day on Smith Field, which is a dandelion enclosure lying west of the Harvard football stadium.

Here at 1:30 in the afternoon came ten of the visiting Yale men, various sets of white and grey gentlemen's pantings, a score-book, and a couple of blazers for the sake of morale. Fifteen minutes later, and 200 yards away, the Harvard team arrived in two old Chevrolets and a Cadillac. They carried the matting out to a weedy airstrip devoid of dandelions; stretched it out and pegged it down; made Indian signs at the glowering Yale men and, discovering that they understood English, formally challenged them to a match; spun a dime, won, and chose to go in first.

The eleventh Yale man was still missing and the Harvard captain, a mellifluous-spoken gentleman from Jamaica, offered to lend them a Harvard man. The Yale captain suspected a trap and said they would wait. Ten minutes later the eleventh man came puffing in, swinging from elm to elm. Everything was set. It was a cloudless day. It had been 92 the day before, but Providence obliged with a 35-degree drop overnight and we nestled down into a perfect English May day – sunny and green, with a clammy wind. The eleven spectators stomped and blew on their hands at the field's edge. And the game began.

Mr. Conboy and Mr. Cheek put on the purchased pads. Conboy took centre and faced the high lobbing off-breaks of Mr. Foster, who delivered six of these nifties and was about to deliver a seventh but saw that Mr. Cheek had turned his back and was off on a stroll around the wicket. This mystery turned into a midfield conference at which it was found out that Yale expected to play an eight-ball over and Harvard a six. An

Englishman on the Harvard side kindly acquainted the Yale men with the later history of cricket, and they settled for a six-ball over.

This shrewd act of gamesmanship effectively rattled the Harvard team for a while, and Conboy was soon out for three and Cheek for a duck. But Frank Davies, from Trinidad, knew a sophisticated ploy that shortly demoralised the Yale men. He came in slowly, hefted his pads, squinted at the coconut matting, patted it, rubbed his right shoulder, exercised his arm, and, while the Yale men were still waiting for him to get set, started to cut and drive the Yale bowling all over the field.

Yale retorted by occasionally bowling an over of seven balls and once an over of five. It had no effect. They were now thoroughly cowed by Davies's professional air. Once he cleverly feigned a muscle spasm and had the Yale side clustered round him terrified at the prospect of a doctor's bill. They were so trembly by now that they thought it only decent to drop any fly ball that came their way. Davies hooked a ball high to leg, but the Yale man obligingly stumbled and pawed the air.

Davies tried another hook with the same result, but the agreement was now so firmly understood that no Yale man would hold anything. Davies accordingly cut with flashing elbows, secure in the new-found knowledge that considered as a slip fielder a Yale man is a superlative bridge player. Davies went on to cut fine and cut square and drive the ball several times crack against the cement wall on which two mystified little boys were sitting. This, it was decided, was a boundary, and the scorer was told to put down four runs.

Davies did some more shrugs and lunges with his shoulder-blades, and, though there was a fairly constant trickle of batting partners at the other end, Davies had scored never less than two-thirds of the total. Suddenly he let go with a clean drive to mid-on for two and the astonished scorer discovered that the total was now sixty-eight and Davies had reached his half-century.

There had been so far a regrettable absence of English spirit but Bruce Cheek, a civil servant, formerly of Peterhouse, Cambridge, was signed up to repair this omission by shouting 'Well played, sir!' – an utterly alien sound to the two Boston small fry on the cement wall. This cued the growing crowd to rise and applaud the incomparable Davies. All fourteen of them joined in the ovation.

Ten minutes later the Rev. Bill Baker, a Baptist from Manchester, went in to receive his baptism of fire from Foster, who had suddenly found his off-break again. The result was that Mr. Baker was walking back right after walking out. Then Davies hit a short ball into a Yale man's hands. He failed to drop it in time. And the whole side was out. Harvard, 102 – Davies, 70.

The two small fry dropped off the cement wall and came into the field to investigate the ritual. One of them stayed in the outfield and the tougher one came on and asked a question of the retreating umpire. It was a simple question. It was: 'What game you playin', mister?' He was told, and turned round and bawled: 'Cricket!' at his pal. The pal shrugged his little shoulders and went off and picked up two Boston terriers from somewhere, for no reason that anyone discovered then or since. They did manage to invade the field during the Yale innings and had to be shooed off.

Meanwhile we had taken tea, from a thermos about the size of a city water tower. From nowhere a parson arrived, wearing an old straw boater. It was a heart-warming sight, and I found myself mumbling through a tear the never-to-be forgotten lines '. . . some corner of a foreign field that is forever Lipton's.'

With a knightliness that cannot be too highly praised, Yale maintained the dogged pretence that they were playing cricket. It entitled their going out to the matting and back again in a slow though spasmodic procession. The continuity of this parade was assured by one Jehingar Mugaseth, a dark supple young man from Bombay, who had one of those long, beautiful, unwinding runs that would have petrified even the nonchalant Mr. Davies. At the other end was a thin, blond man with another long run, an American who distrusted breaks but managed a corkscrew baseball swerve in mid-air.

Between them the Yale team fell apart, and your reporter had no sooner looked down to mark 'McIntosh caught' than he looked up to see Allen's middle stump sailing like a floating coffin past the wicket-keeper's right ear. Yale were suddenly all out – for thirty-four. They followed on, more briskly this time – they were catching on to the essential tempo of the game – and were out the second time in record time for twenty-four runs. It was all over at 6:40.

No excuses were offered from the Yale team. They had fine English names – Grant, West, Allen, Foster, Parker, and Norton – and true to the Old Country traditions they lost magnificently. Nobody mentioned the mean Colonial skill recruited by the Harvard side. Nobody, that is, except a Yale man who dictated to me the exact tribal composition of the Harvard team: one Indian, one Jamaican, one Australian, one Egyptian, one Argentinian, one from Trinidad, one from Barbados, a Swiss New Yorker, two Englishmen, and a stranger from Connecticut.

But after all it's not the winning that matters, is it? Or is it? It's – to coin a word – the amenities that count: the smell of the dandelions, the puff of the pipe, the click of the bat (when Harvard are batting), the rain on the neck, the chill down the spine, the slow, exquisite coming on of sunset and dinner and rheumatism.

An Epic of Courage

September 14, 1951

Sugar Ray Robinson on Wednesday regained his world middle-weight championship from Randolph Turpin, by a technical knock-out after two minutes fifty-two seconds of the tenth round.

No myth dies harder, and none is more regularly debunked by the facts, than the one about international sports contributing to international friendship. White-headed Frenchmen will bear up bravely under the conviction that all the gallantry of France was outraged by pitting the gentle Carpentier against the bruiser Dempsey. The fact that Carpentier was hopelessly outclassed has never been allowed to interfere with the growth of a legend that is now as much a part of French history as the piety of Joan of Arc, another astonishing discovery of hindsight.

Last night Sugar Ray Robinson, tiring to the point of panic before the concrete insensibility of Turpin's massive flesh, wrung everything he had from a brave heart, fought from his finger-tips, and at last had Turpin helpless against the ropes, his arms by his thighs, his stubborn body reeling back and forth like a badly beaten bull when the flags go in. I have never seen a human being receive so much punishment with such dumb bravery. For almost a whole minute Robinson crashed and shot and pounded on him until his head sagged from one side to the other with the flopping rhythm of a broken pendulum.

An old man sitting next to me lit a cigar with precision, keeping his eyes steadily above the flame on the crumbling Turpin. 'Thirty seconds more,' he said quietly, 'and we'll have another Flores on our hands.' Flores was the young boxer killed ten days ago in a similar act of bravery before just such an onslaught. It did seem then that Turpin should be rescued to fight another day. If there had been another minute, I do believe that he would have gone down and out for a long time to come. But pride never lacks pretext, and there were only eight seconds of that round to go when the referee bounded in and scissored his arms to stop the fight. Turpin fell on him in a face-down dive, and it seemed to one no more than twenty feet away that it was a gesture of oxlike gratitude.

Pound for pound, the experts say, Robinson is the best boxer we have seen in many a long year. In victory he is incomparable, in trouble resourceful, in near-defeat – as we saw last night – indomitable. He is Robert E. Lee with the fighting reserves of a Montgomery or a Patton. The point about scoring him, though, is that nothing he does goes unseen or unrecorded.

With Turpin, you have to look beyond the awkward stance, the heavy, harrowing style, and watch for what he's doing when he gets in there. Then you see, if you are close enough, that his short-arm jabs to the belly are faster than the eye and heavier than lead. A flashier fighter than Robinson might appear to be dancing easily around this approach until the sudden moment when the man keeled over, in absolute exhaustion, from the invisible pounding at his middle. Turpin appears to do everything wrong. His left leg is always out, whether his weight is forward, dead centre, or moving over. An undercut consequently sends him down on one knee – this happened twice in the early rounds – but a thoughtful judge might score a point and cancel it when he saw Turpin with his big glass eyes calmly using that knee to rest on.

In the first four rounds the comments of old and young fighters and veteran sports writers sharpened this dilemma, of how to identify as confident pauses what in another man would be helpless postures. 'You can't box this guy,' somebody said, seeing Robinson's long left punching the air to the starboard side of Turpin's right ear. 'He's all flesh,' somebody else said. 'All body, you mean,' another man capped, 'I never did see a man fight more with his body.' You note these good remarks and look up to see Turpin, his gloves somewhere around his thighs, moving in wide open for the sort of murder

Joe Louis used to execute on any man two feet away with one arm down.

But this is Turpin's normal approach to artillery fire in the clinches. Time and again he came on last night, with that modest homely face, and those wide glassy eyes, as untouched by the possibility of human interference as Marley's Ghost clanking up from the cellar, or Boris Karloff wheeling into the petrified drawing-room. 'He's not a man,' an admiring youngster cried. 'He's The Thing.' And the mind winced at the memory of Hollywood's latest terror, the monster that has an arm blown off, then grows another.

This always-moving, never-blinking mechanical man sent anxiety flashing into Robinson's eyes. We saw Robinson's muscles tighten for action, the shower of spittle that grunted out of his mouth after each careful body blow and set the moths darting in terror through the white rectangle of light. And they sucked their teeth and said, 'He's all in. Two more rounds and he's through.' It was then, with an old cut opened, that Robinson summoned up the last cry of courage to brighten the tension of style. He wrung tattoos from his knotted stomach. He missed many times. But he landed many times more.

Even then Turpin tottered, like a man in a nightmare lifting iron legs up an endless flight of stairs, over towards Robinson's corner. There was an ugly misgiving that Turpin was lurching after his conqueror. But he was merely going to embrace him. 'It was,' wrote the New York *Herald Tribune*'s Red Smith this morning, 'a genuine gesture of sportsmanship from a first-class fighting man. There haven't been many better fighters than Turpin seen around here in a long time. There never has been a pluckier loser.' That, I think, is the accurate truth of it.

But recollection in tranquillity, though it may be the making of art, is just as often the death of truth. Turpin may well see the newsreels of those last two minutes and wonder who was that all-in giant who fell into grateful oblivion on the referee's chest. It was Randolph Turpin, a very game young man, nobody else. And all the dressing-room philosophy will not change it.

Turpin's recovery from the event was as dramatic as the right to the chin that sent him down for a count of five and left him panting on one knee for a further count of four. Three minutes after the fight Turpin was standing in mid-ring with his arm around the smiling Robinson. He stood up straight and he was breathing at a normal rate. In the dressing room he admitted to having been 'a little foggy, but I was not hurt. I didn't want to go down again because I knew they would end it.' Without haste or ill will he thought again: 'If I were the referee I probably would have stopped it, too.' He most certainly would.

But out of this act and the reconstruction of it by people with fierce transatlantic loyalties will be built another myth: that Turpin was denied his right, and robbed of the victory, by a referee too susceptible to the home crowd and the howling fringe of Harlemites a mile away against the bright sky. Again the vivid fact remains. Referee Goldstein did as fair a job as I have ever seen. And alone among the judges he gave Turpin four rounds to Robinson's four, with one even. One judge gave Robinson five, Turpin three, and one even. The other gave Robinson five and Turpin four.

My own less confident count was three each and three even, with a footnote to the effect that one or two more rounds and Robinson would have been a ragged frame of flesh, all co-ordination gone, twitching possibly, but from the viscera and nerves, not the mind and will. My doubts about the three even rounds could easily be extended to a fourth and fifth. It is the nasty problem of how you score two men who might have learned their fighting on different planets. How do you compare rare roast beef and crêpes Suzette?

Robinson is still a great and delightful boxer, with the stress on the noun. His stance is the textbook stance drawn in quicksilver. When he jabs with his long slippery left, his neck goes down for cover and the muscles ripple down along the waist. He dances lightly according to the subtle demands of balance. When he comes close he rat-tat-tats in a protective flurry before resting in the clinch. In open fighting he has a left and a right, a wicked hook, a perfect uppercut with belly deflected, and the guard up over his heart.

Finally Turpin came out of a clinch and Robinson flew in like Mercury. Turpin's glazed eyes rolled over – the dragon's last squirm, with the nostrils high and flaring. He pitched forward and Robinson jerked him down, down on to the glaring mat and rolling over. Then he was up on one knee, and up again. Robinson, stretched and taut in the corner, paused for a fraction and came in again to bang him against the ropes. Three more thunderbolts, to the head, the chest, the sagging neck. And Turpin staggered across a right angle to be bounced against another rope.

Turpin seemed almost sick with the concentration of his own frenzy. But he stayed with it and flung all he knew. His left eye was showering blood, so that the four gloves looked as if they had been dipped in paint. Turpin's gloves were up against the hailstorm rattling around his head. Then they were down and limp and gone for ever. Two, three, four more rocketing blows, and Turpin was slipping against the rope, baying mutely at the nearly full moon and the roaring thousands up against it. And then the man in white came in. And it was all over.

Harold Ross's *New Yorker*

December 11, 1951

In the New York *World*, sometime around the end of 1923, there appeared in the daily column of Franklin P. Adams, Manhattan's own Samuel Pepys, an item: 'And to H. Ross's, and we talked about the low state periodical comick literature is sunk into.'

It was true enough. But nobody in America apparently was doing anything about it. There was the old *Life*, and there was *Judge*, two family magazines whose stock-in-trade was deaf old ladies, comic valentines, he-she jokes, and a dreadful series of contributed saloon gags called Krazy Kracks. Sophisticated New Yorkers might wince at this stuff, but the instinct to wince was merely satisfying proof of their own urbanity.

Yet there was one man who winced for a living. He was co-editor of *Judge*, and as he corrected its laughing copy every wince was a stab at his pride, his taste, and his patriotism. He would reach in his drawer and finger the pages of *Punch* and *Simplicissimus* and sigh over the superiority of Europe. He quit his job and turned to improve American humour with the almost suicidal frenzy of a Strindberg hero. He was impossibly cast for this part. He wanted to found a sophisticated, ironic metropolitan weekly. He was a gawky outlander, a runaway from a village in the Rockies, an itinerant newspaperman who had bummed his way to San Francisco, a doughboy who had run an American Army magazine in France, a cantankerous, poker-crazy, all-swearing, all-drinking Westerner — Huck Finn in a slept-in business suit and cracked yellow shoes. He was, however, the H. Ross of 'F. P.'s' little item. He looked for a wealthy backer and found one in the socialite heir to a yeast fortune.

Twenty-five years ago last February he put out a thin, unlikely-looking firstborn. It combined *Punch*'s Charivari with *Judge*'s two-line jokes. It had some comic strips barely dignified as 'panels.' There were a few local advertisements, some caricatures of actors, and art notes by 'Froid.' Its only note of superiority was a derisive promise that it would not be edited for 'the Old Lady in Dubuque.' Ross called it *The New Yorker*.

From that start, it lost 2,000 dollars a week. It took three years and the outpouring of 700,000 unrequited dollars to turn the red ink into black. To-day, we are told, it may be bought by almost anybody with ten million dollars to spare. It has just put out a big twenty-fifth anniversary album of its incomparable stable of cartoonists. A book has just appeared to celebrate the journalistic miracle: *Ross and The New Yorker*, by Dale Kramer. It is not a brilliant book. Its style is pedestrian, but this says nothing – so was Caesar's, but look what he was reporting. Mr. Kramer's raw material is similarly historic. Finishing it, you are ashamed to realise what should have been obvious all along: nothing as distinguished as *The New Yorker* can be made out of the casual recruiting of a few choice urban spirits. It was made out of lava; out of debt; out of Ross's writhing perfectionism, his genius for withholding praise, his diviner's gift for spotting the likeliest prospectors before the gold was struck. Nothing was ever 'good' or 'what we want,' but only 'in the direction of what we want.' 'Comes the revolution,' said Dorothy Parker, 'and it will be everybody against Ross.'

In time he came to be showered with the best from the obscure and the famous. He would look it over and moan, 'We'll just have to print what we dislike the least.' This is, in milder form, a common protective attitude of editors trying to hide their suspicion that they are really most at home with mediocrity and feel bad about it. With Ross it was a genuine, tormented itch for a style and an excellence that had not so far appeared in English. He was never satisfied. He never stopped looking for 'what we want.' He never left a line of copy to anyone else. He pounded around town tracking after unknowns, interviewing great ones, and turning their stuff down flat.

By the turn of the Twenties *The New Yorker* had discovered a language all its own. It had given a transatlantic fame to a crop of local geniuses: Dorothy Parker, Ogden Nash, Benchley, Thurber, Frank Sullivan, E. B. White, Peter Arno, Otto Soglow. With Alva Johnston as first grave-digger, it resurrected the brilliant, intimate character sketch from where John Aubrey had buried it over two centuries ago, and called it a 'profile.' It combed the best reporting talent of the newspapers and established 'A Reporter at Large' as a model of reporting that no newspaper published in English can match. It spawned comic draftsmen by the dozen.

Ross had two bibles: Fowler, and a reprint, which he circulated to the staff, of Mark Twain's devastating diagnosis of the flatulence and related prose disorders of Fenimore Cooper. He brought in Woolcott Gibbs as editor. And, on a chance paragraph or two, E. B. White in his early twenties. No paper has been so painstakingly, so ruthlessly edited. Ross would stay up nights haunting the printers' formes with a flashlight, searching for misprints or suspected errors of fact. Gibbs and White slashed and pared all incoming copy, and set the standard of a clean, lucid, ironic prose. Through these turmoils and with these helpers the gawky Mr. Hyde from Aspen, Colorado, turned out the limpid New York diary of Dr. Jekyll.

To-day it is an American institution, confident, prosperous, unsinkable. Now it enters its dangerous age. For Ross recently complained that when he looked among young men for new ideas, new writing, he found them weaned and bred to write a pallid imitation of the *New Yorker* style. As long as Ross was around looking for the yeast, the thing would ferment. Harold Ross, however, died suddenly last week. And now the day to watch is the day anyone inherits *The New Yorker*, not as an adventure but as a respectable property. When a paper can boast only about its prestige, it had better remember the fate of the *Boston Evening Transcript*, which felt so secure in its prestige one Friday evening that it woke up on Monday morning to find there was no more *Boston Evening Transcript*.

Some of us feared this end over a decade ago. In the autumn of 1938 there appeared a cover drawing that belonged to no *New Yorker* we knew. It was by the ribald Peter Arno. It was not of an investment banker weighing the capital cost of a plunging neckline. It was of a herd of bowed heads, the Nuremberg victims. This had all the bravery of a young Royalist defying the firing squad. It showed at a shocking glance how alien to the on-coming world of violence was *The New Yorker* we cherished. A war, we imagined, would kill it off. For Hitler was outraging urbanity everywhere, like a Dostoievsky madman let loose in a country club.

But 'The Talk of the Town' was being written by E. B. White, and White, who had developed a modern vernacular style as original and influential as any since Steele's, now used it on the great issues of our day. At a perilous time for café society, *The New Yorker* was amazingly led into battle by a man whose grace grew courage, by E. B. White, who wrote like an angel and now felt like a man.

Soviet Light on Baseball

September 25, 1952

Fair-minded Americans were taking a second look today at a game that they have long assumed to be their very own, one moreover that was always supposed to mix gallantry, humour, horseplay, good fellowship, and material rewards in equal proportions. The game however has just been identified, after considerable research by a Soviet youth magazine, as 'lapta.' According to *Smena*, the official periodical of the Young Communist League, Russian peasants played lapta in all its classless purity for many centuries before the game was smuggled into the United States and transformed into a mocking demonstration of the class struggle. In its corrupt American version, according to *Smena*, it is known as beizbol.

In its pristine Russian form, a bol is heet by a better who then ron aronn tree becks of send or bessiz. This is nawn ez a hom ronn. The better then rons hawm an earns great glory but naw kesh. In the United States, on the other hand, *Smena* tells its readers, 'It is a beastly battle, a bloody fight with mayhem and murder.' It is played by 'slaves, bought and sold like sheep.' *Smena* does not explain why the best sheep earn as much as 15,

20, or 30,000 pounds a year. These slaves are 'bought and sold and thrown out the door when they become unnecessary . . . after which, with ruined health and often also crippled, they increase the army of American unemployed.' (*Pravda*'s estimate yesterday of American unemployed was 13 million – 1 million more than in the depth of the depression. The United States Bureau of Labor statistics fall about 12½ million short of this figure.) As an example of the shameless capitalist exploitation of beizbol slaves, *Smena* cites the famous case of the late Babis Rut, known locally as the Babe or the Sultan of Swat. He was 'sold against his wishes to another club for 150,000 dollars.'

The New York Times this morning rather academically notes that there has been 'only one fatality in the entire history of major league baseball.' But the *Herald Tribune* more conscientiously sent a sports writer off to check on the Russian accusations and he regrets to-day to find them well-founded. He attended the game at the polov graundz between the Nieu Uork Djiantz and the Shikago Kubz. The Djiantz were beaten nine to nothing; says Harold Brown, the *Tribune*'s man, 'it was murder all right.'

There were ugly facts to the game the Russians had not mentioned. The slaves were forced to play at night under hot grilling lights. The shoddy official excuse for this torture is that at this season of the year the top teams are trying hard to win the championship of their respective leagues in order to qualify for the test matches and thereby, as Mr. Brown frankly admits, 'make extra money. Players like Boby Tomson and Alvin Dok of the Djiantz have been known to play their hardest because they are motivated by a capitalistic desire for ready cash.' It is a fact that the two winning teams, who meet in the test matches, or lapta series, next month, are given big bonuses. They get even bigger bonuses if they win the series and emerge as the champion team.

Mr. Brown unflinchingly noted regulation barbarities charitably overlooked by *Smena*: the umpire for instance wears 'a mask over his face and a chest protector.' The spectators freely urge the slaves on to petty larceny with such self-explanatory admonitions as 'Steal second base, ya bum.' Mr. Brown positively heard one spectator confidentially advise one player to 'Kill the umpire.'

Englishmen may imagine the ultimate cruelty of the game by pondering *Smena*'s surprising conclusion: 'in the number of maiming wounds and bloodletting, this type of sport is not far behind American football – or rugby'!

Rokbje is, of course, the name of the village in the Ukraine which invented in the fourteenth century the game stolen and patented in England by Doktor Tummaz Arnuld.

The U.S. Negro and the Constitution

Washington, D.C., January 1, 1953

The Fourteenth Amendment to the American Constitution is an historic, and many have thought a dubious, leap in the growth of Federal power over the power of the separate states. Its influential provision repeats the promise of the Fifth Amendment not to deprive anyone of life, liberty, or property 'without due process of law.' But while the Fifth Amendment makes this 'due process' binding on the Federal Government the Fourteenth extends it to State Governments. It is a fine example of the elasticity of creed and action available to countries which take their commandments from the language of the eighteenth century. For the Fourteenth was designed to cure a precise historical ailment – the stateless plight of the defeated Confederates; it soon was presumed to be a charter of centralised power; and after thirty years it was thought of as a pledge of the civil liberties of Negroes.

It was approved in 1868, and in the succeeding decades most test cases tried to reassert the rights of the states, in many matters, against what was taken to be an unfair encroachment of Federal authority. In our own time the mere mention of the Fourteenth Amendment calls up an automatic tableau of the Negro struggling to achieve an absolute equality of citizenship with his neighbouring whites. This reflex would have startled the Thirty-ninth Congress, which wrote the Amendment. For the first test case had nothing to do with Negroes or with the interpretation of 'due process' as the guarantee of civil liberties. It was a case, one of many to follow, which correctly assumed that the new Amendment was designed to secure the citizenship of the truant Confederates and to protect the bankrupt Southern whites against exploitation and oppression from Northern carpetbaggers. To armies that had forsworn allegiance to the Union, to families scattered and impoverished, to businesses disbanded and stripped of their records, the Fourteenth gave a timely reassurance with its new definition of citizenship and its reminder of the citizen's privileges:

'All persons born or naturalized in the United States . . . are citizens of the United States and of the State wherein they reside. No State shall make or enforce any law which shall abridge the privileges or immunities of citizens . . . nor deny to any person within its jurisdiction the equal protection of the laws.'

It is true that after the Civil War the Congress had passed several anti-discrimination laws to safeguard the Negro's new status under the Thirteenth Amendment, which had abolished slavery. But it is curious now to discover how little the Supreme Court assumed that the Fourteenth Amendment was a sequel or rider to the Thirteenth. Sixteen years went by before it was first used for an appeal against a colour bar in theatres, hotels, and trains, and the Court firmly turned it down by eight to one, ruling that the amendment was directed only against state governments, and that no corporation or railway company or individual could be compelled to treat everyone alike. That was in 1883.

Thirteen years later, however, came the test that has since associated the amendment with the social and political status of the coloured race. It was a test of a state's right to pass segregation laws without violating the Constitution. The right was explicitly upheld by the Court on the understanding that Negroes would everywhere enjoy 'separate but equal' facilities. From that year, 1896, until 1950 the Court has backed and filled over the precise definition of an 'equal' facility. But two years ago the Court stiffened and ruled that where a state failed to provide equally well-staffed and equally well-equipped educational facilities Negroes would have to share the regular schools and teachers supported by state taxes. Two years ago also the Court ordered that Negroes were not to be separated in railway dining-cars. Now the Court has just heard arguments on five cases challenging the constitutionality of state laws – which exist in seventeen states – that segregate coloured and white children in the public schools.

For the defence, Mr. John W. Davis, a constitutional lawyer who lost the Presidency as a Democrat in 1924, argued that it is not a question of constitutional right but 'of legislative policy.' South Carolina, which brought the first case, makes segregation in schools compulsory. The interesting variation in the South Carolina case is that, instead of a minority claiming equal rights with the majority, 2,800 Negro children are asking to share the same facilities as the mere 295 white pupils in the same school district. The Negro lawyer, Mr. Thurgood Marshall, maintained that segregation laws are unconstitutional; that they perpetuate the intent of slavery and so violate also the Thirteenth Amendment; that they contradict the accepted mores whereby white and coloured children play together and separate only for their schooling; that they produce lasting humiliation in the minds of coloured children. A Negro lawyer in the Virginia case added that improving physical facilities was no guarantee of equality. He doubted whether the Congress could legally adopt a segregation law under the Fourteenth Amendment.

Justice Robert Jackson, however, questioned Mr. Davis's contention about 'legislative policy' by wondering what would happen if Congress passed a law holding that segregation 'was contrary to public policy.'

The clinching Negro argument went beyond the Constitution of the United States by appealing to the Human Rights section of the United Nations Charter, which pledges all members to promote 'universal respect for, and observance of, human rights and fundamental freedoms for all without distinction as to race, sex, language, or religion.' It is a pledge that has given some embarrassment to American delegates, Mrs. Roosevelt in particular, during debates on 'the dignity of the human being,' in which the Russians have made the most of the actual, to say nothing of the fancied, inequalities of Negroes.

Mr. Davis said that segregation in schools was actually set up under the Fourteenth Amendment and that Congress had never moved to abolish segregation in the District of Columbia, where Congress sits and which is under Federal jurisdiction. He regretted the use of the Fourteenth Amendment as a measuring rod for dividing white and coloured people. To make it so would justify segregation on other grounds, of, for example, sex, age, and mental capacity. 'The great national policy underlying this whole question,' he said, has nothing to do with discrimination. It is the fact that 'the very strength and fibre of our Federal system is local self-government in those matters for which local action is competent.' It was, he thought, 'the height of wisdom' to leave the education of the young to 'the wishes of the parents – both white and coloured' – without forcing their children into 'contacts that may be unwelcome.' He thought that the tensions that arise in mixed schools may be just as harmful as the tensions brought on by segregation.

It is always risky, and probably mischievous, to guess at the Court's views from the questions put to the opposing lawyers.

But it was obvious from one or two interpolations that some Justices were not impressed by the authority given to segregation by the fact that the District of Columbia had so long condoned it. A hint of the resentment and social chaos that might ensue from a Court decision banning segregation came from Mr. Justice Frankfurter, who at one point wondered about the wide possibilities of evasion and said: 'Nothing would be worse in my mind than to have this Court make an abstract declaration that segregation is bad and have it beggared by tricks.' That, however, has been the way with the most famous 'abstract declarations' of the Constitution, and the Court. The climate of public opinion and public policy seems to be moving toward a ruling against segregation, though no one should belittle the social and psychological turmoil it will cause for a time among the first generation in states whose traditions run wholly against it. But if it does not come in a redefinition of the Fourteenth Amendment, it will surely come in the end as a new Amendment to the Constitution.

Traubel Quits *The Ring*

June 12, 1953

Helen Traubel, the celebrated soprano of the Metropolitan Opera, yesterday turned down her pending contract with Mr. Rudolf Bing, the company's manager, because it stipulates that she shall not perform in night clubs during the current opera season.

Miss Traubel is one of the more majestic Wagnerian heroines, and her crooning presence in a jazz basement is as difficult to imagine as that of Mr. Harold Macmillan dispensing pork pies at the *New Statesman*'s annual picnic. But your correspondent was in Chicago recently and saw the miracle of her midnight début with his own eyes. She was about to essay the 'St. Louis Blues' for an audience of liquor salesmen, débutantes, Democratic con men, and other assorted night owls. It was a deeply respectful audience, either from sheer incredulity at Miss Traubel's gracious condescension or honest bafflement at what she was trying to do.

The setting was familiar. The lights were low, the spotlight was pink, the air was reeking, the dawn was in the East, and Miss Traubel was dew-pearled. She hated, as the song prescribes, to see the evening sun go down. But it was the petulance of a hostess who commands flocks of servants but cannot control a short circuit in the chandelier.

Miss Traubel sang on pitch. She swayed like a riven oak over her failure to compete with 'powder and store-bought hair' – a likely story. She rocked her alabaster shoulders in a two-four rhythm to assert her oneness with the common people. But, as Cecilia Ager once wrote about another opera star in the act of humbling her art to our level, 'Her tossing muscles are prim and maintain their inhibitions, no matter how desperately they yearn for abandon.'

This performance brought on in one onlooker a positive nostalgia for dear old Brünnhilde. I guessed that Miss Traubel would be more in evidence than ever at the Metropolitan this year, and that she would probably never again enter a night club, not even as a customer. But Chaplin's hankering to play Hamlet is a hard thing to down. And once a prima donna has experienced the guilty thrill of singing 'She done tole me don't wear no black,' illiteracy must take on in her off-hours the powerful appeal that buttermilk has for a professional champagne taster.

Miss Traubel is now an addict of that good old 'sweet and low down,' and her indignation at Mr. Bing knows no bounds. She has published, without Mr. Bing's permission, an exchange of letters with him. They may never be embalmed with quite the reverence of the Shaw–Terry correspondence but they provide equally instructive lessons in the first principles of art and life.

Mr. Bing referred to her Chicago appearance and reasoned rather uneasily that 'I could so well understand that these two activities [opera and jazz] do not really seem to mix very well.' In fairness to Miss Traubel it should be said she never suggested sneaking 'Ain't Misbehavin'' into *Tristan*. 'Perhaps,' reflected Mr. Bing, who has a pretty talent for intimidation, 'you would prefer to give the Metropolitan a miss for a year or so until you may possibly feel that you want again to change back to the more serious aspects of your art.'

Miss Traubel was too mad to bother returning these subjunctives and conditionals. 'Artistic dignity is not a matter of where one sings,' she laid down. 'The artist of integrity who refuses to compromise her standards is able to imbue whatever place she appears in with dignity.' So *that's* what was happening in Chicago! 'To assert,' she asserted, 'that art can be found in the Metropolitan Opera House but not in a night club is rank snobbery that underrates both the taste of the American public and the talents of its composers.'

Miss Traubel released this letter to the press before Mr. Bing had had it, a procedure he condemned, but with the gallantry of a qualifying adverb, as being 'in not really very good taste.' Mr. Bing said enigmatically yesterday that he could well understand Miss Traubel's desire to seek 'more lucrative' work.

In stark fact, there is very little Wagner at the Met this year — only one part of *The Ring* announced to date – and maybe these letters are only a blind for a credulous public. As a record of an historic artistic upheaval, even, they are less than satisfactory. Neither correspondent can quite get the edge on the other, and the spectacle of Mr. Bing deploring Miss Traubel's tastelessness while she is appalled at his snobbery has an academic tinge bewildering to the layman.

It is rather like two bishops both lamenting that the other hasn't the remotest grasp of the fundamentals of the creed on which they both presumably conduct their lives. It leaves the layman all the more resolved to stay as far away from extremes as possible, and may explain the unflagging popularity of the Air on the G String, Rachmaninov's Prelude, the *Flight of the Bumble Bee* and the whole, calm, cool range of the middle-brow classics.

High Fashion Comes to Texas – and Stays There

July 30, 1953

A hundred years ago there arrived in Dallas, a village founded only twelve years earlier on the Central Texas plain by three families, a dozen Frenchmen in plain long smocks. They were the first of a few hundred who crossed the sea to found La Réunion, one of those many nineteenth-century American Socialist utopias which began alike with common property and ended alike in the sour discovery, unknown to Marxian primers, that some men are shiftless and some women are less than fair.

There are Texans to-day who are proud to claim lineage from these solemn idealists even though any similar expedition of them would nowadays founder on the McCarran Act and run aground at Ellis Island. Nevertheless, every September one or more Frenchmen set out from Paris with Dallas as the goal. This pilgrimage causes no alarm whatsoever and only a little envious pique in New York. The Frenchmen do not wear long smocks, and if they harbour any Socialist ambitions the fact is well suppressed. On the contrary, they are among the hothouse blooms of our capitalist civilisation. They bear such names as Jacques Fath and Christian Dior. They come here not at all to dazzle the back country with the wares of the City of Light. They come rather in the spirit of a Bertrand Russell going to Stockholm for a Nobel Prize, or a Bogart stepping up to a Hollywood rostrum to receive an Oscar. They come here, if they are lucky, to accept an award from Mr. Stanley Marcus and the accolade of the house of Neiman-Marcus, a local store which in forty-five years has managed to sophisticate the prairie matrons to the point where they critically weigh a Neiman-Marcus original against an imported Balenciaga before casting a casual eye over the latest offerings from New York, which in the matter of fashion Dallas resolutely regards as an outer province of Imperial Texas.

In 1905 one Herbert Marcus and his brother-in-law Al Neiman, a graduate of a Midwestern orphan asylum, left Dallas to venture on a small advertising agency in Atlanta, Georgia. In two years they sold it for $25,000. Mr. and Mrs. Neiman took most of the proceeds to New York City, stayed in a boardinghouse and spent $17,000 on a flock of New York dresses and reams of silk and satin. They returned to Dallas, rented a shambling two-storey building, hired a fitter (at their own salary) and a stockgirl, and announced the premature birth of Neiman-Marcus as 'the South's finest and only exclusive women's ready-to-wear shop.'

This pathetic grandiosity is repeated a hundred times every year in every state of the Union and the succeeding bankruptcies are duly filed with the Department of Commerce's Small Business Bureau. Neiman-Marcus, on the contrary, takes in an annual $25 millions. This happy variation is all the more astonishing in view of the time and place at which the gamble was attempted. There would be nothing in the episode (nothing but a mere $25 millions a year, I mean) if its hero and heroine had not been Herbert Marcus and his sister Carrie, and if they had not had the absurd ambition to mass-produce 'high fashion' in a town on the Texas prairie which in 1907 had hardly recovered from the recent depredations of Cole Younger and Sam Bass and the James brothers. Admittedly the town was settling down. Frank James overdid his penitence to the extent of becoming a shoe salesman ten years before Neiman-Marcus opened up shop. But most of the town's 85,000 solid citizens still connected pearls with Belle Starr's pearl-handled pistols. There were 222 saloons crowding the streets along which the first Neiman-Marcus stock girl bravely went to work. The street paving, where there was any, was of wooden blocks. The day of the Neiman-Marcus opening there was a street riot unattended by the cops.

To-day it is a toss-up whether Neiman-Marcus or the Woman's Christian Temperance Union has more thoroughly transformed the town. No liquor is served in any public place. The dominant oil millionaires, like the humblest clerks, go to dine in the best restaurants carrying brown paper bags containing whisky and gin. But their women are not immediately distinguishable. This is the triumph of Carrie Marcus, who was able to imagine styles before she dictated them, and of her brother Herbert, who started with an ideal so perverse that forty-five years later it is dawning on department stores in up-and-coming cities around the world. He said then: 'Any fine store can dress a few women beautifully. Our idea is to dress a whole community that way.'

Granted that Dallas has an outrageously unfair advantage in the comeliness of the female raw material; it was about the only advantage Neiman and Marcus had to start with. Later there was the lucky discovery of oceans of oil bubbling below the bleak landscape. This has diverted into the Neiman-Marcus cash registers a great deal of high and happy spending, and there is hardly a whim of connoisseurship or plain gluttony that Neiman-Marcus will not undertake to satisfy. A Chicago merchant was determined to drape his new wife in the first full-length sapphire mink. Dropping only a hint of a well-bred sigh, Neiman-Marcus obliged for a consideration of $35,000. They have their own mink farm in Colorado and have done pioneer work in developing fine skins of topaz, royal pastel, and latetia. If Wedgwood is your passion, there is an exquisite collection. For moody days, there are little glass tables containing such gems as an antique Italian Book of Hours.

This is the store's conspicuous outer layer, catering to eccentricity or trigger-happy wealth or the hobbies of the cultivated rich. But below that is the legacy of Carrie Marcus Neiman, enough imagination and taste to guarantee fifty thousand charge accounts from women ten miles or ten thousand outside Texas, who live in Paris or Hollywood, on the Blue Train or in the White House. For the purposes of publicity 'chi-chi,' Neiman-Marcus tends to look on this international clientele as a sort of holy sisterhood. But Stanley Marcus is Dallas-bred and he is less concerned over the $2,000 original he imports, at a loss, from Paris for a débutante's eighteenth birthday than over the volume of Neiman-Marcus originals that are selling to local women for $19.95 apiece. This is the nub of Neiman-Marcus's prosperity, as it was once the pivot of Father Marcus's philosophy.

Dallas is a vastly rich town, with oil fortunes sumptuously housed in sedulously watered suburbs. But it is still a ramshackle town, and the backyard of a modern façade or a towering bank may give on to the stripping billboards and alley cats before the yawning prairie takes over. And the wheel of Herbert Marcus's fortune comes full circle in the remarkable fact that in a town of six hundred thousand people on a burning prairie fifty thousand women – one family in three – have a charge account at the store. To give style to the dress of 'a whole community of women': Old Man Marcus converted a sales-talk cliché into a fact and a fortune. Stanley Marcus works at it with all the religious fervour of a man who misunderstood the original mission of Stephen Austin a hundred years ago: 'to redeem Texas from the wilderness.'

Revulsion Against McCarthy

Washington, D.C., June 12, 1954

Senator Joseph McCarthy was all over the front pages again this morning, but the instinct that put him there was for once not his. It looked as if, finally, an impulse of moral revulsion had galvanised the country and braced the backbone of an incongruous variety of his victims. The Department of the Army, a middle-aged coloured woman, the spectators at a session of the Senate's permanent sub-committee on investigations, two Democratic Senators, and a suddenly blithe host of columnists and radio critics were moved to furious protest at the Senator's tactics and his stature.

The Army published a long report, which documented in shocking detail the threats of the young Mr. Roy Cohn, McCarthy's chief counsel, to 'wreck the Army' and break Secretary Robert Stevens if David Schine, a McCarthy investigator, was not given consistently preferential treatment after he had been drafted into the Army as a private.

The report told how Senator McCarthy had directly approached the Army's chief legal counsel to seek a commission for Private Schine; how the Army found him unqualified to receive one; how Senator McCarthy and Mr. Cohn then demanded that Schine be assigned to New York in order to study 'evidence of pro-Communist leanings in West Point text-books,' and how this request was also refused; how, when the Army told Mr. Cohn that after Private Schine had finished his basic training the chances were nine to one that he would be sent overseas, this provoked in Mr. Cohn the threat to wreck the Army and make sure that Mr. Stevens would be 'through' as Secretary of the Army.

The Army insisted at one point that a policy of special treatment for any Army private was not in the national interest, whereupon Mr. Cohn, who is all of twenty-seven, told the Army he would give it 'a little national interest' by showing it up in public 'in its worst light.'

The report listed the many occasions on which Private Schine was given special passes to come to New York, supposedly on the sub-committee's business. Last December the commanding general of his camp complained to the Army's legal counsel that Private Schine was 'becoming increasingly difficult because the soldier was leaving the spot nearly every night,' and usually returning 'very late at night.' The day after this warning Senator McCarthy told the Army that he was no longer interested in having special treatment for Private Schine. But apparently Mr. Cohn was furious and told the Army's counsel that he would show him 'what it meant to go over his head.' Six weeks later the battle to have Private Schine assigned to New York was still going on and Senator McCarthy warned the Army's counsel of the consequences of thwarting young Mr. Cohn.

Two weeks later Senator McCarthy told an assistant to telephone the Army's counsel that he was very angry about the honourable discharge granted to a New York dentist who had claimed his privilege not to answer questions about past associations. Ten days after that General Zwicker, the commanding officer of the dentist's former Army camp, was called to testify before the McCarthy sub-committee. And that, as all the world now knows, was the guerrilla episode that led to the famous 'memorandum of understanding,' or as some say the terms of surrender, between the Army of the United States and Senator McCarthy.

Inevitably there was standing room only in Washington yesterday when the sub-committee called Mrs. Annie Lee Moss, a middle-aged coloured woman, who was suspended by the Army Signal Corps after Senator McCarthy had described her as a 'code clerk' whose 'Communist record' was known to the Army. Mrs. Moss was a cafeteria worker who quietly told the sub-committee yesterday that she had never been in a code room in her life. Mr. Cohn tried to establish her personal connection with a staff member of the *Daily Worker*, but it turned out that the man she knew was a coloured man who happened to have the same name.

The audience was uncommonly ready with applause for Democratic committee members and Mrs. Moss's lawyer, whenever they protested at the tactics of Mr. Cohn. At one point Senator Stuart Symington, Democrat of Missouri, asked if she knew who Karl Marx was. 'Who's that?' she gravely asked, and the crowd laughed itself silly. When she finished her testimony and stepped down from the stand Senator Symington leaned into his microphone and angrily cried: 'I may be sticking my neck out but I think you are telling the truth. And if you're not taken back in your Army job, you come around and see me. I am going to see that you get a job.'

Senator McCarthy was mercifully absent from these rebellious proceedings because he was busy composing a broadcast reply to Adlai Stevenson's condemnation of him at Miami last Saturday, to the first outright attack made on him by a Republican Senator, Ralph Flanders of Vermont, and to a trenchant analysis of his methods televised to a national audience last Tuesday night by the celebrated American commentator, Edward R. Murrow, and sponsored by the Aluminum Corporation of America.

Senator Flanders on Tuesday vindicated the honour of the Republican party on the floor of the Senate by suddenly putting the rhetorical question: 'What party does he belong to? One must conclude that his is a one-man party, and that its name is McCarthyism, a title which he has proudly accepted.' Senator Flanders then launched into the first open attack on McCarthy by a Republican in this session of Congress. He said that McCarthy was diverting the attention of the nation away from 'dangerous problems' abroad and that he was 'doing his best . . . by intention or through ignorance to shatter the Republican party.' Next day President Eisenhower sent a letter of commendation to Senator Flanders and told his news conference that the Senator had done the country 'a service' by calling attention to 'the danger of us engaging in internecine warfare and magnifying certain items of procedure and right and personal aggrandizement.'

But it may be that the spark which has set off this fiery and so righteous explosion of popular indignation was laid, with deliberate courage, by Mr. Murrow. He came to great fame in America during the war through his broadcasts from London. He is a tireless news reporter and, in his weekly television dramatisation of the news, a consummate showman. Last Tuesday night Mr. Murrow gave over his whole half-hour to a pictorial analysis of 'McCarthyism' by projecting visual excerpts from the Senator's speeches and sessions of his subcommittee. It was McCarthy exposed by McCarthy, and Mr. Murrow added only the sparest narrative comment. But at the end, after the huge audience for this programme had seen McCarthy merciless, McCarthy jocular, McCarthy cunning, McCarthy sentimental, Mr. Murrow looked his audience in the eye and ended with these words:

'This is no time for men who oppose Senator McCarthy's methods to keep silent. Or for those who approve. We can deny our heritage and our history but we cannot escape responsibility for the result. There is no way for a citizen of the Republic to abdicate his responsibilities. As a nation we have come into our full inheritance at an early age. We proclaim ourselves – as indeed we are – the defenders of the free world, or what's left of it. We cannot defend freedom abroad by deserting it at home.

'The actions of the junior Senator from Wisconsin have caused alarm and dismay among our allies abroad and given comfort to our enemies. And whose fault is that? Not really his. He didn't create the situation of fear, merely exploited it, and skillfully. Cassius was right: "The fault, dear Brutus, is not in our stars, but in ourselves."'

These words were spoken with the blessing of the Aluminum Corporation of America, which has obviously a lot to lose by taking this stand. The response, however, of televiewers across the country has been a stunning endorsement of Mr. Murrow. So far the comments, by telephone, telegram, and letter, are running about fifteen to one in his favour. Hence the surprising rally of candour in public men who have stayed astutely silent for three years. Hence President Eisenhower's relieved approval of Senator Flanders. Hence a morning chorus of suddenly uninhibited newspaper columnists praising Murrow for 'laying it on the line.' Hence the confident laughter of the big audience at yesterday's sub-committee hearing. Hence the delayed righteousness of Senator Symington, of Missouri. Mr. Murrow may yet make bravery fashionable.

Billy Graham Comes to Babylon

March 10 and 17, 1955

Billy Graham is a deeply modest man. He never minded his obscurity in his native land. He had to wrestle with the devil all over Europe, draw crowds he never dreamed of, and receive a compliment from the Archbishop of Canterbury before it occurred to him that the Lord might be reserving the main bout for Madison Square Garden.

Last night he made it. He came for the first time into the arena of the immortals and took his place with them, with Joe Louis, and Al Smith, with the rodeo and Thomas Edmund Dewey, and the Ringling circus. His debut was held under the tested auspices of The Word of Life Hour, a network radio programme, a weekly offshoot of an established holy enterprise known as The Word of Life Fellowship, Inc. Fifteen years ago this now booming salvation industry had a kitty of only $300, and its original investors were a young couple who felt 'burdened to claim verses like' Jeremiah: xxxiii. 3: 'Call unto me, and I will answer thee, and shew thee great and mighty things.' To-day the weekly budget is a mighty $6,000, and last night's rally was the eighth the Fellowship has been prosperous enough to hold in Madison Square Garden.

But, in a sense, Billy Graham has not yet met the challenge of our town, of the neon-lit Babylon he longs to claim for the Lord. For his audience was built-in. And there was no exact way of knowing how many of the sailors from the Eighth Avenue saloons, the curious cab-drivers, the penitent delicatessen-owners, would have slipped in there if they had not been fairly sure of fusing their identity with a solid nucleus of the saved. It was apparent at once that the multitude was made up of anything but hungry heathens and vagrant Runyonites. They were 'smartly' dressed, as our English idiom has it, meaning they looked clean or tasteless in a respectable way. Some of the old men had an owlish earnestness, and many of the young were bridled colts, sweating with the guilt of delinquent fantasies they were here to prohibit. They all sat so prim and orderly, under three limp Old Glories and a white flag with a red cross, that the curving rows of seats and the dividing aisles were just as they appear in the seating plan. Unsmeared by foul tobacco or smoke or any of the fumes of sin, the air was crystalline, clear enough to count the faithful. *The New York Times* counted 22,000, the *Herald Tribune* 19,000, an Irish cop with his sights on Rome charitably guessed that the assembly of heretics ran to no more than 15,000.

But however many there were, the great bulk of them, it seemed to one sinner, were joyless matrons and their lumpish daughters. Not a smitch or smear of lipstick violated their well-pursed lips. Not a pretty girl or a roguish buck in the lot. But neither were they drab. There is something in the full-time practice of virtue that inclines the female of the species especially to hydrangea blue. It would take a complexion as blooded as Santa Claus and a skin tone as flashing as a Hawaiian to rescue the human face from such an ocean of ghastly blue. Ava Gardner herself would drown incognito in it. Not one, alas, of the grey-faced angels who sported it salvaged her features. They sat, row upon serried row, in a faceless sea, until the music started. Only the smiling ushers, all enrolled servants of The Word of Life Fellowship Inc., exercised that occupational cordiality they share with insurance agents and airline hostesses. It was they, and their similarly radiant brothers on the platform, who – as they say in secular circles only two blocks away – 'had the joint jumpin'.'

Came first Cliff Barrows, the song leader, a friendly professional greeter type with no more diffidence than a radio announcer. His conducting was a mere bow to custom, for the true believers had known these tunes since the day they saw the light and they took off on the upbeat and bellowed in remarkable unison and tunefulness through one majestic hymn by Haydn and two awful caterwaulings by Anon. Then we had your favourite and mine, Beverly Shea, the Graham team's travelling baritone, who modulates a voice of pleasing timbre with a breathing trick or two learned from Crosby. The show moved on as slickly as a Republican rally, the Word of Life quartet next gliding to the microphone. Four slim young men in blue coats and light slacks chanting 'I'm redeemed' in the old-time gospel tempo with crooning overtones. They were accompanied by a girl at an electric organ, and ever afterwards its throbbing tremolo hung on the air to soften the hard-hearted and sicken the musical.

Just before the great man stood up, a very pretty girl walked in, wearing a fitted grey silk blouse and a flaring black skirt that were mated by a twenty-inch waist. She had a Grace Kelly hair-do and a fetching pout, and the cop who piloted her in was as nonplussed as the scowling rows of angels. But she was some relative evidently of the radio technician supervising a tape-recorder and she naturally gravitated to the neutral compound of the press. She had no sort of connection with the official goings-on and was plainly so baffled by it all that she could be instantly discounted as non-union competition. She was joined a few minutes later by a second houri, a strawberry blonde in a black sheath. But by then Billy was in full cry, and if this couple had been hired as decoys of the Devil to test and strengthen the flock, it was a wasted effort. No one paid them any kind of attention, except the long-haired scribblers of the British press.

By Billy's express command there was no clap or salute when he rose. He welcomed them all to Jesus. He declared that Churchill and Eisenhower had both said that the only salvation of the Western world lay in a religious revival, 'and if our intellectual and political leaders say so we as Christians better be about it.' A stalwart coloured man in a port-side gallery let out a resonant 'Yeah!' But Billy turned his pained Apollonian profile, and the ushers dashed to smoke the man out. He never did it again; it was an echo of the honest orgies by the levees and the Mississippi baptisms long ago.

They showed no sign of trance, but maybe they knew that this was only the teaser. Billy would be back. For the present he wanted to say why he was here. New York might not be wickeder than any other place, but it was no better: 'Crime is rampant, juvenile delinquency is out of hand ... church attendance is below the national average.' He stood at a big redwood lectern (he called it a podium), a gift from the president of International Business Machines. It was, said Billy, equipped with 'all sorts of buttons and controls' that timed the speaker and flashed warning lights. The red light glowed, and Billy shrugged an admission that his time was up. At the barest flutter of applause he thundered:

'Every time I see my name up in lights, every time I am patted on the back ... it makes me sick at heart ... for God said He will share His glory with no man. So if you want to stop my ministry, pat *me* on the back.'

No one breathed. His lilting Southern voice rode the steady, well-tempered hum of the air conditioning. He was going to collect the expenses of his coming Scottish campaign. He was going, he said heartrendingly, to help to save Glasgow. There was a rustle and a clinking as many bodies leaned over to reach in their pockets, to dig deep for the unshriven souls of Glasgow.

The Word of Life quartet came back again, ripe now with a barber shop pathos. And again the electric organ spilled its treacly glissandos. It set the tone for a confessional by a former all-American football star, who wanted to know 'Who's coaching you in this great game of life?' The vast audience heaved in again with a mournful melody, wobbling over a wailing counterpoint, to the effect that 'On Christ, the solid rock, I stand; all other ground is sinking sand.'

At last it was time. Time for 'the message.' Time for Billy to give his all. Time, he said, for

'absolute silence, for thirty minutes, there must be no talking, no applause, no whispering, no movement anywhere, time that we have this like a sanctuary and a church service without a sound.'

He must be the only modern performer who can demand silence and get it.

He took from Luke: xiv the 18th verse: 'And they all with one consent began to make excuse.' It was a perfect text for his method, which is not, like the old Salvationists, to threaten hellfire and palpitate the audience with pictures of the brimstone sins, of lust and greed and lust especially, but to sympathise with the modern confusion of the ordinary decent man, to chide with a muscular paternal understanding the twentieth-century sinner: the lie-abed, the procrastinator, the fretted business man, the preoccupied breadwinner, the city dweller fearful of the hydrogen bomb.

'Sure, Billy,' he hears them whine. 'I'll come to Jesus, but not just now.' Meanwhile they go about their pestiferous 'business,' they get 'ulcers and all the other diseases.' To what end? 'Every fourth person here' – he intoned it like a curse – 'will be dead in ten years, if the law of averages works out. Dead!'

So how do we mortals spend our precious time? Yearning

for 'the riches of Wall Street, the gold of Fort Knox, all the pleasures of Hollywood?' Maybe not, but 'You've sold your soul for a little bit of it . . . You don't deny Christ in the flesh, but you won't stand up and accept him.' And you know why? Because 'with one consent they all began to make excuse.' And for why, what are you afraid of? What will the boys at the office say, the men on the football team, the girls in the block, 'what'll the crowd I run with think? Isn't that it?'

He knew there were 'hundreds of people here who have their names on a church list. On Sundays you have a halo around your head, and Monday morning the horns begin to grow.' Well, he was going to tell them, he was going to put it on the line. He had a man come to him and say, 'Billy, I'd have to give up my job. I can't become a Christian.' His job? A bartender. 'You surely can't, Brother, I said to him. And this man earned $45 a week. Well, the Devil couldn't buy *my soul* for forty-five lousy dollars a week.' He was going to tell them right now, to-night, because now was the time. He rocked with the accented syllables: 'You-can't-be-a-Christian-and-live-any-way-you-want-to.'

Amen, breathed a man down front, and a pink-cheeked usher fixed him with his eye. None of that, he seemed to say, none of the old-time vulgar gospel stuff. Where do you think you are, Little Rock, Arkansas? Well, sure enough, we were in Madison Square Garden, spacious and metropolitan, glistening with high floodlights, uniquely clean. We had a pulpit fashioned by International Business Machines, and a switchboard with lights clocking the schedule, and burring tape recorders, and a shepherd in double-breasted blue gabardine. But as he gets into his stride, he is seen to be treading out the vintage with the original God of Wrath. For though his Jesus is no black-browed, bearded Old Testament avenger, he is also not the 'weak, frail, effeminate' hero of the calendars. Billy routs the myth of the Pale Galilean, who he implies could conquer nothing and nobody in this vitamin-packed age. No, He must be put in training and brought up to date. Why, shouts

Billy, angry that the news is not yet an axiom, 'He was a real he-man, talk about your football players . . . He was physically the strongest man on earth.'

Billy is full of surprising information of this sort, and of free-ranging quotations of the words of Christ, of rescued admonitions and snappy warnings and rousing pep talks that must have got lost in all versions of the New Testament later than the Aramaic. It is this bulging image that excites him into something bordering on ecstasy. And now as he talks, and begins to crouch and gesture like a Friday-night football coach, his tenor voice hardens and he falls into a metrical sob. For all his microphone suavity and the gorgeous contour of his hair-do, he is one at last with the grizzled rustics who bark damnation over the hillbillies down by the river. And it is in his voice and tune and phrasing that the old Bible-thumping South claims its own.

'He was a man like you, but He was God. If the chisel should slip in the carpenter's shop, His blood was warm and red, warm like yours, brother, red like yours.' The unmistakable repetitions come in. ('I married a wife and therefore I cannot come. I married a wife. Brother, you got the best excuse right there.') The same over-and-over, syncopated phrasing of the blues. He threw his arms high to mime Christ on the Cross. And in the panting apostrophe of 'Je-sus!' phrased as three syllables, he was not far away from the strain of the Reverend Heck Mosby of Beale Street, Memphis, who used to stump up to his pulpit on a wooden leg, throw his arms high, and chant, 'O Lord, O Boss Man.'

What is modern and superior in his cunning, and it could be wholly unconscious, is the prohibition of all applause. He cages up his audience for thirty minutes and dangles red meat from outside. And when he finally braces his splendid biceps and bends the bars apart, where else can the sprung prisoners go but to him? They are demonstrably free to scatter, but they are just as visibly transfixed by the fear of the Saviour, who has been re-created in the image, however glamorous and clean-limbed, of Big Brother. This Jesus is a snooping, darting detective, spotting you in your mirror, riding in the Underground, watching at the foot of your bed, anticipating the waking excuse, posted at every exit of the Garden if you should dare to bolt for it. The jig is up, the sinners are told.

And when Billy cools off and drops his voice to a whisper, and begs the organ start up its artful gurgle, and says he will stand and pray and wait for the brave to come forward, there is only a momentary pause. And they burst the unbearable silence and shuffle up: the halt and the lame in spirit, surely, but also the pasty-faced, the mean, the careworn, a hangdog sailor, teenagers in desperation, a mountainous mother and her huge sullen daughter, regiments of the awkward and the unloved; and possibly, somewhere in here, a few humble souls holding fast, against all the foregoing seductions, to the mild Man of the New Testament, to that gentle Jesus, no athlete, who 'best to love is and most meek.' But how many have responded to 'the strongest man in the world,' the clean-limbed Superman, something not unlike the 6 ft. 4 in. Billy himself?

Decency will not stay for an answer. It is our time now, time to leave quietly, to exchange the electric organ and its gargling vox humana for the comparative wholesomeness of Eighth Avenue, with its movie houses and pawnshops, drugstores and bars, and cops on clanking horses. For the converted there will be hours, perhaps days or months of peace. For the others there was one flawless jewel to take away: Billy's grateful recollection of Cecil B. De Mille standing last summer on Mount Sinai and crying aloud to his minions — 'Cut out two tablets of stone and carve on them the Ten Commandments and give them to Billy Graham. And they carved out two stones and gave me the Ten Commandments.' Moses did no better.

Change in the Deep South

Jackson, Mississippi, April 28, 1955

The South is one of those kingdoms of the mind, like India or Scotland, that is neat and understandable only to people who have never been there. To the tourist it is that convalescent retreat from modern life that begins appetisingly enough, on the brink of the South, with Maryland's crabcakes. It sweeps down through blossoming cotton fields in which merry Negroes wave at the sleek diesel trains whose elegant travellers, picked exclusively from the pages of *Esquire*, will come to rest at sundown on the colonnade of an old mansion, presided over by a goateed colonel in a string tie dispensing mint juleps in the shade of a live oak tree heavy with Spanish moss.

To the French intellectual, the South is Faulkner's rich charnel-house of vengeance and decay. To the foreign business man, a rumour of shining new factories and low wages, a threat to textile towns everywhere from Massachusetts to Manchester. To the Northern liberal and UNESCO it is the hotbed of Gunnar Myrdal's *American Dilemma*, the complacent region recently described by a touring actor as 'nothing but sowbelly and segregation.' The Southern papers fumed for a day, and the actor's company toured no more.

In the railway stations, big and little, you still see two doors: 'White Waiting Room' and 'Colored Waiting Room.' Some of them are newly painted, to brighten the reminder that the Supreme Court's latest opinion is only a recommendation, not yet a Federal law. But on the train itself, a middle-aged coloured couple sit by day and sleep by night alongside the whites, in the same Pullman car. A detail, perhaps, but a symptom of the revolution already on the way. It is the terms of the social contract that have now to be worked out.

The old Southerners wait and watch and hope, not without guilt, to hit on some legal evasion that will keep the Negroes and the whites apart in school. Four states, at least, still hope to abolish the public school system, to reincorporate it again as a Negro school system entirely, and to charter all the white schools as 'private schools.' But the youngest generation of Southerners know it for what it is: a desperate expedient, the last stand of the old South.

This last paragraph, I realise with some chagrin, is typical of most of the writing that comes out of the North, and out of Washington, about the South. The North tolerates the Negro at its elbow on the bus, over the stove in the kitchen, in the mailing-room of the business office. He can boast up there the dignity of equal contact. But contact is not intimacy; and 'hired help' is not a family servant. The South is bored and angry by turns with the obsessive Northern view that the Negro is 'a social problem' which the South is too lazy or too reactionary to 'solve.' These are harsh, schoolmasterly terms which, like progressive textbooks on sex and marriage, reduce a difficult human relationship, an art at best, to the bloodless simplicity of a graph.

On the train, the steward of the club-car was taking his two-year-old son home from a visit to relatives. He was a tiny, rollicking toy that staggered into white knees, was taken off for a playful interval by a pretty white matron. He bit her ear and nuzzled in her bosom, while his father totted up the bills before the train came into the depot. It would have been an odd sight up North, with the supposedly more tolerant Northerners aghast at their own liberalism. Here it was nothing, a mild affectionate interlude in which all the men and women in the club-car, most of them Southerners, joined with gusto.

It is, I suspect, the Southerner's greater ease, and intimacy, with Negroes that stirs his anxieties about the new order. Where the taboos are tacitly understood on both sides, the affection can be free-ranging, the liberties more safely taken; and alas, the bullying meanness of the rural little Hitlers can express itself without fear of retaliation. Up North it is impossible to imagine a situation that I once ran across in Tallahassee, Florida, where a white man sued his friendly neighbour over some indignity to his coloured yard-man because 'he'd better learn he just can't treat my nigger that way.'

If the taboos, which protect the final intimacies, are now to be abolished, what sort of 'equal' society will replace the privileged inequality of a 300-year-old tradition? The overriding fear, which the gentlest Southerner will confess to only in private, is that of a new scale in which miscegenation leads to acceptable intermarriage and in time to a Southland whose blood-stream is as mixed as is Brazil's. The first signs of it are evident in those pioneering Southern universities where black and white students mix, at a time of life when the heyday in the blood is young. It is a sensible fear and only to be pooh-poohed by people whose daughter is unlikely to marry any male more exotic than a Bradford woollen merchant or an officer in the Coldstream Guards.

The mere act of writing this gives it a false, an almost ridiculous, emphasis in the actual life of the South. Inter-marriage is not on their minds, but it lies under their minds and jumps to the alert on unlikely occasions. Being struck for instance, by the extent of new housing projects for Negroes in several Southern cities, I commented to a garage owner that they were a good deal better than most of the new housing up North. He replied: 'Why, certainly. Ah see no reason why the Nigras shouldn't have just as good homes as anybody. Mah son thinks it's all right for 'em to go to the same schools and colleges. Ah cain't go that far, but we treat 'em pretty good down here. Just don't wanna eat and sleep with them, that's all.'

I quoted this speech to an imposing coloured woman, a mother of three, and a stalwart member of the parent-teachers' association. 'That's right,' she said, 'that's exactly the way we feel, too.'

Mr. Lippmann's First Quarter Century

May 8, 1956

It is a surprise to an Englishman visiting the United States to see that more and more the American papers, not least the tabloids, maintain a strict distinction between the news columns and the editorials.

Reporters who slog along behind Adlai, or mush with Estes, are likely to turn in very similar accounts of their expeditions, no matter whether their publishers are hot for Truman or still convalescing from the rampages of the hated Roosevelt. When an American reporter begins to mistake himself for a seer, or otherwise develops a taste for opining, he can do one of two things. He can grow grey in the service of the news, and hoard his adjectives against the day when he is promoted to the editorial page. Or he can quit and try his hand as a 'columnist.'

The signed column of comment and reflection is the last refuge in America of personal journalism. In the forty years since Don Marquis pretended to come in the office in the morning and file the thoughts of a pet cockroach that worked the night-shift on his typewriter, the American columnist has been all things to all men. Sometimes he is a genuine solo performer, a roving acrobat exploiting for his own audience a trick or two with the language; or like Art Buchwald, a man who sees every place and every problem of the globe with the wry unconcern of a permanently displaced G.I. Often he is a persuasive bigot, either of the Right or Left, who offers his publisher the chance to fulminate vicariously in language that would look too strong on the editorial page.

The columnists are by now a profitable by-product of the newspaper industry; and astute agents breed them like yearlings and sell them in strings for syndication to papers with lots of money and, presumably, no very strong thoughts of their own. In a recent cross-country jaunt, I read scores of papers which printed the most popular columnists of the day in every possible combination. In theory, the reader can discover the truth by hearing every side of a current argument. In practice, his confusion or stamina must be something remarkable.

Of this now venerable breed of journalist, the most singular is Mr. Walter Lippmann, who has just finished his first quarter-century of handing down the oracles and whose retirement would rob innumerable Americans of the most thoughtful and majestic political commentator of their time. There are said to be publishers and editorial writers who have Lippmann's copy flown in at dawn to ensure that their own subsequent versions of him shall preserve for their paper some reputation for judicial opinion. There are certainly admirals and Cabinet officers who bone up on him at breakfast in order to make some sense at the noon briefings in the Pentagon or the White House. His column has been called 'the one continuous act of cerebration' in American daily journalism. And this compliment is just in conveying that though Lippmann's pieces, like those of any self-respecting journalist, are complete in themselves, they are each an interim report on the unending complexities of politics, successive brave stabs at the obscure verities of power, justice, and good government that have boggled philosophers from Plato to Toynbee.

This approach is more familiar in English literary and political comment, and it is doubtful if Lippmann's huge number of readers appreciates the novelty of his disinterestedness any more than they would a close imitation of it. Lippmann is now in his sixties and so much of a national institution that parodies of his grave and speculative style are frequent. They are, all the ones that I have seen, crude stuff: side-swipes at a pompous judge, full of hedging qualifications, open gibes at the sort of teetering, on-the-one-hand, on-the-other-hand mind which passes so often among soldiers, lawyers, professors, and research students for the very act of scholarship. These lampoons miss their mark not because they are crudely done but because they are irrelevant to Lippmann's cast of mind; which is that of a genuine inquirer with no axe to grind, a pioneer researcher who uses great knowledge of the past as a handy but treacherous guide to the present.

There is more of the forest ranger about him than the plant collector, and more of the sceptical judge than either. He takes a lot of kidding with ease and good humour, for he has been a prodigy since childhood and learned to accommodate himself with good grace to that off-hand deprecation, bordering on scurrility, which is the mediocre newspaperman's form of envy.

He was born of the well-to-do offspring of German-Jewish immigrants. The best schools, private libraries, regular trips to the Louvre and Salzburg, a brilliant record at Harvard were matters of course. So, in his younger days, which rumbled with the machinery of sweatshops, the cannon-fire of the Fabians, and the growing pains of American labour, was his early conversion to socialism. He worked, like Attlee, in settlement houses, became a leg-man for the muck-raking Lincoln Steffens, and then a secretary to a Socialist mayor in Schenectady. After two years' daily contact with the grimy politics of city precincts, and the bewilderment of the poor, he decided that Marx was a bad prophet and that there was something 'monotonously trivial' and self-serving about the intellectual's condescension to the working-man. He took at an early age the mature, if unpopular, decision that the intellectual's front line is the war of ideas. Ever since then his critics have seen in his serenity, his sometimes Olympian detachment from the American ferment, a meek retreat into the library and a tractable world of well-groomed ideas and books that do not kick.

But one man's library is another man's battlefield, and Lippmann is more self-searching in the presence of his books and the surrounding silence than a strike-breaker heading for the enemy's factory. In the First World War and after he made famous contributions to the clarifying of labour relations in the Secretary of War's office, he was the secretary of the committee that drafted for President Wilson his Fourteen Points. He has turned out a classic paper on banking policy.

About thirty years ago he conceived the 'trusteeship' system adopted in 1945 by the United Nations. But these were not sallies into 'practical politics' to relieve the imputed guilt of his retreat to writing and brooding. They were the useful fruit of that retreat. It is not so lonely a place as his detractors would like to think. He never has to go after the news, in the mechanical Washington fashion, because so often the news comes to him. He must be the only Washington newsman whose invitation to lunch is accepted as a command by generals, judges, Air Force strategists, and Presidential candidates.

When they are gone he settles to his daily routine, which is as strenuous and unvarying as a professional heavyweight in training for a championship bout. He goes over the column he has written in the morning. He meets – as only the most scrupulous do – the daily temptation to 'coast' on his style, to let his working vocabulary do the thinking for him. He struggles with his memory, his historical analogies, and his conscience. He weighs the justice of this phrase and that. Although innumerable swine will use these pearls to wrap tomorrow's fish, he lets his essay go from him at last as reluctantly and hopefully as if it were a State paper. Sometimes it is.

Segregation Above the Line

Cincinnati, Ohio, May 10, 1956

Let us begin with two respectable clichés which may be none the less true for being familiar. Asia and Africa have waked up and read the Declaration of Independence and found to our chagrin that we declare 'all men are created equal.' Secondly, 'integration' is not a Southern problem exclusively but a challenge to all of the United States to transform the Negro from a traditional servant, a cheap labour pawn, a licensed clown and entertainer into a citizen with equal rights and opportunities before the law.

Having said so much, the Northern liberal, the parson, and civic leader heave a Christian sigh for the benighted South and return with few misgivings to a community life in which the Negro, while technically integrated, is restricted to live in the poorest sections of town, to work at certain well-understood menial jobs, occasionally to enjoy the unreal freedom of a university life, and then to work with whites on a professional level as a marked oddity. In the North the Negro troubles no white man's conscience, since he can be hired and fired as a labour commodity like any other man. In the South he is a ward of a dying tradition of noblesse oblige, a dependant whom the family has deserted. Hence the Northerner, having written laws quietly honoured in the breach, is not nagged by shame for the Negro as a special type of the poor. In the South the Negro's new revolt against old taboos – the separate railway waiting-room, the rear of the bus, the separate school and park – leaves the Southern white dismayed by the abandonment of an old code which, in acknowledging his superiority, allowed familiarities that would astonish a Northerner.

Up to May 17, 1954, the Supreme Court of the United States had cushioned the Southerner's mode of life with the 60-year-old doctrine that the intent of the Constitution, of its Fourteenth Amendment in particular, was to provide 'separate but equal' facilities for education, recreation, and the like. On that day Chief Justice Warren handed down a revolutionary majority opinion to the effect that 'separate but equal' was not enough, that the Negro should go to school with the white. In subsequent rulings the Court has said, and the Interstate Commerce Commission has echoed it, that the Negro should use the same trains and buses as an equal and have equal access to parks, swimming pools, restaurants, theatres, and every other public facility of social life. Since that day, Justice Warren, formerly thought to be no more than an amiable and conservative governor of California, has replaced the late

Justice Holmes in the liberal pantheon. And in the South, where these distinctions were ancient and most keenly preserved, he could not – as a man in Richmond, Virginia, put it – 'run for dog-catcher.' Warren's law, as it is sometimes known in the South, has caused a breeze of pride to blow through the North and an ill wind through the South.

On the maps illustrating segregation customs there is an irregular thick line, running from the south-west border of Texas up to the southern border of New Jersey in the east. It is the line dividing the presumably virtuous North from the sinning South and the wobbling Border states. The 'problem states' are seventeen in number and the District of Columbia is usually added to them. The distinction is a fair one in that it sets apart the great north-east–south-west arc of the country that had laws before 1954 requiring the segregation of Negroes and whites in school. It is misleading in implying that the North lives by a very different tradition. There are many cities of the North which, alarmed by a great influx of Negroes into war-time defence jobs, grew just as eager as Alabama to keep them apart, and achieved strict segregation by iron housing laws and procedures.

Cairo, Illinois, has had a statute on the books since 1874 prohibiting segregation in the public (i.e. the state-financed elementary and high) schools. The law was quietly ignored for seventy-eight years. In 1952, after a brush with the National Association for the Advancement of Colored People (hereafter called the N.A.A.C.P.), and a spurt of public violence, the school board allowed a few Negroes to enroll in white schools, but segregation is the rule. The controlling fact is the same as in the cities of Alabama or Mississippi and Georgia: one-third of the population is coloured. Evansville, Indiana, is another such place which has successfully evaded a 1949 state law requiring complete integration of the schools by 1954. So far about nine per cent of the Negroes go to school with whites.

The Northerner claims that these are aberrations from the decent norm, and that at least the law does not sanction them.

The Southerner, quoting impressive statistics from Los Angeles, Chicago, Philadelphia, and New York, retorts that, sanction or no sanction, they are the inevitable reflex in any place where the proportion of Negroes is high. The rule of thumb, confirmed by the recent *New York Times* survey on segregation, is that integration is harder where there are many Negroes, easier where there are few. The inference must be that in a white society many Negroes constitute an actual or imagined threat to the white man's ease, his sense of power, his control of the job market, and – say the psychologists – his sexual aplomb.

As a law of behaviour this is an important fact. As a conclusion it is too simple. There are other conditions, of geography, social myth, or economic life, that incline a community to the Southern practice. They explain why Cincinnati is the dateline for this first article. It is a solid province of the old Taft domain, Midwestern, conservative, self-reliant. But it lies just north of the Ohio River. Its prosperity has always depended on the river traffic to the south and on a firm alliance with the Southern business men who shipped in the raw materials to manufacture. Its official policy for many decades has been to mix the races in the schools. Its actual practice follows strict segregation in housing. All children must go to school in their own school districts. The well-defined white and coloured sections of town ensure that nearly ninety per cent of the Negroes go to coloured schools. In this way, 'a Northern town with a Southern exposure' need not blush to claim that it is abiding by the Court's order.

How dour is the resistance to integration when it is compelled by law may be seen in small rural towns like Hillsboro, Ohio, where the parents of twenty-one Negro children resolutely led their offspring past the ramshackle coloured school to the handsome white school, and just as resolutely have been turned away every day since September, 1954, while the school board awaited the outcome of its appeal against the Supreme Court order. It has taken nearly two years for the board to see

(85)

its hopes lifted by the state courts and dashed by the United States Appeals Court and at last by the United States Supreme Court's refusal to review the case. It still hoped to postpone the dreadful day by asking the local Federal judge for a specific order. When he incontinently issued it, the board feared first for the suffocation of its pupils, if 21 were added to 850, and then decided that the new-comers, possibly grown stupid in their two years' absence from the schoolroom, would first have to pass an entrance examination. They reckoned without Imogene Curtis, one of the coloured parents, who had privately tutored the children throughout the siege. The papers, the children thought, were not too difficult. And in mid-April the school board gave in.

This example is protected from national publicity by the general assumption of news editors in the North and West that such things happen only in the South. It was one I happened to stumble on while I was here. By luck, my travels took me for a day or two into Michigan, where it was even more of a shock to hear that three cities at least – Dearborn, Wyandotte, and Royal Oak – boast of forbidding any Negroes at all to live within their city limits. Add to this the news that a Northern Governor, a doughty Democratic liberal, recently refused to go south to talk to a segregated audience but spoke in Dearborn with a good conscience, and one begins to see that not the least galling element of the South's ordeal is the offhand complacency of the North.

The Untravelled Road

Montgomery, Alabama, June 7, 1956

Twenty years ago the interest of anyone coming from England in the Southern 'back country' was with the music, the vernacular, and the general pathos of the Negro. On any blinding summer afternoon he could come on a fat coloured wench pausing from the chore of cotton-picking to throw her head high at the sun and whine 'Go down, Ol' Hannah, don't you rise no mo'.' In the scruffy parts of towns he would sit deeply satisfied in dark corners of saloons while bent-over pianists beat out the immortal twelve-bars of the blues. If he was lucky he could go down to Storyville, in New Orleans, at sundown and hear half-naked slatterns reduce their lot to poetry by crooning, from behind the swinging door of their cribs: 'I ain't good lookin' and ma hair ain't curled, but my mother taught me somepn gonna carry me through this world.'

His interest was rarely political in those days, for the New Deal had conveniently shouldered the burden of the poor. There was the C.C.C. for shiftless boys, the W.P.A. for idle hands of any colour, the Government's promise of the 'more abundant life' for all who were heavy-laden. When that the poor had cried, Roosevelt had wept. It was a very satisfactory state of things for those who, having an English background, were artistic connoisseurs of someone else's tragedy. The New Deal was, if we had had the gumption to see it, a menace to this attractive view of the lowly. On his next visit to New Orleans he was apt to find the whores' cribs destroyed, the last transoms of the old sporting houses all pulled down, Basin Street itself turned into a housing project.

To-day his motives would be quite different for seeking out Montgomery's darktown. Twenty years ago he accepted the 'white' and 'colored' signs everywhere as a natural distinction which even Roosevelt would not change. To-day he would be here to see how it was with an embattled city whose whites, mobilised in a Citizens' Council 15,000 strong, were sworn to resist the Supreme Court's order to abolish these distinctions, to send children of any colour to school together, to allow a Negro to sit where he will on a bus or a train. The Negroes of Montgomery were now in the fifth month of their boycott of the city's buses. Useless for the bus company to heed a Circuit Court ruling in South Carolina and order its drivers to seat all passengers as equals. The city commission forbade the change, and the Negroes were enjoying their martyrdom too much to accept a victory by compromise. Some of them walked to work, as to the Crusades. Most were picked up by car-pools. When they were downhearted the militant faithful swarmed, so I heard, to the Mount Zion African Episcopal Methodist Church on Holt Street, to be fortified by the words of thirty-five coloured pastors, most of all by their leader, the Rev. Martin Luther King, Jr.

So I pushed open the doors of the railway station ('White Waiting Room') and hailed a cab and gave the address: '657 South Holt.' The driver dropped me off two blocks away ('Just so you won't be too conspicuous') and when I turned into this frowzy street I heard the blues again. They were coming in spurts from the juke-boxes of small saloons and lunch-counters. Then one of the screen-doors would slam back on its springs again and muffle the licentiousness within.

Even at the church the rhythm of it hung on the air, softened and slowed by religious ardour, no doubt, yet the same minor chords and the same heaving melancholy. It came from five or six hundred people, blacker than the night around them, sitting forward with their hands bunched on their knees. They made little movement and were the best-dressed Methodist audience it has ever been my lot to see. But they were joined in God by memories of long ago, when they wore no clothes at all. Far off, under a brown-painted Gothic window, a sister was 'testifying,' standing and improvising a prayer in many a King James sentence changed through the uvula in strangulated quarter-tones. She went on as long as the spirit moved her, and then a man near me got up and cried, 'Oh, Lord, oh Lord, stay close at hand when my time is come.' Between each solo phrase and incantation the congregation surged in with a mass humming, of the four classic chords of the blues, the Devil's music.

This went on for over an hour before 'Old-Time Religion' was sung as a battle-cry and there was a rustle of people at a side door, and the leaders came out. The Rev. Sims, the Rev. Hays, the Rev. Powell. The Rev. Sims appealed for steadiness 'in travelling this untravelled road.' To put it bluntly, they needed more drivers. The Rev. Powell counselled patience, for 'you can't hurry God.' There was many an obedient 'Yeah' at this, but when they were told that station-wagons had been bought from out of town and would soon be coming in they let out a salvo of applause, and when the Rev. King came forward it was like the Relief of Mafeking.

The leaders, he said with solemnity, had written a constitution for the cause, and he would now submit it to them. He took it in his hand and read it aloud. So far, the only English we had heard had come from the source and textbook of all their peace on earth: from the Bible itself, the only book doubtless that many of them had ever read. Now we were to hear from the Rev. King, an educated man.

This great movement had started, he said, 'without the external and internal attachments in terms of organisational structure.' They listened in awe. If they or their children came to be 'integrated' they too could get to write like this. The Rev. King was indeed a master of Pentagon, or Federal, prose, and the constitution was written almost wholly in it. It was 'implemented' with eight committees, staffed by the leaders, and was heady with executive boards, trustees, public relations committees, provisions for tenure of office, just like General Motors. Its first article was a declaration 'to ensure respect for the dignity of the individual with respect to transportation.' This document was heard in a marvelling silence. And when he had finished the Rev. King hardly paused for a 'moved' and a

(89)

'seconded' to declare the constitution received, approved, and adopted.

Though there had been some violence after the first of these rallies, and a couple of coloured homes burned, the whites now accept them like revival meetings. Before the first one, in December, Mr. Bagley, the bus company's manager, was warned to dissuade his son, a war veteran, from opening up a gas station on the edge of darktown. Mr. Bagley, on the contrary, cornered a coloured friend and suggested that the Rev. King might announce the new ownership in the middle of the rally. So he did, and the Negroes rolled off in droves afterwards to christen the new pump. Eighty per cent of young Bagley's business to-day is from coloured folk filling up their tanks to maintain the boycott of his father's buses. Such is the temper of the 'fight' between the resigned whites and the sassy Negroes of Montgomery, Alabama.

With a final prayer and a rolling hymn, this meeting broke up in ecstasy and good order. I was off down the street as the congregation rose, and a saloon door swung open and let out two Negroes. 'You goin' back home now, boy—' 'Why, sure,' shouted the other, walking fast, 'my old lady weighs two hunnerd and eighty pounds. Man, that's an awful lot of woman.' He cackled insanely, and the bad people went on dancing the blues inside the seedy saloons. And the good people came down the church steps and went home to bed, to strengthen themselves against an early rising, the smooth running of the car-pools, the determination never to faint or yield in upholding the Rev. King, staying off the buses, and so giving glory to God.

The Roman Road

New Orleans, Louisiana, June 14, 1956

It has been 153 years since Napoleon sold Louisiana to the United States. But the French heritage is diffused over innumerable family and street names and concentrated in the shuttered houses, the pink and grey and blue-painted houses of the Vieux Carré. In a garden restaurant here, the waiter strikes a bell and salutes a statue of Bonaparte before he serves a snifter of Napoleon brandy.

If France is vivid in the shapes, names, and smells of the French Quarter, Rome too is a haunting presence: in the Christ figures that dominate the entrance to so many colleges, in the murmurs that float from the Cathedral and sift through the tropical foliage of Jackson Square, in the silent padding of nuns. Some of these nuns are as black as their habits, and the sight of them brings up in a tantalising form the attitude of the Catholic Church towards the Supreme Court's ruling that the segregation of white and coloured school-children must now be considered unconstitutional. Since the Constitution forbids the establishment of a State religion, the Court's order to integrate the public schools is not binding, now or ever, on the Roman Catholic parochial or private schools. Yet the Church has taken a stand hardly less absolute than the National Association for the Advancement of Colored People. The Catholic Committee of the South has set up a commission on human rights whose aims are in bold contrast to those of many a well-wishing citizens' group organised among the laity, and by the Protestant churches, up North. 'We are embarrassed Catholics,' its charter says, and 'the commission is a temporary committee working for its own dissolution.'

The archdiocese of New Orleans is a vast and complicated one, containing half a million Catholics, more than in nine other Southern states together. It has seventy white parishes and fourteen Negro parishes, the pastor of each being responsible for the school, the church hall, and the gymnasium. There are private schools run by different orders. The Jesuits run some superior high schools. There are Negro high schools that answer neither to the parish nor the Archbishop. The Archbishop could certainly lay claim to an embarrassment of local conditions that would justify a long delay, lest a blanket order work injustice on black and white minorities and rudely compel a social revolution in one place that was no more than a social convenience in another.

But for twenty years Archbishop Rummel has been moving with much deliberation towards a declaration of Catholic principle that is now irrevocable. In a famous pastoral letter, read in all his churches in March, 1953, he wrote: 'Let there be no further discrimination or segregation in the pews, at the communion rail, at the confessional and in parish meetings, just as there will be no segregation in heaven.' In another letter last February he went on to announce that 'racial segregation is immoral.' He is an old, blind man speaking only for the Catholic communion of souls, but he has come to share the conclusion of Justice Harlan's celebrated dissent of 1896, that 'the Constitution is colour-blind.'

There are Catholic members of the White Citizens' Councils, which are organised to perpetuate segregation by all means short of violence. But they have been warned by the Archbishop's stand and they take no lead. When three Catholic candidates for the Louisiana legislature suggested that the Catholic schools be brought under the state government, the archdiocesan newspaper reminded Catholics who encouraged the passing of laws that would restrict the dominion of the Church that they might 'under certain conditions . . . incur excommunication.' In the deep ordeal of the South, it is hard to imagine a more exquisite agony than that of sincere white Catholics bred for two centuries in the Southern ways of life.

The Archbishop is sympathetic to this turmoil and, not expecting the millennium or even human redemption by Monday morning, allows for peaceful controversy as a necessary 'purging of the conscience.' Yet the Church has no doubt how the controversy must be settled and for many years has been preparing for the fundamental change. It has encouraged integration 'from the top down,' that is to say first in universities and colleges, then in the high schools. It has shrewdly presumed that even segregationists would consider the mass too solemn a thing, and a sport event too trivial, to bicker about. So fifteen per cent of the Negroes in white parishes have been attending mass at white churches since 1934. Mixed basketball is now a regular thing.

The Jesuits have long been active in promoting interracial councils and getting race relations discussed in parents' clubs, parish meetings, societies pledged to certain devotions. A year ago the Archbishop appointed a committee of clerics and laymen to canvass the sentiment about integration in every unit of the Catholic population. It discovered that the urban parishes were for it, and the country parishes fearfully against it. It discovered much else. 'I am sorry to tell you,' sighed a Jesuit father, 'that the real prejudices of Catholics are no different from those of non-Catholics.' It had to recognise that there is an epidemic of illiterate ideas, which lead a flourishing underground life among some very reputable people: that integrated schools would greatly increase syphilis and illegitimacy and eventually lower the intelligence quotient of white children.

Instead of dismissing these shibboleths, the Church called in psychiatrists, criminologists, bacteriologists, and statisticians to test them scientifically. The results were scattered far and wide among 4,000 Catholic leaders in the form of 130,000 pieces of literature. They are simple handbills that report such home truths as: '1. Income, nutrition, and schooling are the principal factors which account for intelligence differences . . . 2. In the old Army tests, some Northern Negroes scored higher than some Southern whites . . . 3. The bodies of all human beings are composed of units called cells . . . in the cells are chromosomes. Arranged on the chromosomes are unchanging and unblending particles called genes . . . each corresponding cell, regardless of race, has the same number of chromosomes . . . 4. In more than 80,000 investigated cases of venereal disease, there has not been a single case of transmission by inanimate objects . . . 5. Cities which have integrated schools have a lower incidence of venereal disease than cities with segregated school systems.'

The strength of the Church's attitude is in the realism with which it has addressed itself to the hidden but powerful prejudices of Southern whites, the unmentionable forces of tradition. And the importance of its attitude for the whole country is that here is a political issue on which the Catholic Church refuses to argue with the Communists when they are right. It is cutting the ground out from under the Citizens' Councils, the sullen poor whites, the outraged country clubs, who hope to freeze the South in its ancient tracks with the chilling rumour that the Communists are behind the N.A.A.C.P. Such people are frustrated by the position of the Church. They know it, and the language they use here about Archbishop Rummel is terrible to hear. In the echo of their protests, one catches a furious whining admission that the Church may well be the rock on which ultimately all respectable opposition to integration in the South will splinter and crumble.

Look Away, Dixie Land

Jackson, California, June 21, 1956

'State 49' is the well-named highway that runs from north to south through the charming foothills of the Sierras over the Mother Lode, the 120-mile ledge of rock laced with gold that the Forty-Niners panned and plundered and abandoned. One day there was nothing there but the sensuous hills and the live oaks studded on them as in a tapestry design. Next week two or three thousand Yankees, Chinese, Frenchmen, Scots, Swiss, Russians, and Cornish Cousin Jacks came dropping from the snowy passes of the Sierras and lined the streams with wash-bowls on their knees.

To-day the mine shafts rise like rotting redwoods through high weeds. The waterwheels are circles of rust, the rivers run clear again, and nothing hangs over them but the cypresses. The main streets of these ghost towns wobble downhill to wooden hotels with overhanging balconies. There are still some shuttered banks barred by protective iron doors. There are worn plaques with the legend 'Wells, Fargo Company.' And in hilly graveyards a hundred such violent reminders of the heyday as: 'Hans Schmidt, Stuttgart geboren, brutally Murdered, Chinese Camp, May 10th, 1850.'

There are always, as everywhere in the West, the terse poems of the place-names. North of here is Placerville, El Dorado, Fiddletown, Fair Play, Indian Diggins, Michigan Bar, Newcastle, and Penryn. To the south Shinbone Creek, Angels Camp, Murphys, Copperopolis, Chinese Camp, Mount Bullion, Coarsegold, Bogus Thunder, and Lazy Man Canyon. Three miles west is the puzzle of Ione, which is not a Spanish relic but a name clutched from the nearest book (it was Bulwer-Lytton's *Last Days of Pompeii*) when the state refused to accept the town's true name as a postal address. It used to be Bedbug.

In a state with 1,200 new residents every day, the Gold Rush begins to sound like a Boy Scouts' expedition. And after a civic din over San Francisco's juvenile delinquency, and 2,000 university students surging into women's dormitories on a 'panty raid,' it seems a little antiquarian to go dredging for hundred-year-old relics of violence and vice in the Mother Lode.

What drove me out here was a thunderclap from the gold-fields, a true brazen echo of the great days heard in the testimony, before a grand jury in May, 1955, of a lady known alternatively as Dixie Dixon or Anna Beatrice Caplette. She is the last of a distinguished trio of bawdy-house madams that included also two departed sisters called Snow White and Tugboat Annie Schultz. She was, as the detective writers say, 'the state's key witness' in an investigation of local customs that led up to a raid on an unpretentious frame house at the end of March.

The chief of police had sat on the stand through a hot and easygoing day, and the gist of his testimony was that he had seen no evil and thought none. He was too busy most of the time checking the parking meters on Main Street. He was followed by a three-hundred-pounder, a barrel of a man, Constable Gildo Dodero, whom an associate madam had accused of guiding visitors to the houses of dubious fame. To every such aspersion he chuckled and stroked his thigh and allowed, 'That's just great; that's a good one.' Came next the mayor, a plumber who had professionally obliged the madams by keeping their houses in excellent repair. At last the jurors and restless townsfolk got what they were waiting for, the memorable testimony of Dixie.

Dixie is a penitent now, the humble manager of a little café at Aptos, far away on the Coast road. But in 1949 she had a telephone call 'from a nice young girl who used to work for me in a house in Sonora.' The girl was having trouble making a living in a run-down house in Jackson. Dixie saw her duty plain. 'I wasn't busy at the time, I'd retired,' she told a rocking courtroom, 'but in respect to a girl who worked so long and faithfully for me I said okay.' She crossed the Valley and took one look at the girl's house and told her she 'would have to get operating in real style.' This called for 'renovations' and that called for sympathetic patronage from the chief of police. 'So he came over and we began to talk business.' The 'business' included hiring seven carpenters and an understanding whereby the chief would come around 'on the first and third Saturdays of each month to collect $125 a month.' Dixie thought this an equitable arrangement, but she told the Court of the shock to her ethical standards when 'I was also informed by the chief that the house would have to donate to the Community Chest, the Red Cross, the Boy Scouts, as well as wakes and weddings.' The going rate was $25 per wedding of the constabulary, or their kith and kin.

Dixie sighed briefly but admitted that a good sport and citizen gets used to the hardships of inflation. She looked genuinely upset to have to tell on the town of her roaring days and assured the jurors that the carpenters who came 'banging around, building additions on the front and sides of the places' were all local men. 'I did all my trading,' she swore, 'in Jackson. We had Jackson lumber, Jackson nails, Jackson faucets' (supplied by the mayor).

When her testimony was done the courtroom groaned and the grand jury hearing was all but over. It took only a couple of days to bring in the indictments and get out the warrants. The entire police force, three men to be sure, was charged with perjury, the accepting of bribes, or – as a worthy newspaper heir to Mark Twain put it – 'inability to recognise a prostitute at twenty paces.' The chief was hit with the more serious charge of having 'willfully and corruptly' failed to close the houses. Consequently, Jackson woke up one Saturday morning to find the officers of law and order technically in the clink.

This would never do, and the mayor signed a waiver of their shame and put them back on duty till another force of moral guardians could be chosen. The last I saw of them they were diligently patrolling Main Street looking for motorists – prurient tourists by this time – whose parking meters registered a violation. It was a critical day for Jackson, but the cops did not flinch under their heavy cloud. Obviously crime must be made to pay.

The town settled back into the dust of its past. The brisk ladies of the Women's Club issued from their headquarters opposite the County Courthouse and stared at it with all the candour of the hard-working pianist in the song who doesn't know what's going on upstairs.

It was an episode merely and no more suggested a permanent lapse into Gomorrah than a morning shudder of the San Andreas fault, on which much of California precariously slumbers, threatens again the catastrophe of the 1906 earthquake. But, like such small tremors, it was a reminder that the pristine soul of California only sleepeth, that if it tries hard enough Jackson can recapture in a day and a night the spirit of the gaudy days, when it decided to become the Amador County seat by the simple device of raiding the capital town of Double Springs and locking up the county officials in a saloon long enough to swipe the records and strong-boxes from the county clerk's office. Ten years later, an election made it legal.

Making a President

Chicago, Illinois, August 12, 1956

In the confident dawn of the first Federal Government it was assumed that the man best qualified for President would appear as certainly as the North Star. Washington to Adams to Jefferson to Madison to Monroe was the august and acceptable line of what has been called 'the Virginia dynasty.' After that the succession was challenged, and since all great men of affairs, in the enlightened little kingdom of the Atlantic seaboard, were in Congress, the custom grew of letting the Congress choose the Executive. It was a habit radically at variance with the growing realities of a new form of government, in which the Executive, the Legislative arm, and the Courts were separate in function and in leadership.

In 1808 a Mr. Bradley of New York had the offhand inspiration to call a party caucus of the Republicans (later renamed, to confound the English, Democrats) 'to nominate suitable persons as candidates for the office of President and

Vice-President.' It nominated James Madison. John Quincy Adams detested the invention because 'it still places the President in subservience to Congress.' Nevertheless, it was a move towards the direct choice by the people's representatives, and Mr. Bradley's extra-legal audacity was forgiven for the usual American reason: it worked. It turned into the nominating convention when the breaking of the frontier threw up powerful regional leaders who dominated their States on the home ground and did not relish shrinking to little fish in the big pool of Congress. Sooner or later the Congress had to face the rather awful fact, anticipated and spurned by the Founding Fathers, and consequently never mentioned in the Constitution, that Americans would develop rival political parties, even as the benighted Europeans; but, unlike the Europeans, these parties would function on a national scale, apart from the work of Congress in remote Washington. From this recognition sprang the sturdiest and most original of American political institutions, which to-day summons 1,372 party workers from every county in the nation to participate in a chess tournament disguised as a circus.

The nominating convention is the only American parliament, and its feverish but subtle life lasts only for about five days. Having laboured and delivered the candidate, it goes into hibernation for four years, but will surely spring up again in the summer of 1960, clattering in its accustomed armour of rhetoric to hide its usual Italianate cunning. Its whole purpose is to win the November election battle, not to choose the most chivalrous general. All discussion, rumours, and weighing of rival candidates in terms of statesmanship, moral character, or political wisdom are suddenly very academic in the convention city. To the delegates, the farmers, lawyers, county chairmen, small bankers, labour union organisers, road commissioners, trucking company managers, ward heelers, precinct captains, feminists, and local 'characters,' the leader they yearn for is a man who has the knack of getting votes. Stevenson's eloquence simply gave a burnish to the well-remembered fact that in 1948 he had won more votes in Illinois in running for the Governorship than Harry Truman did for the Presidency. In 1948, Thomas Dewey defied the strong prejudice against nominating a man who had lost last time because in the off-year elections of 1946 he had swept into the Governorship of New York with a record majority.

The ideal candidate has been precisely defined by Professor D. W. Brogan as 'male, Gentile, white, Protestant, from a large and doubtful state,' preferably a Governor, almost always a man who has not come from the Congress. Governors start with powerful advantages. They have whole granaries of patronage at their disposal. The details of their administrative skill do not usually fan far beyond their own borders, so that they become in the popular imagination reasonable, fair-minded – that is to say, pliable and uncommitted – men. It is curious to see how, every four years, the Washington correspondents start considering the chances of this senator and that. A Washington man is naturally close to the political parties as legislative instruments. However, the choice of the nation's chief executive is not the privilege of Congress but of the brief Parliament whose power testifies, by the act of a resounding assertion, to the vitality of party life in the three thousand counties of the United States. These men, who compose the delegations and have their finest hour on the day of balloting, are the last to equate a political party with its elected representatives in Congress. They have long held to the prejudice that a United States Senator is almost disqualified *de facto* as a Presidential candidate.

A Senator is a committed man. He has given terrible hostages to a Presidential fortune. He has taken up positions and registered his vote, on foreign policy, race issues, the tariff, immigration, all the things that may succour one region of the country and offend another. Also, as a practical matter when you are looking for a leader who is also the keeper of the Federal payroll, a Senator is a man whose powers of patronage are very modest compared with those of a Governor. Only two

Senators have made the White House this century, and both of them were freaks. Harding was pulled from the bottom of the barrel as a malleable weakling when the two strong contenders refused to agree which one would settle for the Vice-Presidency. Truman was dictated by Roosevelt as a compromise Vice-President to mollify the convention's distrust of Wallace, and death alone, not the convention, crowned him.

Next time or the time after, the convention will no doubt give the lie to this rule, for it is part of the system's maddening fascination that no two conventions are exactly alike and that, as Freud said about human conduct, the unthinkable is always likely to happen. No Democrat has been nominated from the South since the Civil War. At the moment, this prejudice seems as inviolable as did the seventy-year-old habit of never nominating a man who could not win a majority of the delegates from his own State – until Franklin Roosevelt broke it in 1932. No man has ever come to the convention as an obscure worker for a Titan and displaced him as the candidate; no man, that is, except James Garfield, who began as the floor manager for the mighty Senator John Sherman and ended up, even after protesting against the placing of his name in nomination, as the President.

What is not disputed, by the forty or fifty men who do the serious business of the convention, is that everything decisive is done behind the scenes and in the precious scheming pause between ballots. The absent politico, no matter how powerful, is impotent at a distance. Perhaps the crucial convention anecdote is that of David Davis, Lincoln's manager, sweating for the soul of Pennsylvania with an industrialist who controlled the state's delegation. The man agreed to arrest the swing to Seward and go for Lincoln if he could be promised a Cabinet post. Some such suggestion was telegraphed to Lincoln and he wired back: 'Make no bargains for me.' The tycoon thought the deal was off until Mr. Davis, looking askance at the telegram, said: 'Hell, we are here and he is not.' The man got his Cabinet post, without – the biographers are desperate to insist — Lincoln's prior knowledge of the deal. And Lincoln was the nominee and the President.

This story shocks some people. But it is of the sort to inspire a delegate with the reassurance that, while Presidents and pundits and Cabinet officers may be there, he is here. And it is here, for a few tumultuous days, that Bottom is translated and wooed by the fairest in the land. And it is here that a farmer from Froggy Bottom, Louisiana, or a postmaster from Thunderbird, New Mexico, turns into a dictator and a kingmaker.

Senator Kennedy Looks Ahead

Washington, D.C., July 11, 1957

Whenever an American politician announces that his devotion to a foreign land has become acute, his rivals count the number of voters in his state who come from the beloved country, either by immigrant ship or an earlier collateral line.

Let Scandinavia be ravished by an invader and the Senators from Wisconsin and Minnesota enlist at once in the non-combatant brigade of mourners. If the turban'd Turk shakes a fist at Greece he will be denounced overnight by the senior Senator from Nevada, and the Congressman from the First District of Florida will hasten to share a handkerchief with the Greek sponge-fishers of Tarpon Springs. Since white Protestants are a minority group in New York, no mayor in the city's history is on record as ever having gone brass-rubbing in England or seeking out the birth-place of Martin Luther. But when the Israelis, the Italians, or the Irish cry out, the Mayor of New York thunders.

Alarmed by Senator John Kennedy's moving concern for Algeria, it is natural that the foreigner should wonder how many divisions the Algerians could muster in Massachusetts.

The answer is puzzling. The Bay State abounds in tooth-sucking Yankees, Italians, Poles, Finns, Czechs, and Catholic French Canadians. It positively swarms with Irishmen, well instructed in the sins of the British up to the third and fourth generation, which makes it no surprise at all that Senator Kennedy, a practising liberal and a man definitely against sin, kept his mouth shut during the long dark night of McCarthy.

But if, as *Le Monde* was quick to surmise, Kennedy is now running for the Presidency, why should he open his mouth about a country that will neither win nor lose him a single vote in his native state? For if there are ten Algerians in Massachusetts, they came in as stowaways. The flat, unsatisfying answer is to say that Senator Kennedy is a sincere student of foreign affairs, a London School of Economics alumnus, a former foreign correspondent who specialises in the early symptoms of European decay (he once wrote a book called *Why England Slept*), an internationalist with a French-extracted wife who deeply feels for France. This answer, which is already on the lips of Kennedy's boosters in Congress, is naive in the extreme. Consider his past record and the present cut of his jib.

At birth he was the wealthy son of the substantial second generation of Irish with whom the Cabots, the Adamses, and the Saltonstalls had to come to terms in order to share the rule of Massachusetts; at twenty-three, a graduate of Harvard *cum laude*. At twenty-six a naval hero in the Solomons; at twenty-nine elected to the House of Representatives, and again at thirty-one and thirty-three; in his thirty-seventh year a United States Senator, the winner over the redoubtable Henry Cabot Lodge. In the 1952 campaign, he was the Frank Sinatra of the Democratic party, bringing to the platforms of bigger men a boyish pompadour crowning a handsome grin, a reputation for party loyalty and a gift of appropriate sweet-talk, before audiences both big and scattered, which is the political equivalent of perfect pitch in a crooner.

In 1956 he would have toured the land as Stevenson's

vice-presidential running mate had not the Southerners at the convention seen in him the bobby-soxers' emissary from the Pope. In the moment that he conceded the nomination to Kefauver, he heard the rafters ring and saw the Presidential lightning. It may not have burned him yet, but he is among the four or five others who were singed by it at the last convention and whose actions will never be reasonably accountable again – Nixon and Knowland among the palace guard who live in the daily dazzle of the Presidency. Senator Lyndon Johnson, Senator Hubert Humphrey, and Kennedy are among the Democrats who are beginning to bare their bosoms and call upon the Lord to turn the next thunderbolt their way.

The Algerian sortie shows that Kennedy may be the most accomplished of the supplicants in sight. His protocol was ably written, by Kennedy, no less, and carefully documented by two foreign affairs assistants. As chairman of the subcommittee on United Nations affairs of the Senate Foreign Relations Committee, the junior senator from Massachusetts has such experts easily on tap. And, *Le Figaro* to the contrary, he is a very well-informed man.

Senator Kennedy is too shrewd to make a hobby out of Algeria. It has brilliantly served its purpose of pitching him into centre-stage, from where this week he will deliver a lament for the barbarities of the Russians in Poland. This is as safe a mode of indignation as any man from Massachusetts could express. The choice of Algeria was a careful one. Precisely because it is a country that knows neither friend nor enemy in Massachusetts it is no liability to his own constituents. But it has nicely suggested to his newspaper supporters that the Senator is a statesman, something like Stevenson, of majestic disinterestedness. From his own point of view, a gratuitous but bold pamphlet on Algeria written by a Democratic Senator could be trusted to do two things: to astound the French and infuriate the White House. Ergo, the Senator's shadowy figure is suddenly spotlighted in Europe. At home he has made himself at a bound the Democrat whom the President must 'do something about,' the next Presidential hopeful the Republicans will delight to scorn. It is a form of running martyrdom the Senators Humphrey and Johnson may come to envy.

There are Democrats who coolly admire the Senator's strategy but fear that he marched flat-footed into a terrain that must be very delicately explored at the next United Nations General Assembly. Kennedy is smarter than they thought. As chairman of the aforementioned subcommittee, he is well-informed also on the tentative agenda of the next Assembly. He will be hard to pass by as the Democrats' Algerian 'expert' on the next United States delegations. The Assembly, indeed, might bring him the rare fruit of the plant he seeded. He could choose to oppose – or arbitrate – the Administration's position on Algeria, according to the pulse of popular opinion, and in so doing make Ambassador Lodge hit the dirt a second time at the hands of his brash young conqueror.

All this is not to say that Presidential ambitions can ever be so minutely or consciously planned. But not every boy who aims at Bisley does his target practice there. Senator Kennedy is setting up a bottle or two in his own back yard for the admiration of the home folks and the astonishment of foreigners beyond the pale.

America Discovers Mr. Muggeridge

October 24, 1957

Like a proconsul summoned to Rome to explain the riots in East Anglia Mr. Malcolm Muggeridge flew into New York last night to account for his views on the British monarchy to Mike Wallace, the public prosecutor of American television.

In one year Mr. Wallace has bounded from obscurity to portentous fame. He is a handsome, coltish young man seated in a black void, whose shady secrets he will expose before the night is through. *Night Beat* was the title of the show that made him celebrated; a title that carries powerful ambiguous associations with a cop on the prowl, dirty work at the crossroads, the midnight pounding of the stubborn suspect in the interest, of course, of all good men and true.

Strong men have quailed and wept when exposed to Mike Wallace's cross-examination. Fast women have stuttered and stumbled. The average sensual man never fails to wonder why anybody not besotted with a lust for publicity would expose himself to Wallace's approach, which combines a Boy Scout's zeal for good deeds with Bogart's professional sadism. Once in a while, Mr. Wallace meets a character who is immune to insult, who reacts to the needle as to a pleasant sedative. Such a character is Mr. Muggeridge.

Mr. Wallace came at him like the Hound of the Baskervilles, and Mr. Muggeridge said: 'There, there.' Mr. Wallace bayed to heaven to bear witness to Muggeridge's *lèse-majesté*, to his 'carefully designed attempt to create a sensation.' Mr. Muggeridge said not so, and mocked him with a roguish smile. Mr. Wallace leaped to his full height to maul the abominable no-man, and Mr. Muggeridge tugged his ear. No matter how threateningly Mr. Wallace shifted his inflections, narrowed his eyes, drained smoke from his nostrils, he still was as adorable as a puppy to Mr. Muggeridge. In the end he was eating out of the enemy's hand.

Come now, Muggeridge, he began, how do you justify your attack on the Queen at the very moment she appears in America? A few pleasant cracks appeared in Muggeridge's granite face. 'An attack?' He had never attacked anybody. He has accepted a commission from a conservative family magazine long before the Queen's visit was planned, to write 'a considered piece on the present state of a popular monarchy.' He could think of 'nothing more useful in connection with the Queen's visit.' Mr. Wallace tossed at him the three or four wounding phrases isolated by the news agencies from their context. Mr. Muggeridge quietly pointed out this routine dishonesty and confessed to having attempted only 'a sincere, genuine analysis' of an institution that had its faults but had also many advantages, not least that provided by 'the image of a happy, virtuous family' with which the Queen had endowed it. In fact, he thought 'the present incumbent is a delightful exponent of the institution' as well as 'a most charming woman.'

How about that crack, Muggeridge, that duchesses thought her 'dowdy, frumpish, and banal'? No attack here? 'Not at all,' said Muggeridge, simply a proof of his theory that 'criticism of the Queen came rather from the upper echelons than the lower.'

Mr. Muggeridge paused occasionally and fixed on his chubby accuser the glittering kindly eye of a patient old headmaster. It was a splendid thing, he seemed to think, to have boys of such fire and impulse even if they should not distinguish an adjective from an idea. Every time Mr. Wallace tossed him an insult to defend, Mr. Muggeridge would show it was not an insult but a thoughtful item in a thesis. He addressed his pupil's attention to the general idea that 'free speech is an admirable thing in free societies . . . and the benefit of living in one is that you say what you think.' You think 'that Britain is a free society,' barked Mr. Wallace. Suspecting for a moment the wiliness of youth, Mr. Muggeridge pretended to be wrestling with Plato. Let's put it this way, he said: 'I like to *think* it is.' Well, snapped the young man, if it's so free 'why were you fired as a columnist for the *Sunday Dispatch*' and cancelled by the B.B.C.? 'Ah,' sighed Mr. Muggeridge, 'those are episodes for which I blush and do indeed reflect on the freedom we claim.' It was an interesting reflection on American freedom, he thought, that the Washington station had banned this interview. Very interesting, said Mr. Wallace.

This was as close as they ever came to an equal exchange. Mr. Wallace always has in front of him a stack of 'research,' a body of knowledge as inflexible as a crib, a neat list of leading questions expecting snappy answers. And what does this character offer in reply? Philosophy, ideas, speculation, the unsatisfying sound of grave good sense. All right, then, he would try one final four-square tack. Okay, Mr. Muggeridge, you are a very smart cookie, but if the monarchy is in such a bad way, what are you going to do about it? Mr. Muggeridge was afraid he was 'much too modest to offer a complete solution,' but he would dare to pose the working problem: 'In so far as the monarchy is identified with an obsolete class structure the object should be to detach it from that structure.' This was obvious Greek to Wallace, but he thought Mr. Muggeridge might like to volunteer for the job. 'I'm much too old, nor do I think it very likely it would be offered me.'

Mr. Wallace fell back on his reserves, which include the Astors, no less. Mr. Michael Astor, he noted, wrote this past week in the New York *Herald Tribune* that 'you have a pathological contempt for your fellow human beings.' How about that, Muggeridge? No chance for evasion there, eh? 'If my fellow human beings were all Astors, there might be some truth in it,' but he was relieved to note that the human fellowship was not wholly composed of the Astors. ('By the way,' said Mr. Muggeridge, 'have you still got any of them or did they all come to England?') Consequently, he found the vast majority of his fellow beings to be interesting, 'congenial and lovable.'

Mike Wallace had been tearing around in circles after his own tail. It was twenty-five minutes past ten. The Queen was unscathed and Muggeridge was not even breathing hard. Better try for some quick Muggeridge-type insults. How about Churchill, Mr. M.? Answer: 'In the period when the Germans occupied the Channel ports, he fulfilled a role as great as any in our history . . . Without him we might well have collapsed. I will honour him for that as long as I live . . .' Unfortunately 'he is an appallingly bad politician who held on to power long after he should have done . . . his post-war administration was a disaster.'

The present Prime Minister, Mr. Macmillan? 'A very

interesting man,' Mr. Muggeridge mused, 'who achieved supreme power too late, as politicians so often do. They differ from ladies of easy virtue in that they get *their* pleasures too early.'

How about Sir Anthony Eden? Answer: 'The most disastrous Prime Minister in our history, and I am not forgetting Lord North.'

There was no scaring Muggeridge on the home front. With two minutes to go, it might be possible to have him shed a sneer on the local heroes. Or would he dare? Mr. Muggeridge cocked a formidable chin and kept his eyes unblinkingly on Wallace. He is obviously a man beyond daring, or caring, for the television audience or any other crowd in the great beyond that suffers from frequent bouts of middle-class morality. He is therefore easily assailed but unassailable by the ordinary strategy of spite, malice, or popular uproar. He positively nestled for the kill into Mr. Wallace's embrace.

Mr. Dulles? Mr. Muggeridge hesitated, seeming actually to be choosing his words. 'I do not think he is equipped – by nature – to deal with the situation in our world. He strikes me as portentous, sincere, honest, and rather stupid.'

Mr. Wallace unveiled his last idol and, short of Lincoln in his memorial, it could not have been a figure more sacrosanct in American life. It was none other than Eisenhower himself. Mr. Muggeridge did not stir. He took a long pleasurable pull on his cigarette and said: 'He did the most marvellous job in the war, not a military job but a public relations job when it was essential to have a public relations job done.' But (the inevitable, the delicious but) 'like Macmillan, his power came too late. I do not think he is on the wavelength of the dreadful time we live in.'

Wallace was bewitched, bothered, and bewildered. Since no human known to sainthood intimidated him, maybe Sputnik had him by the ears? Alas, Mr. Muggeridge found himself belonging to a tiny minority that was 'neither interested nor frightened' by the satellite. Because the things that interested him had nothing to do with trips to the moon. He thought that 'if the founder of the Christian religion had been conducted on a tour of Rome or flown in a jet plane, the Sermon on the Mount would have been neither more nor less profound than it is.'

Mr. Wallace lifted one limp paw and yielded his last tiny bone. Wasn't there a great amount of anti-Americanism in Europe, and how did he explain *that*? Yes, there was, and it was 'simply that Americans are very rich and very powerful. People always loathe the rich and powerful. The difference seems to be that in the nineteenth century the English liked being loathed, whereas it appears that Americans rather dislike it.'

Mr. Wallace looked wistfully into the camera. All but brainwashed by now, he could only thank Mr. Muggeridge for coming and exercising the freedom of his speech, which, said Mr. Wallace, sounding like Churchill, was 'one of our ancient freedoms.' Mr. Muggeridge thought the half-hour had gone by 'like a flash.' It had gone by like a mushroom cloud for Mr. Wallace and in the boom and smoke of it he must have gathered scant consolation from the fact that, like every other human being except the Astors, Mr. Muggeridge found him 'congenial and lovable.'

The End of Reticence

June 15, 1958

In all the sad and sympathetic speculation about Mr. Dulles, and the effect of his illness on the foreign policies of the West, no mention has been made in this country of the unique break with tradition implicit in the publication last Sunday of his doctors' bulletin. It announced, in the plainest clinical terms, that the Secretary of State had a grave type of cancer which had metastasised. It all but declared that further surgery was useless. And in the stark phrase, 'Radiation therapy will be used,' it admitted that the brave old man is now reduced to the desperate and exhausting resort of massive shots of X-ray.

The New York *Daily News* printed a banner headline on Sunday morning, which was warranted by the published results of the biopsy and which was more shocking than most only because it more clearly recognised the truth and printed it: 'Dulles Has Incurable Cancer.' The *News* indeed, in its dispatch from Washington, interpreted the doctors' bulletin with more accuracy, and less pussyfooting confusion, than its so-called serious rivals. It went on to the fair presumption that 'in general, patients with cancers [so] advanced and widespread . . . begin to decline rapidly. Death often comes within a matter of months or a year. There are sometimes exceptions, however, and [cancer experts] did not rule out the possibility of Mr. Dulles's returning briefly to his desk before further inevitable complications set in.'

We have come a long way since the day that Congress heard of Jefferson suffering in Monticello from 'a debility'; or from the last days of any of the eighteenth-century celebrities who succumbed to such mysteries, which public taste did not care to unravel, as 'a violent ague' (Washington), a 'swelling dropsy' (Dr. Johnson), an 'asthma in the chest' (Pope). But what has not been remarked on is that, in one bulletin issued from Walter Reed Hospital a week ago, we have come almost as far from the last days of Franklin Roosevelt and Senator Robert Taft. Medical knowledge obviously varies greatly from age to age, to say nothing of the nomenclature that sometimes masks the ignorance of the learned. And it may be that Johnson's friends, catching the coffee-house gossip about an 'ague,' had their hopes as thoroughly dashed as ours have been by the note that 'a small nodular implant on the hernia sac . . . proved to be an adenocarcinoma.' But in Johnson's time no public man's last affliction was proclaimed in the press before he died of it; nor was it the custom in our time until last Sunday.

From Seattle, in the summer of 1923, an agency message said

that 'President Harding has been sent into collapse by a heart attack.' The public was given nothing more to go on until August 2, when a second and fatal attack killed him in San Francisco. The classic example of official reticence, blandly maintained for eighteen months, was that which surrounded Woodrow Wilson after his collapse in September, 1919, and protected the American people from knowing that they had in the White House a President virtually incompetent for high office. The stroke that paralysed him paralysed as much as anything else the hope that the United States would join the League of Nations. Yet the tasteless suggestion was never made that a sustained nervous collapse might invoke the 'disability' clause of the Constitution as fairly as the madness of George III, which was the only sort of disability the Founding Fathers had in mind. 'The President,' wrote the White House usher in his memoirs published in the 1930s, 'was sicker than the world ever knew; he lived on, but oh, what a wreck!' James Truslow Adams comments, without protest, that after the autumn of 1919 Wilson was 'more or less shrouded in the mystery of a sickroom for the remainder of his term.' 'The mystery of the sickroom' is the precious nicety that we have now exploded. It is an honourable cliché that was never challenged, so far as I can discover, until the murky day in Denver in September, 1955, when the press bristled with suspicions that President Eisenhower had suffered something more serious than the 'digestive upset' his press secretary gave out. Once the specialists had confirmed and published the diagnosis of Dr. Howard Snyder, who alone knew the truth as he sat with the President through the first night, the newspaper editors and the Congress clamoured for all the details. They did so because, in the waiting interval between the hint of indigestion and the account of a coronary thrombosis, the pundits of the press recognised a kind of crisis that had not so far afflicted the United States in its first flush of world power. The researchers recalled Wilson, and the Republicans with more alarm remembered Franklin Roosevelt.

Without a doubt it was the memory of Roosevelt's well-disguised decline which forced the White House to the elaborate and painful displays of honesty that may now be studied in the huge, clinical lectures of Dr. Paul Dudley White. There were rumours, both frivolous and malign, about Roosevelt's strokes long before he had any. But the country was shocked by the wan skeleton that appeared as Roosevelt in the newsreels of the Yalta conference that were withheld until after his death. Since then there is a mass of evidence, in the memoirs of everyone from Mrs. Roosevelt to Presidential acquaintances, that Roosevelt was sinking fast in the two months before the end. During that time he roused himself to go before Congress and expound the Yalta settlement in terms that Congress cheered without a dissenting grumble. But as soon as Roosevelt had died, the news came out of the secret agreement with Russia about voting procedure in the Security Council; and when the Russians implied that their hand-picked Lublin regime would have satisfied Roosevelt's view of a representative Polish Government, the Republicans suspected that Roosevelt's weakness had trapped him at Yalta. With the publication of Stalin's bargain over Chiang Kai-shek, the Republican outcry strengthened to a charge of near-treason. To this day, to the Right-wing Republicans, Yalta is 'the great betrayal.'

Yalta, indeed, may be the valid passport to the sickroom of any ailing President, or of any Secretary of State who, like Mr. Dulles, virtually annexes the Presidential prerogative of deciding the foreign policy of the United States. Mr. Dulles has done this by nothing more improper than his own knowledge and devotion; and he has paid the price of his mastery by forfeiting the privilege that is given to the obscure and the doomed: to be allowed to face the world at the end with the dignity of a man who keeps his death-warrant to himself.

Frank Lloyd Wright

April 16, 1959

I met him first on a winter's afternoon in what I almost slipped into calling the vestry of his suite at the Plaza hotel in New York. I pressed the electric button at first timorously, then boldly, then incessantly, and was about to turn away when the door was opened by a pretty young woman, a secretary, or granddaughter, or vestal virgin perhaps, who beckoned me into the hushed gloom behind her through which I expected to see sacramental tapers. Then she nodded and vanished down the corridor.

It is difficult to avoid these theological images in introducing him because his reputation, his public pronouncements, his photographs – the majestic head, the marble serenity, the Miltonic collars, the cape of Superman – all conspired to suggest a sort of exiled Buddha, a high priest scuttled from his temple by the barbarians, one of those deposed monarchs so frequently seen around New York who gamely try to convey that a free-wheeling democracy is just their speed. The room he sat in was seedy, in a lavish Edwardian way, and no single furnishing – no chair, fabric, window casement, carpet, lintel, or door knob – appeared to have been invented much later than the June of 1867 in which he was born. He lay stretched out on a sofa, his fine hands folded on his lap, a shawl precisely draped around his shoulders.

He looked like Merlin posing as Whistler's Mother. Indeed, there was always a curiously feminine grace about him, but it was nothing frail or skittish. He looked more like a matriarch of a pioneer family, one of those massive Western gentlewomen who shipped the piano from Boston round the Horn, settled in the Sacramento Valley, defied the Argonauts as they set fire to the cattle barns, and, having finally reclaimed their Spanish land grants, came into their own again as the proud upholders of old manners against the derision and ribaldry of the new rich.

In writing about him as a character delineated by Henry James, or sentimentalised by Gertrude Atherton, I hope that I am not so much arranging a suitable atmosphere as conveying a psychological shock. One expected a tyrant, a man constantly caricatured by the press as a bellowing iconoclast. And here was a genial sceptic whose habitual tone was one of pianissimo raillery.

It may be that I knew him too late, when the fire and brimstone were all spent, when whatever lava had been in him in the turbulent days had cooled and hardened in the enormous, firm dewlaps that started at his nostrils and seemed to be tucked away not far above the clavicle. There must be some explanation for the discrepancy between the legend and the man. Perhaps his long decade of neglect in his sixties, when he had to borrow from friends to retrieve a mortgage on his own home, is as good as any.

At any rate, all my apprehension vanished as he threw me, from a seniority of forty-odd years, the flattery of calling me 'young man' and asking what was on my mind. It was a project that was to waver and die and come alive again in his eventual appearance on a television programme. He dismissed it at once as an absurdity, since it involved a medium only slightly less debased than the movies. I told him that no sponsors would interrupt his sermon, the models he used would be of his own choosing, he could say exactly what he pleased.

He wafted the whole vision aside as a bit of vulgarity for which he would not hold me responsible. Then he slipped, from total and inexplicable free association, into a diatribe against Franklin Roosevelt. In some dim but infuriating way, Roosevelt, it seemed, was responsible for the triumph of the rabble, for the 'agony of our cities,' for skyscrapers, for the United Nations building ('an anti-hill for a thousand ants'), for the whole mushroom fashion of what he called 'Nuremberg Fascist Modern,' and for the coming destruction of the Edwardian pile we were sitting in ('the only beautiful hotel,' he said bafflingly, 'in all of this god-awful New York').

About two hours later, by which time he had murmured most of the slogans from his latest book, he chuckled and said: 'Tell me, Alistair boy, did you ever meet an executive, a president of a corporation, a button-pusher, who had a smitch of aesthetic in his make-up?' I said I never had.

'Very well, then, when do you want me to appear and where?'

We blocked out the feature and arranged rehearsals, and went around for weeks in euphoria, which was shattered when he passed down an ultimatum through an emissary: 'No rehearsals! Rehearsals freeze the natural flow of the human personality.' This sounds awful in print, but all such sententiae were delivered, either in person or over the 'phone, in the delicate and warmly modulated voice which had for fifty years seduced wax manufacturers, oil tycoons, bishops, university boards of trustees, and at least one Emperor of Japan into commissioning cantilevered Aztec structures most of which were later rescinded, condemned as unsafe, or merely paid for and deplored.

On the day of the show, we asked to pick him up after his midday nap and brought him to the studio well ahead of time. He had evidently forgotten all about the fiat against rehearsals, and stood by a model of his Bartlesville, Oklahoma, building and watched the stage manager chalk in a position for him on the floor. 'What is this?' he asked, pointing down at the tiny prison yard he was meant to move in. I recalled to him the actor's famous crack about television ('Someone stuck in an iron lung') and he smiled and seemed to be pacified again. The director's voice came squawking over the loud-speaker: 'Mr. Wright, will you turn and face the model?' He must have thought it was God's commandment, for he raised his head and said to the air the appalling syllable, 'No.'

He thereupon sauntered off to get his hat, cane, and cape. I chased him and got him off for a stroll around the dark cavern of the studio that lay beyond the lighted set. It was a tight moment. He needed to be coaxed, but he could spot a fawn at twenty paces, and flattery got you nowhere. We had only an hour to go, but he took my arm and we pattered in circles in the gloom while the director watched the minute hand of the clock. I agreed that television was a catch-as-catch-can business but suggested it was hardest of all on the camera men, 'the real craftsmen.' I mentioned that they could not trust to luck, they had to block their shots and know where the prima donnas intended to move. Five minutes later, he was back on the set, as malleable as an ageing cat. The scripted outline was forgotten. We simply sat and talked, and to comatose or apoplectic millions he trotted out such unashamed ad libs as: 'The interior decorator is simply an inferior desecrator of the work of an artist'; 'we are all victims of the rectangle and the slab, we go on living in boxes of stone and brick, while the modern world is crying to be born in the discovery that concrete and steel can sleep together'; 'we should learn from the snail – it has devised a home that is both exquisite and functional.'

After this first bout with the most highly advertised ego of our time I ran into him in various places or was asked to call on him, and I probably presume in saying that my failure to discern any conceit in him but only a harmless vanity, penetrating observation, and always his beautifully cadenced good sense was due to one of those accidents of personal chemistry that seal confidence in an instant and dissolve mountains of fear or antagonism that can never be argued away by two uncongenial people.

The last time I saw him, a year ago, I was to 'moderate' a debate in Chicago on the present condition of our cities. The panel consisted of real-estate men, a housing commissioner, a young professor of architecture, and Wright. It was sponsored by a steel company that legitimately hoped to popularise 'the steel curtain,' which is now the first constituent of most of the skyscrapers going up. Wright outraged his sponsors, and almost broke up the forum, first by professing boredom over the arguments of the buildings and real-estate men and consequently walking out to take a nap; and later by indicating a diorama advertising the steel curtain and saying: 'These steel frames are just the old log cabin, they are all built from the outside in, first a steel frame, then they bring in the paper hanger, and what have you got? — a box with steel for horizontals instead of lumber.'

Driving back along the Chicago lakefront he had done most to glorify, he ridiculed the glinting skyscrapers and the whizzing automobiles ('rectangles on wheels'), but he could work up no steam or bile. His only genuine sigh was for the universal misuse of steel, 'this beautiful material that spins like a spider and produces a tension so perfect that you can balance a monolith on a pinpoint.' I felt that this lament of the city he secretly adored was a little recitation for Buncombe. In his ninetieth year, he could afford to be agreeable to everybody, though he tried valiantly to resist the inclination. After all, it had been forty-eight years since he had pioneered the sweeping horizontals of the first 'prairie house' (which would pass creditably anywhere as a distinguished 'contemporary' house), fifty-one years since he built the first air-conditioned building, fifty-four years since the first metal-bound plate-glass door, forty-eight years since the cantilevered floor, poured concrete, and all the other explosive solecisms that are now the grammar of the modern architect.

One imagines him arriving this week-end in Heaven, tapping his malacca cane against the pearly gates to test the strength of the carbonate of lime, and greeting Saint Peter with the disarming tranquil gaze and the snowy head held high. He will ask to see the 'many mansions I've been hearing about for nearly ninety years,' and will be taken on an obsequious tour only to discover, without surprise and without regret, that there is a distressing reliance on Gothic, that there is nothing so bold as the cantilevered balcony over the waterfall in Bear Run, Pennsylvania; that nothing has been done to dampen with coloured glass the enormous glare of the light that never was on land or sea. He will say as he turns away in boredom from his guide: 'The principle of floating all these structures on a more or less stable mass of cumulus clouds is no newer than the cushion of mud I put under the Imperial Hotel in Tokyo in 1922, with the express purpose of withstanding (as it did) the wrath of God. I understand He has been sulking ever since.'

New Ways in English Life

July 16, 1959

No one knows exactly when the first Englishman sounded the alarm against the arrival of corrupting imports from America. But Francis Moore, an adventurer who went to Georgia in 1735 as a storekeeper to the colony, has a powerful claim. Mencken gives him first place of honour in his history of the American language because he was the first recorded Englishman to notice a new coining 'and what is better to the point, the first to denounce it.' Describing the new village of Savannah, he mentions 'the bank of the river (which they in barbarous English call a *bluff*).' This note, published in his journal in London nine years later, conditioned a reflex that has been for two centuries as dependable as any other in the relations of Americans and Britons.

But there are signs that the Englishman is losing his power to wince as the crackle of American words and ways over England attains the mass and charge of a thunderstorm. Twenty-four years ago, in a talk given over the B.B.C., I reconstructed, from the researches of Whitney, Sheldon, Orbeck, Kenyon, and the New England town records, the pattern of speech that most likely belonged to cultivated Londoners of the late eighteenth century, when the two countries chose their separate ways. In the course of this pilot-project, I noted the many strong characteristics of Southern English speech, rounded vowels especially, which have since vanished in the native land and are characteristically retained in the speech of most Americans. I remarked that 'that brilliantly malicious little man-about-town, Alexander Pope, probably spoke more like the late John Dillinger and less like Noel Coward.' This speculation provoked a tidal wave of protesting mail, the least of whose insults suggested that I would soon be saying that Shakespeare was an American.

If English pronunciation has managed to resist the fate predicted for it by early bemoaners of 'the talkies,' the English vocabulary seems to have succumbed to Americanisms since the war at an unprecedented rate. Of course, everyone believes that Americanisms were invented in his youth. But there is the humbling fact that most Little Englanders protest their purity in a language already mongrelised by ten generations of new blood. It is hard to believe to-day that Lamb objected to 'awful,' that 'reliable' was long banned from respectable English journals, that seventy years ago the London *Daily News* should have warned its readers against 'an ignoble Americanism' – the word 'scientist.' Every time an Englishman opens his mouth either to prove his own raciness or deplore that of the Americans, he is quite likely to talk about a has-been, a down-and-out, or about horse sense, barking up the wrong tree, facing the music, or keeping a stiff upper lip – all of which barbarisms were first admitted into England practically, as William Archer said, at the point of a bayonet.

The first shock came on the first English train, where 'W.C.' has given way to 'toilet.' I am told that this is very non-U, but I have noticed that this line has become a sort of last-ditch argument against American habits impossible to resist. It shows a willingness to surrender but a refusal to reveal one's serial number. (I could be properly humiliated by the U–non-U line if I had not noticed that an obsession with what is U in itself is a suspiciously non-U characteristic.) The next surprise is the advertisements in popular and even highbrow magazines. Most of the copy is unashamedly American in style, and no apology or note of dissociation is printed to explain the photographs of well-known American models enthusing over

English toothpastes and hair rinses. I see the 'season ticket holder' has collapsed before the onrush of 'commuters.' Even *The Times* has given up 'black-coated' workers in favour of 'white-collar' workers.

I discovered that the Etonians assembled for the Fourth could no longer maintain the pretension of a 'shooting brake.' The hock was served from the 'boot' of 'a station wagon.' When a thunderhead threatened to stop play, some people yelled (in a well-bred way) for a mackintosh, but many others were glad to have brought their raincoats. It would be wearisome to go on picking out examples, a chore (or odd-job, as Britons used to say) that begins to resemble untangling the warp from the woof. In three weeks of travel and reading I noticed, in all, three or four hundred words, about which no one seemed to protest, most of which were unused in England in the 1930s or were then isolated in the quarantine of quotation marks.

I have not mentioned the wholesale importation of 'beat' slang, dress, and mannerisms, for this is a full-blown fad. It has had its predecessors, and the addicts – whether in Glasgow or in Oxford – make a point of being as American as they know how. Even so, the beatniks seem to have engulfed the teddy-boys and, because they add to the general air of social protest an advanced literary tone, have captured a more pretentious following. The young men and women strolling through Trinity Great Court or sprawling on the Backs at Cambridge were indistinguishable from the student body at Berkeley, California, except possibly for the more strident patterns of the girls' shirts and the Mansfield cut of their toreador pants. They bore no imagined resemblance to any English undergraduates I had known, and I can only say that an old fogey like myself (if you will permit the Americanism) could not conceive what their appearance would have done to the dons twenty years ago. At the Cambridge Arts Theatre in the evening I had no sense of the social origins of anyone around me, but I gathered, from the variety of accents that emerged from under a standard

Tony Curtis haircut, that the social ideal of Harrow and Blackburn Grammar School are now as one. Half the skits in the 'Footlights Revue' were played, with surprising skill, in American and for no better reason I could discover than that they sounded more modish that way.

If the fads of the young follow their usual practice and pass over into the settled habits of middle age, attributable to no country but to the period they were learned in, then in another quarter-century England indeed will be the fifty-first state. For the most compelling social characteristic of the British people to-day is not the wide gamut of native qualities and habits but the greater range of American habits, customs, and conventions they seem to have incorporated, without complaint, since the war. It is time for someone to add another volume to the 'Legacy' series of the Oxford University Press. The legacy of America started with a turkey and the full inheritance is only now beginning to be enjoyed by the people it was willed to: namely, the lower middle class. It is easy, and it is traditional, for the upper middle class, with a garden to cultivate and a maid on call, to pooh-pooh the mass introduction of the suburban house with a garage, the electric toaster, the washing machine and the 'fridge,' the cake-mix, and the frozen vegetables. But these and the shoal of other boons that are coming in the wake symbolise the floodtide of a liberty most men in most countries have never known. More convincingly than nationalisation schemes or the local promises of politicians, they constitute the Social Contract of the common man flexing his muscles in the century he has been told is his.

The Unexplained Mr. Nixon

July 21, 1960

Franklin Roosevelt was not the first Democrat to pin on the Republicans the stigma of 'the party of privilege' as distinct from the 'party of the people,' three of whose last quartet of nominees have been a Hudson Valley patroon, a prairie patrician from Illinois, and now the millionaire·son of a Boston multimillionaire. Like most recent nominees of the party of privilege (Willkie, the boy from the tomato canneries of Elwood, Indiana; Dewey, the Sunday school baritone from Owosso, Michigan; Eisenhower, the farm boy from Abilene, Kansas) Richard Milhous Nixon was born poor.

His father, a street-car conductor who failed at a lemon grove, opened a small general store in Whittier, California, a humble mecca of Quaker pioneers from the East. He married one of those gentle and now legendary matriarchs of the Western settlements: a mother who baked the bread before dawn, taught her five sons Bible verses, helped itinerant Negroes and Mexicans to scrape a living in the bean fields and sat them down at the table as the family's social equals. Richard, a husky studious boy, worked in the store, made pin money for his education by being in turn a gas-station worker, a grocer's delivery boy, handyman, a janitor in a fruit-packing house – a familiar American stereotype of the early twentieth century, a source of inspiration in *Saturday Evening Post* stories and later, of jokes and skits by Jewish vaudeville comedians whose own origins were usually as humble but much seedier. With his strong religious background, his acute sense of thrift, his natural assumption that a sixteen-hour day is the normal human lot, Nixon is a good example of the log-cabin bright boy in the era of the Great Depression. To this day he owns no stocks or shares and earmarks a part of his salary to pay off the mortgage on the only house he has ever owned.

It is worth dwelling on his early poverty and the proved daily belief of such as his people that hustling energy and family prayers are the minimum recipe for salvation in this or any other life. For in the later American society, of a huge secular and prosperous middle class, this sort of heritage is mooned over by rich Republicans and kidded as a corny cliché by Democrats rich and poor alike. There is a good deal of inverted snobbery in the Welfare-State assumption that Roosevelt came along to make such personal histories obsolete. Only a week ago a French editor, standing apart from a Beverly Hills gathering of rich Democrats, was baffled by his own question: 'What or who is a rich Democrat?' The answer, in this place anyway, seemed to be – 'generous intellectuals who are secretly embarrassed by the poor.' The theme of social guilt has been too little explored in the history of the New Deal and Roosevelt's prescription of 'the more abundant life'; and though it explains only a small element of the conflict between the two ancient parties it is a persistent one and throws a discerning light on the fury with which they disagree about the working premises of American prosperity.

Nixon says that in college, during the depression, he became 'a liberal' and his heroes were Brandeis and Cardozo. It could explain his view, which is strikingly typical of industrious American boys with high ambition, that the law is a holy calling. At any rate he put himself through the small Whittier College, married a miner's daughter, and in 1936, at the age of 23, went to New York resolved to join 'a great law firm.' He graduated from law school, failed to land a job with the FBI (which was in those days a band of popular heroes, led by a Zorro), and went back to Whittier. He started his own law office and became a big man in civic projects and the Quaker church. After a stint in the Navy he went into politics. His tough campaigning in California, first against the incumbent Democrat Jerry Voorhis and then Mrs. Helen Gahagan Douglas, is now a part of history and a necessary part of the Democratic legend which ascribes Machiavellian electioneering gifts to Nixon that few Democrats, when challenged, are able to document.

The great puzzle about Nixon, and the only one that foreigners care to have solved, is why he arouses such dislike, why he is the only man in public life that Stevenson actively hates. The Democratic indictment turns on the word 'chameleon.' He certainly exploited the McCarthy terror for all it was worth as a surefire method of getting out the popular vote. He impulsively crowed over the frustration of the British and French armies at Suez and then quickly adjusted himself to Dulles's more judicial afterthought that it was no time to exasperate America's best allies. It is even possible to say that he is – in the Dewey, Willkie, Eisenhower tradition – a practitioner of continuous 'me-tooism,' that he has followed one step behind the Democrats and now, as Kennedy's writers put it, 'has the courage of our convictions.' But this is campaign quippery, and we shall have a bellyful of it before the winter. What is still unexplained is the instinctive Nixon, what kind of man he really is and would be if he was on his own.

People who know him well and who can look at, without gagging, Herblock's ferocious caricature of him (an unshaven witch over a cauldron of hate) say that he is essentially an introspective man whom politics has forced into a public show of energy and optimism, and that much of his uneasy cordiality is a defence against the Democrats' slick view of him as an all-American Uriah Heep. Fairminded men who have talked over with him his past, his ideas, his political philosophy come away with the uneasy feeling that he is the least known of American politicians, that he is as lonely as Stevenson, and that by much self-questioning and an unflagging capacity for the sixteen-hour day he is now the most conscientious Vice-President there has ever been, a statesman of considerably more astuteness and tact than Eisenhower, and the best informed member of the National Security Council.

For myself, I can only fall back on the first impressions I took of him when he sat on the House Committee on Un-American Activities. I see, from the running notes I kept at the time, that I was immediately struck by his probing intelligence, his obvious distinction among a committee of mediocre witch hunters and high-school debaters. He was the only one who trusted his instinct enough to suspect that Chambers was either a scoundrel or a flounderer who had made a ghastly mistake of identity. He opened his eyes and ears impartially to Hiss's story, noted an early discrepancy and correctly diagnosed Hiss's legal pedantries as a systematic protection against the possibility of his case being brought to trial. Once he felt for sure that Hiss was a consummate liar he went after him with merciless skill.

These generalities do little to strip the chameleon's skin, to show what political stance matches his true character, what political colour he instinctively prefers. But at least it may induce doubts in people who have swallowed whole the Machiavelli legend; and it may clear the air for a steadier look at him when he marches out to do battle with Kennedy. If we do not know him by November 8, we never will.

The Man Who Defeated McCarthy

October 13, 1960

Yesterday morning on Cape Cod, 'Joe' Welch died on the eve of his seventieth birthday. If he had died seven years ago his long and successful career in a distinguished Boston law firm would have earned him short obituaries under the probable headline 'Joseph N. Welch, an attorney.'

As it is, Mr. Punch's sad and mischievous smile looks out at us today from a thousand front pages, and there can hardly be an American adult over thirty who does not recognise St. George, who killed McCarthy, with kindness. On the spring day in 1954 when a mysterious but authoritative voice came over the telephone to Mr. Welch in Boston, he was an ageing and anonymous lawyer, whose origins on an Iowa farm, whose poor English parents, whose scraping to go to college, and whose subsequent acceptance as the very model of a proper Bostonian were his own business, matters for reminiscence, meditation, and quiet self-esteem. Six weeks later he was a national idol. For Mr. Welch responded to the telephone call, came in a daze to New York, and was flattered and alarmed to learn he had been chosen by a former Republican presidential candidate to carry the army's legal case against the unconquerable McCarthy.

Mr. Welch stayed overnight at the Harvard Club in New York and was then flown to Washington and the Secretary of the Army. Two months later the Harvard Club sent him a bill for six weeks' residence. He treasured this episode as a reassurance 'that only Harvard could go its way and be so supremely, so serenely, oblivious of the headlines and the fact of my absence in their service.'

In those six weeks, the working population of America came to desert its desks, feign illness in the factories, and head for the nearest television set to watch McCarthy paralyse his witnesses, reduce the Secretary of the Army to an apologetic dither, and, in the fullness of time, collapse and wither before the touch of Mr. Welch's velvet glove. It is now a part of American folklore that McCarthy's moment of truth was the moment that Mr. Welch took off his glove and pierced the Senator's backbone with a single trembling thrust.

The Senator had affected boredom verging on nausea over Mr. Welch's 'clowning,' his considerable theatrical powers, his gift for 'burlesquing this hearing' while all the time, the Senator whined, communism ran rampant over American society, reaching even into Mr. Welch's own law office and snatching a young man who 'has been for a number of years a member of an organisation which was named, oh years and years ago, as the legal bulwark of the Communist Party.' This bulwark was in truth a floundering lawyers' guild to which the 'young man' had very briefly belonged. He had told Mr. Welch all about it when the old man came to pick his staff for the Army hearings, and Mr. Welch gently excused him on the principle that his own team must be beyond suspicion.

At the unveiling of this old scar, Mr. Welch dropped his many Dickensian disguises and sat mute and naked with rage. He leaned into the microphone and steadied a querulous voice long enough to say: 'Until this moment, Senator, I think I never really gauged your cruelty or your recklessness . . . I like to think I am a gentleman, but your forgiveness will have to come from someone other than me.' He would not hear any more of McCarthy's blustering charges and left the room rubbing his eyes with a knuckle.

In no longer than two minutes, Mr. Welch had opposed McCarthy's heavy artillery with a short outburst of human decency. It divested the McCarthy crisis of its political cunning and brought millions of confused people to their elementary senses. Tonight the New York *Post* wrote Joe Welch's best epitaph: 'Rarely has any man served his country so well with a single act.'

Mr. Kennedy Takes Over

Washington, D.C., January 26, 1961

Snow swirling from high winds and twelve degrees of frost, the worst inaugural weather in fifty-two years, did not ruffle the smooth succession of John Fitzgerald Kennedy to the presidency today or prevent the American people thousands of miles from Washington, millions of them in snow-bound homes in the East, from seeing a presidential inauguration more intimately than all the dignitaries present.

Most of the Washington press corps were also either compelled by the overnight storm or persuaded by their memories of television's earlier conquests to stay in their homes and share the privilege of the ordinary American householder to switch a knob and hop around as a fly on the wall of history.

From the moment in mid-morning when we saw some of the rumply thirty-five White House staff members, who had been marooned in the White House overnight, join President Eisenhower at a coffee break in the Navy mess, the cameras of three networks kept up an unbroken scrutiny of every move of the Eisenhowers, the Nixons, the Lyndon Johnsons, the Kennedys leaving their house, the ride to the White House, the ride from the White House, the bland demeanour of the Diplomatic corps exchanging compliments on each other's hats, the close-up of a saturnine Justice Felix Frankfurter and an expansive William Douglas, the lifted eyebrows of Eisenhower and Mrs. Kennedy as a rabbi burst into a Jewish prayer, the restrained alarm of the marines and Senator John Sparkman (the inauguration host) when the smoking breath of the principals grew dense and was seen to be a separate cloud issuing from a fire that had broken out in a heater under the lectern.

This momentary fright, and a mix-up in the seating, delayed the taking of the oath for a full half hour. But Kennedy was sitting on the left hand of Eisenhower, and Eisenhower is a famous talker, and Ike regaled the new man with anecdotes and reflections and busy gestures for twenty minutes or more while we went through the traditional rituals of patriotic selections played, as always since 1801, by the band of the Marine Corps, while various rattled officials sniffed at the fire and argued with it.

The people could share, in fully amplified sound, the boredom of the famous as they listened to long prayers being intoned or rasped out by a Catholic cardinal, a Greek orthodox archbishop, a Protestant clergyman, and a rabbi, who always prolong their finest hour by turning these supplications into their own variation of the inaugural address.

While the invocations and beseechings barked or droned on the winter air, the cameras put together a portrait gallery of the victors and the falling in action: Adlai Stevenson, the only member of the Executive branch in a felt hat instead of a topper, chewing the cud of his two defeats and talking to no one; Harry Truman, in unbelievable Christian fettle chatting affably with the enemy Nixon; the features, trenched with age, of a little old lady nestled close to the peach bloom fuzz of Mrs. Kennedy's pretty face; Chief Justice Earl Warren, sitting at the alert immediately behind Kennedy and preserving at all times the impassivity of a melon; and all the time Kennedy inclining over to the voluble Ike and listening without a fidget, his fine hands slightly clasped.

At last, old Sam Rayburn rose to administer the Vice-Presidential oath to his fellow Texan, Lyndon Johnson, whom he had laboured so to install on the President's throne. Then there was a prayer, handsomely praising the earthly capacities of Mr. Johnson, by a Texas clergyman.

Then old Robert Frost was summoned to read an old poem with a new introduction composed specially for this day. The sun flashed wounding reflections on his failing eyes and he stumbled through the introduction, threw in a despairing aside ('I'm not in a good light . . . I can't get through this thing'), abandoned his text, and spoke the poem loud and strong, but with his fingers kneading his palms in a secret fury and his white hair lapping in waves against his forehead. Kennedy was the first to tap his shoulder and reassure him with a grasp of the hand.

After that Chief Justice Warren stood to the right of the lectern. Kennedy put his left hand on a family Bible, raised his right, and repeated the immemorial oath to 'preserve, protect, and defend the Constitution of the United States, so help me God.'

Then with never a quaver he delivered the simple, rolling cadences of what is certainly one of the simplest and most eloquent of inaugural addresses. 'This is not a victory of party but a celebration of freedom . . . let every nation know whether it wishes us well or ill that we are here to assure the survival and the success of liberty . . . To those old allies we pledge the loyalty of faithful friends . . . To those in huts and villages of half the globe we pledge our best efforts to help men help themselves . . . If we cannot help the many who are poor, we cannot help the few who are rich . . . This hemisphere intends to remain the master of its own house.'

At the end, when the cheers rose from the shivering crowd, Eisenhower gave two slaps, tweaked his nose, shook Kennedy's hand. And Kennedy walked out as cool, but alive to small courtesies and distant nods, as an admiral being piped aboard. That, in a way, is what was happening, for the Marine band, which had been interspersing the oaths and prayers with homely but traditional ruffles and flourishes, now burst with new zest into the presidential tune, 'Hail to the Chief!' The cameras roamed over a huge square packed with thousands of ordered dots. Beyond these frozen 'eye-witnesses' was Constitution Plaza and the Hill and Pennsylvania Avenue – a continuous ribbon of bare highway, the only naked street in Washington.

Beyond that were the houses slumped in snowbanks and a frozen landscape for thousands of miles housing the warm, remote population that had seen Robert Frost's moment of misery, and Mrs. Kennedy's smooth throat twitch for a second as the 'unbearable office' passed over from the oldest President to the youngest.

The Legend of Gary Cooper

May 18, 1961

When the word got out that Gary Cooper (who died on Saturday, aged 60) was mortally ill, a spontaneous process arose in high places not unlike the first moves to sanctify a remote peasant. The Queen of England dispatched a sympathetic cable. The President of the United States called him on the telephone. A cardinal ordered public prayers. Messages came to his house in Beverly Hills from the unlikeliest fans, from foreign ministers and retired soldiers who never knew him, as also from Ernest Hemingway, his old Pygmalion who had kept him in mind, through at least two novels, as the archetype of the Hemingway hero: the self-sufficient male animal, the best kind of hunter, the silent infantryman padding dutifully forward to perform the soldier's most poignant ritual in 'the ultimate loneliness of contact.'

It did not happen to Ronald Colman, or Clark Gable, or – heaven knows – John Barrymore. Why, we may well ask, should it have happened to Frank James Cooper, the rather untypical American type of the son of a Bedfordshire lawyer, a boy brought up in the Rockies among horses and cattle to be sure, but only as they compose the unavoidable backdrop of life in those parts; a schoolboy in Dunstable, England, a college boy in Iowa, a middling student, then a failing cartoonist, failed salesman, an 'extra' in Hollywood who in time had his break and mooned in a lanky, handsome way through a score or more of 'horse operas'? Well, his friends most certainly mourn the gentle, shambling 'Coop,' but what the world mourns is the death of Mr. Longfellow Deeds, who resisted and defeated the corruption of the big city; the snuffing out of the sheriff, in *High Noon*, heading back to duty along the railroad tracks with that precise mince of the cowboy's tread and that rancher's squint that sniffs mischief in a creosote bush, sees through suns, and is never fooled. What the world mourns is its lost innocence, or a favourite fantasy of it fleshed out in the most durable and heroic of American myths: that of the taut but merciful plainsman, who dispenses justice with a worried conscience, a single syllable, a blurred reflex action to the hip, and who must face death in the afternoon as regularly as the matador, but on Main Street and for no pay.

Mr. Deeds Goes to Town marks the first jelling of this fame, and *The Plainsman* the best delineation of the character that fixed his legend. These two films retrieved Cooper from a run of agreeable and handsome parts, some of them (in the

Lubitsch films for instance) too chic and metropolitan for his own good. At the time of *Mr. Deeds*, an English critic wrote that 'the conception of the wise underdog, the shrewd hick, is probably too western, too American in its fusion of irony and sentimentality, to travel far.' He was as wrong as could be, for the film was a sensation in Poland, the Middle East, and other barbaric regions whose sense of what is elementary in human goodness is something we are just discovering, perhaps a little late.

It is easy to forget now, as always with artists who have matured a recognisable style, that for at least the first dozen years of his film career Gary Cooper was the lowbrow's comfort and the highbrow's butt. However, he lasted long enough, as all great talents do, to weather the four stages of the highbrow treatment: first, he was derided, then ignored, then accepted, then discovered. We had seen this happen many times before; and looking back, one is always shocked to recognise the people it has happened to. To-day the intellectual would deny, for instance, that Katharine Hepburn was ever anything but a lovely if haggard exotic, with a personal style which might enchant some people and grate on others, but would insist she was at all times what we call a 'serious' talent. This opinion was in fact a highly sophisticated second thought, one which took about a decade to ripen and squelch the memory of Dorothy Parker's little tribute to Miss Hepburn's first starring appearance on Broadway: 'Miss Hepburn ran the gamut of human emotions from A to B.'

Marilyn Monroe is a grosser example still. Universally accepted as a candy bar or cream puff, she presented a galling challenge to the intelligentsia when she married Arthur Miller, a very sombre playwright and indubitably *un homme sérieux*. The question arose whether there had been serious miscalculation about a girly calendar that could marry a man who defied the House Un-American Activities Committee. The doubt was decided in Miss Monroe's favour when she delivered pointed ripostes to dumb questions at a London press conference.

At least until the mid-thirties there was no debate about Gary Cooper because he presented no issue. He belonged to the reveries of the middle-class woman. He reminded grieving mothers of the upright son shot down on the Somme; devoted sisters, of the brother sheep-ranching in Australia; the New York divorcee, of the handsome ranch hand with whom she is so often tempted to contract a ruinous second marriage in the process of dissolving her first. To the moviegoer, Cooper was the matinee idol toughened and tanned, in the era of the outdoors, into something at once glamorous and primitive. He was notoriously known as the actor who couldn't act. Only the directors who handled him had daily proof of the theory that the irresistible 'stars' are simply behaviourists who, by some nervous immunity to the basilisk glare and hiss of the camera, appear to be nobody but themselves. Very soon the box-offices, from Tokyo to Carlisle, confirmed this theory in hard cash. Then the intellectuals sat up and took notice. Then the Cooper legend took over.

For the past quarter-century, Cooper's worldwide image had grown so rounded, so heroically elongated rather, that only some very crass public behaviour could have smudged it. There was none. After a short separation he was happily re-united with his only wife. He spoke out, during the McCarthy obscenity, with resounding pointlessness and flourished the banner of 'Americanism' in a heated way. Most recently, there has been a low-pressure debate in progress in fan magazines and newspaper columns about whether his 'yup-nope' approach was his own or a press agent's inspiration, like the malapropisms of Sam Goldwyn, another happy device for blinding mockers to the knowledge that they were losing their shirts. This was decided a week or two ago by the New York *Post*, which concluded after a series of exclusive interviews with his friends, that Cooper's inarticulateness was natural when he was in the presence of gabby strangers, that gabbiness was his natural bent with close friends.

He could probably have transcended, or dimmed, bigger

scandals or more public foolishness than he was capable of, because he was of the company of Chaplin, Groucho Marx, W. C. Fields, Bogart, Louis Jouvet, two or three others, give or take a personal favourite. He filled an empty niche in the world pantheon of essential gods. If no cowboy was ever like him, so much the worse for the cattle kingdom. He was Eisenhower's glowing, and glowingly false, picture of Wyatt Earp. He was one of Walt Whitman's troop of democratic knights, 'bright eyed as hawks with their swarthy complexions and their broad-brimmed hats, with loose arms slightly raised and swinging as they ride.' He represented every man's best secret image of himself: the honourable man slicing clean through the broiling world of morals and machines. He isolated and enlarged to six-feet-three an untainted strain of goodness in a very male specimen of the male of the species.

A Woman of Integrity
Marilyn Monroe
August 9, 1962

Marilyn Monroe was found dead in bed this morning in her home in Hollywood, only a physical mile or two, but a social universe, away from the place where she was born 36 years ago as Norma Jean Baker. She died with a row of medicines and an empty bottle of barbiturates at her elbow.

These stony sentences, which read like the epitaph of a Raymond Chandler victim, will confirm for too many millions of movie fans the usual melodrama of a humble girl, cursed by physical beauty, to be dazed and doomed by the fame that was too much for her. For Americans, the last chapter was written on the weekend that a respectable national picture magazine printed for the delectation of her troubled fans a confessional piece called 'Marilyn Monroe Pours Out Her Soul.' The plot of her early life is as seedy as anything in the pulp magazines, and to go into the details now would be as tasteless as prying into the clinical file of any other pretty woman whose beauty has crumbled overnight. It is enough, for summoning the necessary compassion, to recall her miserable parents, her being shuttled like a nuisance from foster home to orphanage, the subsequent knockabout years in a war factory, her short independence as a sailor's wife, the unsuspected first rung of the ladder provided by a posing job for a nude calendar.

She talked easily about all this, when people had the gall to ask her, not as someone reconciled to a wretched childhood but as a wide-eyed outsider, an innocent as foreign to the subject under discussion as Chaplin is when he stands off and analyses the appeal of 'The Little Man.'

Then she wiggled briefly past the lecherous gaze of Louis Calhern in John Huston's *Asphalt Jungle*, and his appraising whinny echoed round the globe. Within two years she was the enthroned sexpot of the Western world. She completed the first phase of the American dream by marrying the immortal Joe DiMaggio, the loping hero of the New York Yankees; and the second phase by marrying Arthur Miller and so redeeming his suspect Americanism at the moment it was in question before a House committee.

To say that Marilyn Monroe was a charming, shrewd, and pathetic woman of tragic integrity will sound as preposterous to the outsider as William Empson's Freudian analysis of *Alice in Wonderland*. It is nevertheless true. We restrict the word 'integrity' to people either simple or complex, who have a strong sense of righteousness or, if they are public men, of self-righteousness. Yet it surely means no more than what it says: wholeness, being free to be spontaneous, without reck of consistency or moral appearances. It can be true of forlorn and bewildered people as of the disciplined and the solemn.

In this sense, Marilyn Monroe was all of a piece. She was confused, pathologically shy, a straw on the ocean of her compulsions (to pout, to wisecrack, to love a stranger, to be six hours late or lock herself in a room). She was a sweet and humorous person increasingly terrified by the huge stereotype of herself she saw plastered all around her. The exploitation of this pneumatic, mocking, liquid-lipped goddess gave the world a simple picture of the Lorelei. She was about as much of a Lorelei as Bridget, the housemaid.

This orphan of the rootless City of the Angels at last could feel no other identity than the one she saw in the mirror: a baffled, honest girl forever haunted by the nightmare of herself, sixty feet tall and naked before a howling mob. She could never learn to acquire the lacquered shell of the prima donna or the armour of sophistication. So in the end she found the ultimate oblivion, of which her chronic latecomings and desperate retreats to her room were tokens.

The U.S. Science Pavilion

Seattle, Washington, October 18, 1962

The Seattle World's Fair is closing down and in its six months' existence the United States Science Pavilion has towered over every other exhibit in popularity as it does in distinction. It is as much of a pleasure to salute this single achievement at the end of the Fair as it was a pain to decry the rest of it on opening day.

It lies, happily, along the south-western edge of the Fair, away from the main architectural babel, but one appreciates its dominance best from an airplane: five high slender aluminium Gothic arches rising above graceful plots of buildings enclosing a court of pools punctuated by jetting fountains. The six flanking buildings are slabs of pre-stressed concrete of such crystalline purity that even on the dull days their reflection was as difficult to bear as Alpine snows. Their façades are evenly broken up with continuous Gothic arches used as a kind of filigree. The terraces between the buildings are enclosed with nothing but the arches themselves. The motif is repeated in miniature in the grille work of the iron fences that rail off the stone platforms which bridge the pools and lead from one building to another. The terraces swirl with indented Moorish circles.

The distant effect on the newcomer is that of a cluster of King's College Chapels over-exposed by an ecstatic photographer on a brilliant day. As you come closer and are surrounded by the concrete surfaces everywhere, and the delicate and rippling interplay of light and water, arches and scintillating stone, it is as if the Gothic style had passed without a break through the Renaissance and the eighteenth century, in and out of Spain, and had achieved a final sensuous purity in the twentieth century. It is as if Venice had just been built.

This most moving pavilion is the work of Minoru Yamasaki, who was born in Seattle forty-nine years ago, was a humble instructor in watercolour at New York University in the depression, who then moved into architectural design, became the chief designer to Raymond Loewy, and has since been sweeping up awards across the country, most notably for the splendid new airport at St. Louis.

It is not possible, you say to yourself, that his pavilion could begin to match inside the beauty of its exterior. You are wrong. For inside, five great halls using every known and some novel techniques of demonstration present a history of science designed by Raymond Loewy, George Nelson, and by Charles Eames, the Mozart of the applied sciences. When you consider the pressures that shape any project sponsored by the executive branch of the Government (this is under the Department of Commerce) and subject to the approval of Congress to the tune of $9.5 millions, it is a marvel that what should have emerged is a single philosophical conception of remarkable majesty and disinterestedness. It can be sensed only dimly by its official definition: 'To present the role of man in a search for truth and science.' To inch towards a description only a little more adequate, it is a place designed to register the shocks of the physical universe, both terrible and exquisite, on the human mind; and to trace in sequence the attempts of men to explain and use them, from the Egyptians to Einstein and beyond.

We begin where the primitive began, agape before huge dioramas of the elemental natural phenomena: twenty panels showing the rising and setting of the sun; a tornado; the Northern Lights; a comet; the visual splendour of the New England fall; an electrical storm; the spawning of a trout.

Next we pass through a corridor that demonstrates some sophisticated illusions of the senses. Two suns swinging back and forth into the line of vision are seen, close up, to be quite stationary, being merely inflating and deflating balloons within the same plane. A Western street scene has the houses and trees hitched at an angle uniformly sharper than forty-five degrees. The street itself is plumb flat, but weaving along it you have the sense of going both uphill and down, and you are lucky not to end in nausea.

So far we have experienced the natural and contrived phenomena of the world we live in. The remaining halls illustrate (through murals, dioramas, calculators, beautifully designed working models) the successive ways in which men have tried to explain them. Mathematics begins in Egypt with the shrewd primitive observation that three trees and three horses have some knotty thing in common, and ends with determining the temperature of a distant star. Electromagnetics starts with Galvani's dead frog twitching in brine and ends with the behaviour of Hertzian waves. We grope our way into genetics by walking through a corridor of panels that stylise the rain forest. Inset against their proper flora are coloured motion pictures of the animals – the armadillo, the tiger, and the rest – whose wild variety baffled Darwin. Its puzzle is then taken up by Mendel, first in a panel of experimental formulae, and then in a winking model of his pea-plant experiment that he would have given two brown eyes to own. So we pass on to Morgan and the 'crossing over' of chromosomes, and then to Muller and Beadle and Tatum, and Watson and Crick's D.N.A. molecule, and to a final or perhaps only provisional, generalisation: 'Life is the control of increasing orders of complexity.'

And so it goes, with halls devoted to the Methods of Science, the Horizons of Science, and the Human Being. Shakespeare's image of man as a forked radish is articulated in a huge magnification of the incredibly complicated structure of a salamander's spermatozoa. It stands at the entrance of the hall that deals with the human organism, and, to put it mildly, it would give pause to the most riproaring fundamentalist. An hour later we leave this place with a nervous backward look at a monkey embracing a comfortable artificial mother, made of terry cloth, to the denial of its food, planted in another 'mother' made of scratchy wire mesh. We came in to the sound and sight of a thunderstorm and went out pondering the connection of motherhood, food, and affection. Through the two or three hours it takes to follow this show, we appreciate at last that we have been the faltering but graceful Watson and Holmes – tracking Galileo and Faraday and Avogadro and Chadwick and all the others.

There is one dizzy interruption to their humbling journey. It is a central hall, a circle of darkness underneath a mammoth saucer dome, which turns into the screen for a visual journey into space. The spectator first holds then clutches a rail and sees Canaveral fade away, and then the Florida peninsula and then the Americas. The ghastly moon looms up, is suddenly the whole of the sky, is about to engulf us when it veers off overhead. Leo and Virgo and Libra and Scorpio float by. The sun streams its millions of miles of flame and recedes into a cinder, as negligible as a glow-worm in the Grand Canyon. The rest of this passage through a trillion light years is a wonderful nightmare of rattling meteorites, asteroids, snarling gases, the ringed planet, the mystery of Mars, before we touch Pluto and the limit of the solar system. On the way back to cosy Canaveral I thought of Empson's witty emendation of Pascal: 'Spaces between stars seem to say what common sense has seen.' It is not true. The only dead spaces between stars, it turns out, are those huge ones between Mars and Saturn. All the others seem to say what giants dare not think. Poor old common sense is not the same interval between epigrams but a space as humdrum as a parking lot.

At the last, this dazed layman went back to the beginning, to a beautiful curving entrance hall to the Pavilion, and watched again Charles Eames's exquisite twelve-minute film – or rather nine films projected simultaneously on a composite screen – called *The House of Science*. Here from a comic animation of the first man and the first cave, the house grew into a Victorian mansion of all the modern specialities and then dissolved into a fly's-eye view of their function: the slitting of a muscle, the building of a cyclotron, the isolation of a virus, the marvel that is the eyeball of a salmon, the vein of a maple leaf.

When Handel, writing the *Messiah* through those fifteen nights and days in his Dublin garret, came to the Hallelujah Chorus, he wrote that it was 'as if the Lord God Almighty had appeared before me.' Something of this sublimity comes to the layman who, transported for an hour or two out of his single culture of the humanities, finishes the magic trek through this Pavilion. He knows he has been initiated into that humble awe before the mysteries of the universe which, until so lately, was thought to be the prerogative of the poet and the priest. And if, as he moves off into the jungle of the Fair, he looks back at Yamasaki's masterpiece, he can hardly stifle a chuckle at the thought that here and now, in the high noon of the abstractionists and the steel and glass honeycombs, one modern architect has made the blinding discovery that a Gothic arch does, after all, seem to express the aspiration of men to reach beyond the earth they live on.

Maker of a President

Eleanor Roosevelt

November 13, 1962

Mrs. Franklin D. Roosevelt, the widow of the thirty-second President of the United States, died last week in New York City where she was born seventy-eight years ago. Except for increasing deafness in old age, she had never been troubled with anything much more bothersome than a cold or a broken ankle until she took to a hospital bed a few weeks ago with a pestiferous condition that was eventually diagnosed as anaemia complicated by a lung infection. 'Eleanor,' Franklin Roosevelt used to say, watching her and her notebook whirl continuously around the United States to check on soil erosion, unemployment, sick leave among nurses, or silicosis among miners, 'has time for everybody's troubles but her own.'

It was a proud complaint which, in the missionary days of the New Deal, the newspaper cartoonists turned into a national joke. Until Mrs. Roosevelt, First Ladies were supposed to be the most gracious furnishing of the White House. They kept the silver polished and the fires burning against the unpredictable return of the great man and from the crushing appointments of his office. It is a tradition honoured up to 1933 and since 1945. The twelve intervening years turned the White House into a sort of national hotel operating under emergency conditions. Protocol was packed off with the bags of Mr. and Mrs. Hoover. The President's bedroom was invaded at breakfast by the Brain Trust. Lunch was a sandwich on a tray dispensed to visiting Governors, labour leaders, national committeemen. Birthdays, national holidays, and most Sunday evenings were the occasion of the famous and inedible Roosevelt buffets.

This genial chaos was the logical extension, on a national scale, of the domestic free-for-all which Franklin and Eleanor Roosevelt had developed at Hyde Park and Campobello, and at their house in New York, as the boisterous childhood of five children coincided with the effort of Mrs. Roosevelt and Louis Howe to boost her paralysed husband into national politics and to save him from the fate which his mother prescribed with such grim resolve: 'My son must come home to live in Hyde Park: he's going to be an invalid the rest of his life and he needs rest and complete quiet.'

Even now, forty-one years after the famous chill at Campobello and the black two years during which Roosevelt agonised over the hardest task of a lifetime ('trying to move one toe'), the transformation of Franklin and Eleanor Roosevelt from an upper-class couple of no particular personal distinction into two iron characters who have left their permanent brand on history appears to be nothing less than a human miracle.

Eleanor's childhood and youth seemed a pathetic prelude to a life of social martyrdom. Her father was a gallant drunk, her mother the spoiled and beautiful daughter of a beauty more petulant still. She was a nuisance and butt. From earliest girlhood her mother mocked her for her gravity, her prominent teeth and shapeless mouth. She comforted herself in her journal with the thought that 'no matter how plain we may be, if we have virtue and trust, they will show in our faces.' She went to work in a settlement house and came to know the daily aspect of poverty, a running sore on the body politic that astonished and embarrassed Franklin.

Then came New York State politics in Albany, and the dreadful summer, and the dedicated battle with his mother, and soon his discovery that if he listened more and tossed his head less, he could like people and they could like him. Eleanor took night classes in government and sociology and fed her lessons to Franklin, while Louis Howe massaged his legs for hours on end. It is the symbolic picture of the rest of their lives. In the White House, when the steel braces grew too heavy, he took them off and Eleanor, fresh from the Midwest or the Deep South, read over the compassionate statistics she learned on the road with such unflagging and humourless devotion.

'This concept of duty,' writes her biographer, 'was Victorian, soft-headed, and entirely un-American, in the brassy 1920s. But Eleanor Roosevelt had it and it guided her entire existence.' It transmuted an ugly duckling school-ma'am into a great woman, and it planed away the emotional fat in a feckless, generous man, knotted his fibre, and produced a great president. There are few women in the history of great nations who could claim such a personal achievement, and none less likely to make the claim. The people, though, sensed it and year after year, to the annoyance of her chuckling detractors, she was voted, in a national poll, the First Lady of the World.

For herself she simply listed in the *Who's Who* entry only three or four of the offices she filled on her own account. She might have recorded the sum of her great life with nothing more than her vital statistics and the single entry: 'Created the Thirty-second President of the United States.'

Scourge of the Book-burners

April 25, 1963

Dr. A. Whitney Griswold, one of the most civilised leaders and critics of contemporary education, died on Friday evening of cancer, on the campus of Yale University of which he had been President since 1950. He was 56.

The fitness of 'Whit' Griswold to preside with conspicuous courage and humour over a great university in the McCarthy era was a very well-kept secret until the moment he was appointed. True, he was a direct descendant of three Governors of Connecticut, and a collateral descendant of Eli Whitney of the cotton gin, but these proofs that he was of the blood royal were known only to a handful of friends.

The university had known him, barely, as a nervous freshman, a stringy student, and a contributor of sassy verse to the university daily. Wall Street knew him briefly as a clerk in a brokerage firm. He moved from Yale into the financial world modestly in the summer of 1929 and deserted it, like thousands more, in the clatter of the following October. Like other bright and swiftly disillusioned boys, he preferred to teach history rather than endure it.

He went back to Yale to get his Ph.D., and became an instructor in the history department. From then until his forty-fourth year he was known to the campus as a modest expert on the Far Eastern policy of the United States and a lecturer with a sardonic strain. His wildest admirers would have bet on a lifetime professorship agreeably relieved by a gift for dialect stories. The notion of a college presidency apparently never crossed his mind, for in this country a university president is above all a money-raiser, and Whit Griswold was, on the contrary, a scholar and a teacher.

On a certain weekend he was lunching in New York with the president of a small college who was elaborating on the striking resemblance of his job to that of a community chest chairman. Griswold no sooner thanked the Lord he was 'not in that racket' than, as in a Cary Grant film, he was called to the telephone and told that the Yale Corporation had just picked him unanimously to succeed Dr. Charles Seymour, the historian. The corporation included the then Secretary of State, Dean Acheson, and the late Senator Robert Taft. Their choice of Griswold, it emerged, was as inspired a bit of bipartisanship as they ever achieved.

He surprised everybody, possibly including himself, from the start. He began rapidly to change the university curriculum and quieted his critics with a slogan picked up from a bottle of mayonnaise: 'Keep cool, but do not freeze.' As a simple act of belated justice, he doubled the faculty pay scale. He developed a remarkable ability to raise money, and in his twelve years tripled the university's endowment fund. But this, he made clear to everyone around him, was a vulgar, if vital, necessity to survival in a teeming world of taxes and real estate.

A university president above all, he said, must speak for the best values he knows in the society he inhabits. This can guarantee a droning sort of fame in a quiet time, but Dr. Griswold was matched with the McCarthy hour, and for five or six years at least he was a thorn in the side of the book-burners and the loyalty-oath-takers: 'Books won't stay banned. They won't burn. Ideas won't go to gaol. In the long run, the censor and the inquisitor have always lost. The only cure for bad ideas is better ideas.'

When the university's financial position was still very shaky, he was urged to commit it to a Federal programme that gave loans to poor students. But the Federal Government required a loyalty oath and an affidavit disclaiming membership in any subversive society. To Griswold 'this negative affidavit' was like 'the oppressive religious and political test oaths of history,' and was too much to swallow. He took Yale out of the general programme and sought money from similarly high-minded men who were also millionaires and unafraid of McCarthyism. In the mid-fifties this was a fairly rare combination.

The free-wheeling temperament is often acceptable in a scholar provided he does not indulge it as an administrator. But this thin, insistent, courteous man went cheerfully on the rampage against the whole committee approach to running a university and its departments. The normal faculty broodings in committee he called 'endless, sterile, stultifying. Could Hamlet have been written by a committee or the Mona Lisa painted by a club? The divine spark leaps from the finger of God to the finger of Adam.'

That sentence might well be his epitaph. In 1950 he looked like a springy, rather earnest, young idealist who would soon crack his skull on a Congressional committee at worst, a board of trustees at best. When he died on Friday he was known throughout the Western world as a brilliant administrator, but also, and better, a man of salt who had good wounds to show for his defence of freedom in a high place in the early 1950s.

The Thirty-sixth President

November 28, 1963

It is hard to describe the appearance and personality of President Lyndon Baines Johnson in any words that would mean the same thing to readers of different nationalities or, indeed, of different States. To say that he is 55, just under 200 lbs., 6 ft 3 in., clean-shaven, has crinkly, quizzical eyes, and a blue-rimmed chin, is about as objective and blank a description as one could give. It only begins to acquire life through the lens of the observer's preconceptions.

Thus, in a French paper, he is an 'earthy yet dapper son of the Far West.' In a score of Northern tabloids he is a 'a rangy, back-slapping Texan.' To an English politician he is 'one of those ingratiating, shrewd Southern types the Senate seems to breed.' Because he decided, ten years ago, that 'segregation is doomed,' most Southern conservatives look on him darkly as the native son who betrayed the Southland. To Texans of liberal bent, and there are many, he is an easy combination of sentimental New Dealer and smooth operator in oil, ranching, natural gas, and insurance. To the Congress, he is quite simply 'Lyndon, the supreme strategist of the Senate,' an alternately engaging and terrifying figure on Capitol Hill who, in the ironical progression of American politics, achieved the honour of the vice-presidency and got lost in its tomblike vacuum; although every succeeding President swears to transform the office into that of an active deputy commander, somehow the system can accommodate only one leader, and the Vice-President becomes a powerless Pooh-Bah, a ceremonial courier, a certain attender of funerals in Addis Ababa.

It is from this hallowed void that, like seven other 'accidental' Presidents before him, Lyndon Johnson has now been plucked to assume the supreme command. He comes to it from a background about as far removed from that of John Fitzgerald Kennedy as Boston, the Cunard terminal for immigrant Irishmen, is from Stonewall, Texas, where, until very recently, the shooting of an unarmed man 'who made threats' was legally interpreted as justifiable self-defence. Both of them, however, were the grandsons of practising politicians, and the gap between the farmer's son and the second-generation Ivy Leaguer was bridged when they came to Washington by the politician's code of teamsmanship and party loyalty. The contrast between a boy who taught school to Mexicans and Negroes and a boy who had his own car in Palm Beach shrivelled before the same tough facts of political life: the means whereby campaign funds are raised, a city machine is disciplined, a winning coalition is forged at the expense of personal friendships. It was this bond that made them close and admiring allies in the Senate. It was the reason why Kennedy, surveying the disorder and dissension of the South in 1960, picked Johnson to save it by wheedling, cajoling, and bullying its leaders in the last weeks of the campaign.

Johnson was born to a small farm and few comforts. At the age of nine, he was a shoe-shine boy in a barber's shop, at fifteen he had left school for a road-building gang, and went from there to California by way of odd jobs in garages, lunch counters, and hotels. He came back to Texas having been convinced in his odd moments that formal education was not the sissy frill he had been led to think. He worked his way through the Southwest State Teachers College, at San Marcos, Texas, and three and a half years later took a B.S. degree. One endowment that simply required polishing was his gift of the gab; and it should be no surprise to anyone who has seen him woo and win an audience that in his early twenties he was a teacher of public speaking and debating.

In 1931 he decided to go into politics as a political secretary to a Texas Congressman. In Washington the engaging young man with the dark eyes and the energy of a mustang came under the eye of Franklin Roosevelt, who became from then on, in Johnson's special phrase, 'a daddy to me.' In 1937 he scraped into the Congressional seat of a dead Congressman and the next year was elected to his own term. In 1948, the year of Harry Truman's miraculous reincarnation, he slipped into the Senate by eighty-seven votes. The rest is the story of his rise as Democratic whip to the leadership of the party on the Senate floor. To those who had watched him calculate the possible and contrive the impossible, it was the inevitable mating of a round peg with a round hole.

At this moment of hasty recall, political reporters remember him most vividly as the Senate leader who kept a mental file on the men who balked him, who yet liquidated old enmities in an unflagging gift for compromise. They reflect that there are not many Senators, even now, who are not beholden to him. And they hope that in some way, never yet discovered by a Congressman translated to the White House, he will be able to mesmerise the legislative arm of government that was set up as his watchdog.

What is more plausible to anticipate is the strengthening of his instinct for compromise, for his whole professional life has been lived in the rooted belief that politics is 'one long accommodation of competing forces.' This conviction has often made him contemptuous of the liberal Jeremiahs. What matters, he used to swear, is not the throbbing speech (though no one can throb in better iambic pentameter) but the bill that emerges, not the scarifying abuse of McCarthy but the contriving of his censure on the floor of the Senate; on what he honestly regards as the supreme American issue of the day – the civil rights of the Negro – not the flaming sword but the guarantee that it shall not cleave the nation in two.

So, to look over the last chapter of his active record with a cold eye, he catered to the North by steering through the Senate, with considerable courage, the first Civil Rights Bill in a hundred years; and while he first tried to redeem himself in the horrified South by protecting its rights to filibuster, he saw, with the same delayed but irrevocable honesty, that the filibuster must soon go, and so he incensed his fellow-Southerners again by cautiously restricting the right of unlimited debate.

Until a few years ago, his glaring liability as a president for the 1960s seemed to be his vague, baffled view of foreign affairs. Indo-China he thought to be a 'futile war.' Algeria was a remote nuisance, Quemoy and Matsu the proud ramparts we must watch, Africa and Asia were 'growing suburbs.' But nothing could be more unfair than to leave him with this air of a petulant provincial onlooker. In the last three years he saw President Kennedy through all the worst hours of the Bay of Pigs, Berlin, the missile crisis, South Vietnam, the McNamara—Pentagon feud, and the rest. 'The President,' he said a couple of years ago, 'carries heavier burdens than I ever envisioned. You feel goose pimples coming up on your back.' Because he is a doggedly untheoretical man, he has a capacity to digest unpleasant facts beyond his early experience. 'I hate this thing as much as you do,' he once shouted at a Senate colleague, 'but this is what is happening.'

What he has lately discovered 'is happening' is the enfranchisement of Africa, the revolt of Asia against the white man, the feudal upheaval of Latin America, the yearning of democratic Europe for self-reliance. Luckily, in ceremonial line of duty, he has visited most of the allies, as also Scandinavia and the Middle East, and is personally acquainted with some of the African leaders. He has declared himself most pungently on three great issues:

On civil rights – 'The words of the Declaration of Independence do not need to be further interpreted. They need to be implemented for all Americans.'
On the United Nations – 'It is very necessary. We would be at war without it.'
On peace – 'Reciprocity is the key. If the Soviets want America's co-operation, they can earn it. If the Soviets want America's hostility, they can certainly provoke it.'

In the melancholy waiting interval between the requiem and the inauguration, there are few certainties about the Johnson

Administration. One of them is that he will take hold. And though the high style of the Kennedy regime is gone forever, as the White House reverts to the folksier manner of the county courthouse square, it will not surprise the friends of Lyndon Johnson if he emerges as a second Harry Truman, who arrived blinking in the White House one day, a failed haberdasher needing all our prayers, and the next sprang fully armed as an irascible all-American legionnaire and, more astonishing still, a twentieth-century statesman.

Rally in the Valley

Van Nuys, California, May 17, 1964

Twenty years ago the way out to what they used to call this 'bustling' valley settlement would have been through two-lane roads rippling through small canyons between the characteristic mountains of the Coast Range, the green or gold breasts of hills dotted with live oaks as in a medieval tapestry.

Then we should have wound down the eastern slopes and looked on a most typical California scene: the table-flat valley with its fanning groves of orange trees or lemon or peach or avocado, the long fields guarded by battalions of eucalyptus trees in single file, and very far off to the east the ramparts of the Sierras, so high in the skyline that their snowy crests were mistaken for drifts of stratus clouds. It was a California not much wept over at the time, but it is long gone. It was a California beloved by Senator Goldwater and by me.

Tonight, our seat belts tight and our car slotted into one of the eight lanes of the roaring Freeway, we whizz between the crummy brown hills from which the live oaks, the eucalyptus, and the pepper trees have gone for a hundred hillside housing developments ('Veterans no down payment'). After four minutes (or six miles) we unwind off the Freeway and thread through bungalow boulevards to the place in the valley where

Senator Goldwater will no doubt tonight lament the passing of Geronimo and Wells Fargo and bemoan the arrival of the 'planned economy' and Johnson's 'boon-doggle' of an electioneering 'war' against poverty. It is a huge race track, or athletics field or open-air stadium of the 'Valley' college, yet another state college in a State that must now build one school a day to keep up with the baby boom and the additional 8,000-odd permanent settlers who come into California every week.

It is a chill night for these parts, and as three or four thousand people gather in the stands and the high grid of lights goes on, the Valley Youth Band peers from under its shakos and stamps on the grass for circulation.

It is darkening now and the Senator is late. So evidently are the young 'fascists,' the bullyboy Birchers, the protective S.S. men we had been warned about by muttering liberals. No, there come the S.S. men now: blue-uniformed highway cops with breeches stiff as starch, ferocious goggles, leathery faces, and motorbikes like landborne rockets. They whine and rip around in formation. In fact, their formations are so audacious, involving men doing handstands and cradling their heads in the driver's lap, that you fear some mistake. They turn out to be not cops at all, but Victor McLaglen's Motor Corps, which seized the trick-riding championship from Mexico City twenty years ago and has held it ever since.

Here he comes, convoyed by the McLaglen boys in arrowhead formation.

Everything is fitting into place. Then the really sinister notes, as thousands of heads are bowed (and you notice that the young bow low – no rowdies, these); and a parson with a blood-curdling baritone begs the Lord 'to keep us from the deadly folly of coexistence. Thou, Oh Lord, knowest that we have every weapon for victory except one – the will to win.' It was the first time I ever heard the opening prayer applauded.

Now we must get through the joking palaver that is compulsory at these rallies. The band flashes and stomps. Ronald

Reagan, the movie-star, delivers rousing cracks from cue cards: 'They say the Republicans belong with the McKinley administration. Not a bad idea that; under McKinley we freed Cuba.' Soaring, helpless laughter. Finally, the idol, the Führer, the man Goldwater.

We really ought to end here, for the comfort of anyone who wishes to preserve the stirring picture of southern California as a vast Dallas with eucalyptus trees and freeways, a place where all Republicans are Far Rightists whose crackpot private militias stash rifles in the hills against the arrival of the Russians — from the Aleutians, maybe?

The crowd rises at him and you look around and try to gauge their types. The thousand or so I got a glimpse of seemed singularly unembittered. They are in all the clothes that ranchers and drug-store cowboys and the early timid beatniks wore, by now standard uniform for the young of all countries. To anyone over forty they look like garage mechanics gone to the ball game. They are young husbands with well-cared-for children, chemistry students, second-year agriculture or Eng-Lit pupils, retired small farmers, shopkeepers, real estate agents, bank clerks.

Two beanpole youths have furtively waited for this moment. As a thousand 'Goldwater for President' signs are waved against the purple sky, these two unfurl a home-made banner, a bed sheet, perhaps, and reveal the legend: 'Fight Extremism.' There is a little gasp, a high-rumped boy dashes to tear it down, fails, it is unfurled again and it stays sagging in the chill wind through most of the leader's speech.

The crowd is alternately depressed and amused by it. It turns for comfort and for inspiration to the leader himself. He stands there in a grey suit, no politician's gestures, his hands in his pockets, his profile firm but unprojected. He is without question the handsomest, the most modest, the most graceful and impressive presidential candidate of our time, from the brain down. Goldwater has been called everything from an old cowhand to Wyatt Earp, to the Chairman of the Board of '18th

Century Fox.' The last crack was supposedly coined by Hubert Humphrey, but there is shrewd evidence that it might have come from Barry himself. At any rate, he repeats the joke, for he is in many ways an eighteenth-century man and most of his photographs suggest a Jefferson with horn-rimmed glasses. Indeed, much of Goldwater's favourite campaign literature echoes ideas that might well have come out of Jefferson's hand-made printing press at Monticello, and his speeches sigh with echoes of the man 'whose ways I learned from my Uncle Morris.' To wit:

'I have always stood for government that is limited and balanced and against every concentration of government in Washington . . . Social security is a contract between the Government and the people and should be so honoured . . . The real division in the world is not between liberals and totalitarians but between those who believe in a transcendent order of things and those who would treat man as a creature of appetite, self-created, to be ordered as social planners desire.'

Not to qualify him too soon for the American Parthenon, it should be added that he also believes that the income tax is a necessary evil, that no man should be compelled to join a union, that the Federal Government should keep its hands absolutely off education, that the late Senator McCarthy's 'selfless service will forever redound to the credit of Wisconsin,' that the Birch Society is 'anti-Communist, and I don't see how we can be against that.'

He is a very difficult 'conservative' to pin down under a label. He wants the Government to match the States with funds for the care of the ageing sick. He is against large Federal public works, but he voted for the St. Lawrence Seaway. He thinks integration should be left to the States, but if the States resist a Federal Court order, they violate the law.

To compel integration in restaurants and hotels is a sin against 'an inherent right of property,' but in Arizona he helped to integrate the National Guard, the public schools, and airport restaurants; and in the department store he inherited from his father he started employing Negroes long before the thing was an issue.

What Goldwater offers, he has said, is 'a choice and not an echo.' He said it again, once he got under way before this glowing, attentive crowd. But he said very little else that was new, except to suggest – as thousands paid reverent attention to his military expertise – that Secretary Robert McNamara is full of 'statistical razzle-dazzle' and had neither the guts nor the sense to bomb the Vietcong's 'supply bases' in Red China, Cambodia, and Laos.

But for the rest, he ground through familiar platitudes about fiscal responsibility, morality in government, 'law and order in civil rights.' Most of the time his hands stayed in his pockets and so did his voice. The most interesting thing about him is the unreconciled contrast between his manner and his words on paper, between the firebrand reputation and the palpably good man and true. Some excellent citizens (Eisenhower's former Cabinet officers George Humphrey and Arthur Summerfield) speak of him as an abler, civilian Eisenhower. Near-Nazis, suburban rowdies, and iron-clad tycoons put amplifiers to his wilder ideas and boom him as a Führer.

The rally is over. The good-natured crowd disperses to its Cokes and T.V.s, and plans to collect 'bucks for Barry.' The night closes in and leaves us still with the galling contradiction between the Goldwater character and the Goldwater mania. He has no strain of demagoguery in him. He detests racial discrimination, but the ingrate South listens and sees the Negro foiled. He thinks of Jefferson, and his audience looks on Caesar.

How It Happened in Watts

Los Angeles, California, August 19, 1965

To-day Watts, one of the eighty or a hundred small towns that interlock across the beach meadows, the mountains, and inland valleys of Southern California to form the weird urban complex known as Los Angeles, was said to be becalmed or cowed or smouldering, according to the colour and the temperament of one's informant. At any rate, it is at bay, which is only to be expected of any small town between Cyprus and South Vietnam where you have ten thousand soldiers patrolling, manning machine-gun emplacements, and erupting out of 'staging areas.' In the sooty pall of uncounted fires and the rubble of a thousand looted stores, the Californians are, in their energetic fashion, calling in their heads of police, their Governor and his cabinet, their State Senate, their sociologists (in a city whose university school of sociology is especially distinguished) to find out how it happened, and why.

It is very early to isolate first causes or assign blame, but there has been no foot-dragging among resident civil rights spokesmen, institutional psychiatrists, and liberals, who overnight have put together these 'reasons' for the explosion of a routine drunken driving charge into the most mindless orgy of race-rioting that has happened in this country since the Second World War, or in California since the anti-Chinese riots of the last century.

Watts has the lowest per capita income of any part of Los Angeles, except its downtown 'Skid Row' section for chronic drunks. Its population is ninety per cent Negro. Its crime rate is the highest of the Los Angeles suburbs: it had a record of close to 200 murders, rapes, and felonious assaults, and 800 other crimes, in the last three months. Unemployment is, if anything, worse than the usual Negro rate. The school drop-outs are about normal for a Negro community. These statistics are, however, hardly explanations. They are parallel or chronic facts about an undiagnosed disease which, in the past four days, flared into an acute attack. There are other figures, given as fair cause for burnings, stabbings, and lootings, which a European may find odd, since they report a social-educational situation rather better than hundreds of big city neighbourhoods in any country that remains peaceable if resigned to their lot. To wit: two thirds of the adult population of Watts did not have a secondary school education (imagine, they left school at fifteen or sixteen!). One eighth of the population is illiterate. Eighty-seven per cent of the houses of the town are 'over twenty-five years old'! The place, not unlike Dublin, Chelsea, or San Francisco, has its share of prostitutes, drug addicts, and alcoholics.

More promising as a guess of a contributing cause is the news that more than five hundred criminals on parole from California prisons live in Watts and would be most apt to 'give direction' to a mood of public anger or a single act of violence. But, unless there comes to light a ringleader, a plot, or proof that the sparking incident was arranged, the known and well-attested origin of the riots is disturbingly simple.

First, Wednesday night in Los Angeles was very hot and humid. (A humdrum detail, true also of Chicago and Springfield, Massachusetts – the two other most recent delinquent cities; but it is worth a note, since the Justice Department's very useful study of last summer's seven most serious city riots warned the police that great heat with high humidity is the climate most provocative of civil disturbance.) Watts, like every other suburb west of the Coast Range in the City of the Angels, had the additional grievance of eye-burning smog. Sometime around eight o'clock in the evening a highway policeman saw a car wobbling and weaving along a Watts boulevard. He waved it down and gave the driver a sobriety test, while twenty or thirty people looked on. The first essential fact is that the policeman was white and the drunk was a Negro. (Four of the seven looting orgies of 1964's 'long hot summer' started with this unfortunate fact, for wherever a white policeman arrests a Negro in the United States, with coloured people looking on, the chances of a shambles are acute.)

There was no trouble until the mother of the 21-year-old driver came on the scene, upbraided him and goaded him not into shame but into rage, which he then turned on the cop. A bigger crowd was gathering now and the cop asked, or radioed, for help. He meanwhile drew his gun. The young Negro let off a howl of defiance, the mother jumped the policeman, and there was a scuffle of onlookers, many of whom – a Negro resident remarked later – were from out of town. The policeman got his help, and the mother and son were taken to the station house. At what is usually a welcome moment, when the tension sags and the crowd breaks up grumbling or cackling, the crowd grew, was excited by rumours of 'police brutality,' and suddenly consolidated into an army carrying stones and bottles and some guns. Their original protagonist had gone, so the first targets of its rage were the city buses and the shop windows of stores both white and coloured, and protesters of any colour. Eighty policemen were sent in to try and confine the uproar to the few blocks where it had all started.

It was now about ten o'clock, and this will be the fruitful time for the State and city investigators, and the sociologists, to dig. Nobody knows how the crowd was so swiftly mobilised into a howling mob of purposeful and systematic looters and firebugs. All through Thursday the rampage spread and by Friday took in the whole 150 streets of the suburb. By Friday, too, the indiscriminate beatings and firings concentrated in a racial campaign to 'get whitey,' any and every white man or white property in sight.

What should be recalled are the stages of a city disaster: when the curiosity of a handful of bystanders turned into a mob vowing vengeance; when the vengeful mob turned into guerrilla fighters (last night and today) against all law and property as the symbols of the white man's Establishment, however modest that Establishment may be in a suburb like Watts, whose three-bedroom houses and little lawns, by the way, would look like a dream city to the slum dwellers of Glasgow or Manchester or Harlem.

At this point there is little that can be said dogmatically, except to note that a public demand for civil rights had nothing to do with these horrors. It is doubtful if last summer's Harlem, Rochester, Philadelphia, and the rest had much to do either, except that the great and true emphasis given to the progress of civil rights legislation may taunt the lowest depths of Negro life with the reminder that precious little of these freedoms and new dignities can ever touch them. For it is a bitter, and perhaps hopeless, irony of the Watts episode that it should have happened at the end of a decade which did more for the American Negro than the three hundred years that went before, and at the end of one year that did more for him than that decade, and only a few days after the President signed the historic Federal Voting Rights Act of 1965.

It is a great and liberating law, but it can only liberate the next generation. It cannot yet separate gangsters from their gangs, or addicts from their drugs, or drop-outs from the shiftlessness that, on hot evenings in poky towns, moves them to vice and, nowadays, since the Negro has been encouraged to stand up and be a man, moves the witless to go on rampages and shatter windows and grab on the run some of the goodies of the good life that the telly so seductively exposes and which Hollywood, the near-by dream city, so tantalisingly holds just beyond reach.

Hasty Marriage
Better Part of Valour

September 2, 1965

For the first time since anyone could remember, the President of the United States yesterday signed an executive order urging young men to get married before midnight. This unusual advice was not in the text of the order in precisely that form, but if it had been it could not have set off such a stampede for the marriage bed. What the President signed was a series of amendments to the Draft (Conscription) Act, which in the first place is passed by Congress but is then left to the President to carry out according to his judgment of the country's military needs. Evidently, he is bracing the nation for a long slow haul in Vietnam.

Nineteen to twenty-six is still the range over which local draft boards must fill their quota of conscripts. Within it, married men with children are exempt. So are childless men who were married before August 27, 1965. That is the rub of yesterday's Presidential order. The clause that rang the alarm bell through all the back porches, ocean beaches, parked cars, and other havens of the lovelorn was the specific warning that men between the ages of nineteen and twenty-six who got married 'later than midnight of August 26' would be just as liable to the draft call as single men. It was possible to find out from the Defense Department and from local draft boards that no vengeful or dramatic change in conscription policy was intended. The boards would still try to exhaust their pool of eligible single men before intruding on holy matrimony. But thousands of lovesick couples who have been thinking of setting a date set it very fast. The trouble was getting society to co-operate.

The word came over the radio at precisely 5 p.m. Eastern Daylight Time, just when the marriage licence bureaus here were closing their doors. However, it was only four o'clock in Chicago, three o'clock in Denver, and two o'clock in California. San Francisco's bureau was besieged within the half hour and licences were issued like, as they say, hot cakes. But they could not be acted on unless the reckless couple could already show proof of a negative Wassermann. The District of Columbia and all the states but three (Maryland, Nevada, and South Carolina) require a blood test, and usually a three-day wait for its authentication. So thousands with the most honourable intentions were foiled by the President's 5 p.m. dateline.

Elkton, Maryland, occurred to many in the East as the perfect and fairly convenient sanctuary from the draft. For Elkton has long been famous (notorious?) as a slap-happy Gretna Green, where desperate or slightly squiffy couples could stagger to a Justice of the Peace at midnight and wake up at eight astounded to find themselves married. Within an hour of the broadcasting of the President's order, Elkton police had had innumerable calls from inside Maryland but twenty-five also from patriotic lovers in New York, Connecticut, and New Jersey. These love calls were eventually turned over to the man who runs the fire alarm system at the police station. Some didn't wait for the bad word but headed for Elkton and got it in person and in disillusion. It seems that Elkton has lately been polishing up its rather squalid national 'image.' It has now instituted a forty-eight-hour wait after the filing of an application for the licence. So Elkton last evening was just as hopelessly respectable as New York City, Salt Lake City, Dallas, Seattle, or Conception, California, where certificates noting the absence of communicable syphilis are a *sine qua non* of wedding bells.

The only happy story given to our own (*Guardian*) bureau is that of a young couple on Long Island who had got a licence weeks ago and dillied and dallied till finally the young man was browbeaten into a Sunday date. Last evening, it was he – not the girl – who heard the radio and called a Nassau County district court judge. The boy said he was 'desperate.' Forty minutes later he was safe from the Vietcong for, say, a year or so.

For what the Presidential order did not mention was the series of advices from Defense Secretary McNamara and the national head of the conscription system about the alarming drain Vietnam has caused in the manpower pool. Two years ago only 6,000 men a month were being drafted. This month the figure is 17,000. Next month it will be 27,000 and 33,600 in October. When the Defense Department planned this steep increase a month or so ago, Mr. McNamara told the President there would have to be a drastic change in the rules about married men. The President has harboured this knowledge for a month. He told nobody about it till the marriage licence bureaus were closing in the East last evening.

As for the Westerners who beat the clock in Nevada – the Army, Navy, Air Force, and Marine Corps no doubt wished them good riddance. Nevada does not require a moment's wait, not for meditation, parental permission, or even a guarantee against syphilis. All it requires is the presence of a male and female and five dollars. Just under a thousand such quickies were solemnised in Las Vegas before the witching hour.

The Coronation
of Miss Oklahoma

September 15, 1966

Although the Jeffersonian Law ('All men are created equal') is the first article of the American faith, the facts of American life have demonstrated for some time now that it is an irksome faith to live by. The Robber Barons, especially the ones who started out as office boys or ferry captains, made no bones about transplanting Norman castles to Chicago and to Fifth

Avenue, in the hope of being mistaken for eighteenth earls. To-day the inequality principle flourishes in such studied insults to the plebs as automobile licence plates bearing the owner's initials and airline lounges reserved for the V.I.P. (that is, a man who can afford to travel first on the company's money, carry a black pigskin brief-case, and wear coat-sleeve buttons that are actually unbuttoned).

But it is a universal itch, nagging most at the three countries which most profess their equality and fraternity. The Russians, once they got the hang of the quality syndrome, developed a blue book for the behaviour of the military that would not shame the Brigade of Guards; de Gaulle talks of himself in the third person as a Supreme Being indistinguishable from La France. America bespangles the breasts of her soldiers, whether of the combat or quartermaster supply divisions, with more ribbons and medals than Napoleon wore to his coronation.

For the female, America preserves a crown. It was balanced at midnight last night on the high bee-hive hairdo of Jane Jayroe, and Miss Oklahoma began the national reign which millions of American girls covet far more than they would hope to become Miss Truman or even Jackie Kennedy.

It all started in 1921 in a naïve and fumbling way as a 'bathing beauty' contest. By now the process of succession has become as complicated as the rights to the Spanish throne. The civic fathers of every county of every state choose a comely girl, who must be certified as a practising spinster, a high school graduate, and an idealist who ignores her smashing beauty in the search for some admirable 'goal': to be a nurse, a sociologist, a concert pianist, or an archbishop.

Miss New Hampshire, who appeared to be cast by nature for a king's boudoir, insisted last night that she wanted to be a graduate student in international affairs, which, after all, was Madame Pompadour's specialty. Miss California, a nifty mermaid in a one-piece bathing suit, rattled off a Chopin *étude* with more aplomb than most festival finalists.

The coronation ritual itself is by this time as formal as a Greek tragedy. The stand-in for the Archbishop of Canterbury is a breezy, glossy-haired M.C. in white tie and tails known, in all humbleness, as Bert Parks. He carries white cards from which he reads uplifting prose. His minister is the forever regal Bess Myerson, the queen in 1945. From time to time she tries to explain the magic that creates a natural queen ('she must be compassionate and concerned about others in the American tradition') and this chore leads easily into a series of television catechisms which suggest that a hair rinse, a cola drink, and an automobile have something to do with it.

Just before the witching hour itself, the judges announced themselves satisfied, or at least in public agreement. The five finalists are now called and sit, a blaze of teeth, heads held high, white gloves shimmering way above their delicious elbows. They are not to change expression by an eyelash until one of them is allowed to crumble onto the bosom of the runner-up.

The fourth runner-up is announced: New Hampshire's International Affairs Specialist. The third: Miss Ohio, whose 'goal' is, shamelessly, a husband. The second, Miss Tennessee, a ravishing, graceful blonde who sent the audience into a tumult of obvious dissatisfaction with the judges. Now the two heirs-apparent take a refined breath, gently undulating their adorable bosoms, and try to look as apparent as possible.

'Remember,' warned Archbishop Parks, 'that if for any reason Miss America is unable to fulfil her duties, this girl will be her true successor.' It is Miss California, the trim mermaid, and she duly receives the speechless bowed head of the lonely Miss Oklahoma, the Queen herself. The four losers sweep into minuet positions as a court of honour. Archbishop Parks lets loose a tenor aria: 'There she goes, Miss America!' And, wearing her crown as tenderly as it might be a brimful glass of beer, she floats with proper majesty along the runway and all the length of the looped silk curtain.

It is noticeable that there is not a flat chest, a bandy leg, a bird's-nest haircut, a craggy knee, a mini skirt, a mackerel foot in the lot. Is this bad? Well, fellow Americans, I dare to say it is. It reveals America back in the thirties, forties, and early fifties, resting on her laurels on long thighs, and unashamed bosoms; an America smugly disdainful of knobby knees and bloodless lips; an America content with clothes cut only for females, and with piles of glistening hair, superb figures, and the carriage of a Gibson Girl. Not only do they look in superlative health. They are – ugh! – physically clean! They restore us by a process of dangerous, perhaps subversive, nostalgia to an America where women had legs like pillars of gold, bellies like bushels of wheat, breasts like meringues.

If allowed to go on, this could undermine everything the nineteen-sixties have been working for: which is, I guess, the triumph of the neuter and the revival of tuberculosis.

The Rise and Fall of
J. Robert Oppenheimer

February 27, 1967

Dr. J. Robert Oppenheimer, the most eminent and controversial of nuclear physicists, has died in Princeton, New Jersey, at the age of 62, after a long failing bout with cancer of the throat.

There were three dates in his life that marked the rise, fall, and resurrection of his great reputation. The first was July, 1945, when from a mountain in New Mexico he watched the first explosion of the atomic bomb whose manufacture he had supervised. The second was April, 1954, when President Eisenhower directed that 'a blank wall be placed between Dr. Oppenheimer and any secret data' on suspicion of association with Communists and resisting the development of the hydrogen bomb. The third was December, 1963, when President Johnson bestowed on him the Fermi award, the highest honour at the disposal of the Atomic Energy Commission, which nine years before had voted by four to one to discharge him as its chief consultant because of 'fundamental defects in his character' and 'associations with persons known to him to be Communists [that] have extended far beyond the limits of prudence and self-restraint.'

'In the Case of J. Robert Oppenheimer' has remained down the years a political episode as inflammatory as the Dreyfus and Hiss cases, and one that similarly excites people – pamphleteers, novelists, and playwrights – who have only a passing acquaintance with the testimony against the accused, including his own. Oppenheimer's name may have to wait a long time for an historical judgment to settle on it, but in the meantime we can only be sure that at the time of his trials the Atomic Energy Commission judged him fairly as a dependable Government servant and harshly as a man; and that it later made it up to him with laudable generosity.

J. Robert Oppenheimer was born in New York City on April 22, 1904, the son of an uncommonly prosperous type of German immigrant, a textile importer, who indulged his son's early passions for rocks, poetry, painting, and chemistry by flooding him with books, rigging up his own lab, securing his admission to the Mineralogical Club of New York at the age of 11, and decorating his home with several early Impressionists. By the time he went to Harvard he was almost a one-man research team, and he remained a 'loner' throughout a brilliant college career and, perhaps, throughout his life. He graduated with highest honours in the natural sciences (having also acquired Latin, Greek, and Dutch on the side) and went at once to Cambridge to work under Ernest Rutherford in the early complexities of atomic physics. He whirled on to other researches in Europe and America, and came to pause and consolidate his findings at the University of California at Berkeley. There he stayed from 1929 to 1947 and there he laid the ground of his special reputation as the contemporary master of theoretical physics and, a little later, of his popular reputation as a mystic and a mystery. It was inevitable that when Roosevelt's scientific advisers looked around for 'the man to make the bomb,' he should have been that man.

Until the middle 1930s, Oppenheimer took no interest whatsoever in politics. But he became engaged to one active Communist and married a former one and was soon a knowing figure in smart Left-wing quarters. One of his few close friends was a lecturer in Romance Languages, one Haakon Chevalier, and an unwitting cause of Oppenheimer's downfall and his own.

In late 1942 or early 1943, Chevalier mentioned to Oppenheimer that an English chemical engineer in San Francisco felt that since 'the Soviet Union and the United States were now brothers-in-arms' there were Russians who felt that exchanges of strategical information would be 'highly desirable.' The implication was that Oppenheimer might become the link. He was shocked at the suggestion, thought it a 'frightful' if not 'treasonable' thing, and both friends dismissed the idea. But it preyed on Oppenheimer when he shortly went off to exile in New Mexico to supervise the most secret and awesome job of the war.

By a fatal slip, he returned to San Francisco to spend a night with his old Communist girlfriend, and thereafter he was unknowingly trailed every hour by security agents. His security file was quietly opened, but when he was called in by army intelligence it was to be warned about the number of Communists who were rumoured to have infiltrated the bomb project. Whether it was panic over the San Francisco indiscretion, or worry over a student of his with Communist leanings, we shall now never know. But when he was questioned, he plunged gratuitously into an account of the English chemical engineer's approach that he elaborated into an actual subversive movement involving three men, microfilms, and the Russian Embassy. This was news to Army intelligence and the tragedy was that it was fantasy to Oppenheimer. Eleven years later, before the Atomic Energy Commission, he confessed that 'it was a cock and bull story . . . a piece of idiocy . . . a whole fabrication and tissue of lies in great circumstantial detail.' At the time of his questioning, afraid that Army intelligence was ahead of him, he had given the name of Chevalier, who was dismissed without stated cause from his teaching job, had some rough years, and emigrated to Paris where, in 1954, he was thunderstruck to read his name in a newspaper as the missing link in a dire plot that never was.

This small, grotesque incident, buried in the 992 pages of the Atomic Energy Commission's hearings, was the one that guaranteed the fate of Oppenheimer as that of a fallen angel. In the past few years, he retired to the job he had held after the war as Director of the Institute for Advanced Studies at Princeton. A year ago he retired as an invalid. He gave himself, with unquestioned loyalty, to the making of the bomb and the subsequent researches on the hydrogen bomb. When all the bother was over, his sin was seen to be one that happens every day. Unfortunately, he was Caesar's wife, raised superbly above the common lot, and therefore he was a dazzling figure for a Government to call to account, and for little men to demean.

Henry Luce
His Time, Life, and Fortune
March 2, 1967

As it must to all men, death came this morning to the man who made this the standard lead for all obituaries: Henry Robinson Luce, the founder and ruler of the empire of Time Inc., and quite possibly the most universally influential figure in twentieth-century journalism. He was 68.

His kind of life story is so familiar as to have become a stock American myth. It is a genteel variation on the more primitive log-cabin-to-White House routine and it was diligently followed also by such other towering moral figures as Elihu Root,

Henry L. Stimson, and John Foster Dulles. It is the story, usually, of the first born of a well-bred frugal family of ascetic Christian faith and a steady devotion to books and good works. But just as an urban middle-class America is unlikely to be led again by a frontier farm boy like Lyndon Johnson, so it seems improbable that any more $271 million publishing empires will emerge from two college boys with one bright idea, one small rented room, and $30 a week.

It is difficult now to believe that the six magazines (*Time, Life, Fortune, Architectural Forum, House and Home,* and *Sports Illustrated*), housed in their own gleaming skyscraper on Sixth Avenue, were hatched by the wits of two schoolboys who had the mad idea that what America needed was a weekly 'news magazine' and the madder notion that it should be written in a new style of inverted sentences and Homeric compound adjectives.

Balding, beetle-browed, sardonic Luce (as his own 'staffers' might have labelled him) was born in 1898, the son of a Presbyterian missionary, in Tengchow, Shantung Province, China, in a house that was proudly described as 'severe and forbidding but attractively decorated.' He spent four years at a British boarding school in Northern China, then a bare year at St. Albans, and arrived in the United States as a scholarship boy at Hotchkiss, one of the crack New England prep (i.e., public) schools. The records of his scholarship and his Horatio Alger performance as a waiter and janitor are dimmed by his friendship with a gay young blade who swam into his life like a comet. He was one Britton Hadden, who had a passion for Homer as Luce had an early passion for giving the people what he thought they ought to have. They passed on together to Yale, edited the college daily, enlisted together, returned to graduate together, and dreamed together.

Luce had a year at Oxford and a spell as a Chicago newspaper reporter and then joined Hadden again on the Baltimore *News*. Pretty soon they quit their paper and decided they would need $100,000 to float the dream paper, *Time.* They badgered every well-heeled acquaintance and relation in sight and raised $86,000. They put out, in March, 1923, a first issue of 12,000 copies. From that moment to the employment of a staff of 300, a weekly circulation of nearly 3 millions, and another 2 millions in international editions, is a painless success story; and so it has been with all the other ventures. Throughout three decades, in the words of Woolcott Gibbs' immortal parody, 'backward ran sentences until reeled the mind . . . where it will all end, knows God.' Sobered by the Second World War, the sentences ran forward, the exotic coinings (cinemaddict, tycoon) had either been banished or naturalised. The Luce staff was no longer a nest of skylarking college rebels but a palace guard of the American Establishment, conservative, tough-minded, scholarly, unfooled. But the last phase of Henry Luce was even more familiar than the first. As a son of the Americans who knew the Chinese converts and knew not at all the Manchus, he preserved and intensified the missionary zeal which has so often informed, and misinformed, American policy towards China.

He looked on his publications as the tablets given to the people in the interest of their 'right thinking.' Like John Foster Dulles, he regarded himself, with terrifying modesty, as a soldier in the army of Christ; that is to say, as a warrior to whom the nation's wars, once they are begun, are holy wars.

Mary McCarthy in Vietnam

September 26, 1967

Mary McCarthy in Vietnam! It holds the promise of a secret weapon or the threat of a crash programme by the doves. Once her visa was granted, you can imagine the general beefing-up procedure for the military (alert the ambassador, suspend the tortures, hide the napalm); the swift roundup of p.r. officers who had read Kafka – or seen *The Group* at least; even a series of night briefings for Gen. Westmoreland ('General, we are about to receive the toughest of the resistance leaders, the Pasionaria of the *New York Review of Books*. This woman, General, could menace the whole war effort. She makes fun of counterinsurgency, the hospitals, the Staley plan, the P.C. infrastructure, everything. She'll probably want to poke into other refugee camps than Phu Cuong. General, she'll stop at nothing'). Stations, everyone. Now hear this!

Well, either G.H.Q. never heard of her or the telex got scrambled and the confidential bulletin – 'McCarthy on the way' – suggested the arrival of a co-operative witness. In any case, her tour of what she calls this 'looney' power struggle, 'a war of incredible blunders,' must have been a disaster to the press relations office and an embarrassment to the American command. It also presents yet another whanging knife between the shoulder blades of Our Leader and an occasion for revelry to the New Left, the Vietniks, and draft-card burners.

She begins by exercising the familiar scalpel of her intelligence on what we have done to Saigon: 'an American city, a very shoddy West Coast one . . . a gigantic P.X. . . . a stewing Los Angeles, shading into Hollywood, Venice Beach and Watts.' She notes, with no indignation, the mocking discrepancy between the briefing charts about New Life Hamlets, Constructed Hamlets, and their reality in the field. In a Saigon 'backgrounder' she is impressed, as loads of other visiting journalists have been, by an account of 'public health measures undertaken by Free World Forces.' Without leaving the room, she deduces from the statistics and 'a slightly irritated official' that few civilian casualties ever seem to reach a hospital. She later learns that the 'improvement of hospital facilities' includes donating drugs and antibiotics which 'in turn are *sold* by the local nurses to the patients for whom they are prescribed.' Nobody before Miss McCarthy, it appears, has raised the question of what they do with the Viet Cong wounded. She simply remarks on the disparity between the official estimate of 30,000 or 35,000 V.C. wounded in five months and the office figure of 225 of them being treated in U.S. hospitals in one month.

If she was a nuisance to the briefing officers, she must have been a plague in the field. She looks into the Pacification Programme and is struck by jealous relations between the Spanish, American, and German medical teams. She takes a dim view of the 'springy, zesty, burning-eyed' American zealots distributing canned goods and chewing gum and teaching crop rotation with 'Civics 101.' She passes on to the 'grim town of Phu Cuong,' which houses the enforced 'refugees' from hamlets we burned and levelled: 6,000 men, women and children taking their pots and pans and sacks of rice into their tin-roof camp, ready to be taught about free enterprise and permitted to build and *buy* their own homes. In a temporary refugee camp, a stagnant duckpond is revealed as the only water source, for all purposes, of 700 persons. In the delta, she comes on the little schoolhouse John Steinbeck wrote about with such pride; she stops long enough to debunk it as a place with no materials and no teachers.

The flight to Hue is not wasted: she hears the pilot and co-pilot hoping, when the war is over, to make a killing in Vietnamese real estate. The Marines tenderly making it up to a child wounded by their bullets are not to be forgiven ('to spoil a child you have injured and send her back to her parent, with her dolls as souvenirs, is pharisee virtue').

Then on to observe the bombing. 'The Air Force seems inescapable, like the eye of God,' and she reflects that 'at the present rate of destruction there will be no place left for them [the Viet Cong] to hide, not even under water, breathing through a straw.' Yet her vivid example of a bombing mission is that of the pilot of an F.A.C. plane who responded to the sight of a lone bicyclist pointing his rifle skyward by letting him have it 'with the whole bombload of napalm – enough for a platoon.'

From Saigon to the delta, up in the air, on the foul ground, in hospitals and press tents, in hamlets and at headquarters she sees the evidence of nothing but 'a totalitarian' blueprint for teaching the people democracy. She makes patently absurd the official claim to be building up a democratic front against 'Communist aggression.' A sullen refugee may be a V.C. spy. The families so lovingly protected are far from their sons and husbands fighting for the Viet Cong. A captive girl may be beaten up for her own good. A young American hates having to shoot a wounded Viet Cong. Tubercular V.C. defectors are apparently trained as missionaries for our side and then turned loose to browbeat 'our' natives. The C.I.A. is in there in the shadows, subsidising God knows what, backing and training 'a right-wing movement, against Prince Sihanouk' of Cambodia. Everywhere she sees corruption, half-baked do-goodism, and 'relentless priggery' fostering the distrust of a people rendered apathetic by malnutrition and the application of sales-conference ethics to the ordeals of the Old Testament.

Now she turns to, or on, the big boys back home, the presidential advisers and political scientists and their scouts in Vietnam who devise the blueprints and the lingo of military – i.e., democratic – government. The 'Intellectuals,' she calls them, who move with mounting excitement from the Strategic Hamlet idea to Rural Construction and now to Revolutionary Development. These are the 'motivated' theorists who hold 'structured' conversations about 'the cultural basis' of land reform and who hammer away at 'rooting out the paramilitary infrastructure.' (In any other time and place, an 'infra-structure' was the underground or, more simply, two sneaks and a spy.)

Miss McCarthy is on her own ground here. The clinical examination of adipose mental tissue was her first and best specialty, and in this she is oddly more convincing than in the reporting chapters, where there is always the suspicion that she is a professional knocker, an intellectual Pegler willing to grant that an occasional poor slob of an American is doing his best but is, on the whole, the victim of an enormous racket. In this chapter, too, she is also more depressing, for the articulation of our aims and hopes in Vietnam seems to rest with men going back to Kennedy's graduate scholars, who turned a committee into 'a task force' and a memo into 'a position paper.' One sees this vast tragedy being briskly organised at 8,000 miles by deskbound enthusiasts whom the Navy used to call ball-bearing admirals.

At least, you may say, we have had the prudence not to bomb the port of Haiphong and we have had the steady humanity not to use The Bomb. Miss McCarthy won't have it so. On the contrary, we have exploited these restraints to develop more adhesive napalm, anti-personnel bombs (that means you are blasted apart), a blower that raises the temperature in a V.C. tunnel to 1,000 degrees Fahrenheit: weapons, which, on the whole, seem less humane than The Bomb.

In short, her Vietnam is a Hieronymus Bosch bedlam run by the Pentagon. So, a thousand other protesters have moaned and deplored, but they always excuse themselves from the vulgarity of suggesting what is to be done. Miss McCarthy is a welcome exception. At the end of this withering indictment — of our original motives and our subsequent policy, intelligence, and inhumanity — she reverts to a prose as terse and outraged as Tom Paine's and invites her readers to total defiance of the war. She suggests 'self-immolation . . . tax refusal . . . the operation of underground railroads for protesting draftees . . . simple boycotts of key war industries . . . the "hard thinking" about this war needs to begin at home, with the critic asking himself what *he* can do against it, modestly or grandly, with friends or alone. From each according to his abilities, but to be in the town jail, as Thoreau knew, can relieve any sense of imaginary imprisonment.'

'Get Out!' she says. And when the Establishment, military or civilian, says, 'Ah, but how?' she replies that that is up to Johnson and the generals. 'Not being a military specialist, I cannot plot the logistics of withdrawing 464,000 American boys from Vietnam, but I know that it can be done, if necessary, and Johnson knows it too.' The French schoolteachers who told de Gaulle to get out of Algeria 'did not supply him with a ten-point programme . . . that was de Gaulle's business.'

We have been so used to Miss McCarthy's intelligence as a surgical weapon purely that it is a shock to find it suddenly warmed by compassion and courage. She wants to go to jail. She wants *you* to go to jail. It is the healthiest breakthrough in the whole dove movement, whose spokesmen – Fulbright, Galbraith, Schlesinger, the New York *Post* – she damns as weak-kneed apologists for a limited war. Heretofore, the secret agony of the dove, muffled by the noisy assertion of all sorts of 'rights,' has been how to despise the war and impede it *and yet stay out of jail*. It is something that one liberal is clear-minded enough to see, and say, that everyone has a right to burn his draft card as a man, and the government has the right to jail him as a citizen.

The Permissive Society

October 26, 1967

If the 'permissive society,' as the phrase is now used, has a manifesto, John Dewey's *The School and Society*, published in 1899, is it. And the Teachers College of Columbia University was its seedbed.

Naturally, there had been rebels against traditional education before Dewey, notably Horace Mann, who died in 1859, the year Dewey was born. But the turn of the century heard the first piping cries of 'progressive education,' so called, and its midwife was Dewey. By the late 1930s, the word 'permissive' had come into American English bearing a special meaning. It was pronounced in a low, proud tone by Dalton and other progressive teachers. It was an invocation that banished slavery from education and promised enlightenment, spontaneity, the 'identification' of the child with his studies in a new and passionate way. It implied that the three Rs, parrot teaching, learning dates, getting poetry by rote, boning up on Euclid, or the battle of Austerlitz, had been exposed as the symptoms of an authoritarian system. God said, 'Let Dewey be!' and there was light.

From then on, happy pupils would bound like kangaroos to schools where 'expression' (expressed with astounding and illiterate verbosity) was encouraged; where handicraft gave way to rubbing the soul in 'textures,' and the study of historical periods was supplanted by trips into the Fenimore Cooper country to bring home to the budding New Yorker the very touch and smell of the life of the Algonquin Indians. To be truthful, I have known such children who really did leave school with a vivid and accurate knowledge of the way the earliest inhabitants of Manhattan lived and ordered society, even if they had never heard of the Bill of Rights, a hanging participle, or the Thirty Years' War. Of course, it is easy now to mock the later absurdities of progressive education, which came under brutal attack in the early 1950s, so much so that rednecks from Louisiana to Southern California, egged on by the late Senator Joseph McCarthy, howled for a return to the rod and the little red schoolhouse. But progressive education had already done its duty, or its mischief, and not in the private school either. Its reforming course had so changed the elementary schools that many a McCarthyite, screaming for the blood of the progressives, was unaware that his own strong belief in unit teaching, school projects, individual attention, and compulsory courses in a life science and civics had come from nowhere but Columbia and nobody but Dewey. The Progressive Education Association, founded as a standard bearer in 1915, had done its work so well that it was dissolved in 1955.

This stress on the origins of permissive learning and teaching is worth making because, outside the United States certainly, so many bewildered parents, conservatives, and reactionaries talk as if the permissive society had sprung up spontaneously on a signal out of Millbrook, N.Y., from Doctor Timothy Leary under the influence.

I am not, on the contrary, saying that it all goes back in an orderly and sinister fashion to John Dewey, or to Marx, or Freud, though much that now passes for individual expression, freedom, and constitutional rights derives from a mass misinterpretation of all three. But the actual vehemence and universality of the beatnik, hippy, teeny-bopper, acid-head revolution is harder to explain. It cannot be said to be a revolt against authority, for authority has been crumbling in all Western societies, as it has been stiffening in Communist countries, since the First World War.

But it is, I take it, the free-wheeling young we are talking about. Who are the hippies? Lamentably little scientific work has been done on their genes and their social history, though a limited New York psychiatric study asserts that as many as sixty per cent are seriously sick, mostly with schizophrenia. But we do know that they tend to come from better rather than worse educated families, that their parents are rarely impoverished but have a high incidence either of divorce or of rigid morality (perhaps a sure sign of Freud's revolutionary discovery that, in the unconscious, opposites are the same). We know also that the children of Catholics and religious Jews are very much in the minority among the new rebels. And – a saving statistic – that hippies and their vagabond variations account for less than ten per cent of the young.

Drug addiction, however, widely overlaps the 'squares.' Nor are hippiedom, sexual licence, the flower phenomenon, merely indigenous to metropolises that have always tolerated a Bohemian quarter. Of course, they flourish there in most conspicuous anonymity. The provincial strictness of the Old South and the farming Midwest covers up, for the time being, the more outlandish forms of hippiedom. But their children too are off to the cities; and cities across the whole continent have their proportionate quota. The draft card burners know no geographical limits. The mystery, which no mere perambulating journalist should try to solve, is how it comes about that the rebel young appear, in East Berlin and East St. Louis, in the same international uniform, that they profess the same half-baked 'philosophies' and rustle as indistinguishable as cockroaches over three or four continents.

The mass media take the blame for everything these days. And until a better theory comes along, it will have to do to wonder why the children of Nigeria have forgotten their native songs and echoed the Beatles; why a sit-down in the London School of Economics is inspired by the same types (and the same ringleaders?) as organised the shenanigans at Berkeley. We can be sure of only one thing: that he who runs no longer has to read. He can simply see a Californian smoking pot on the telly, rush out into a Wimbledon backyard, grab a handful of the stuff, and do the same.

Reagan's Reasons

Sacramento, California, December 28, 1967

The road to Ronald Reagan goes north-east across San Francisco Bay, up through the postwar industrial litter of the San Pablo shore, over the brown foothills of the Coast Range, out across the broad farmlands of the Sacramento Valley, and along by the Sacramento River to its confluence with the American River, where Sutter's boss carpenter, James Marshall, sat down on a January day in 1848 and examined some little yellow particles that had flaked through the tailrace of Sutter's sawmill. They were gold.

It is an appropriate introduction to the hero of *Death Valley Days*, the decent young pioneer of many a B-Western who now finds himself the Governor of California, the first choice of California, the first choice of Republican county chairmen, and the second choice of Republican voters for the Presidency.

You are taken to him through corridors of exhibits extolling the bounty of the California counties, and then through a Cabinet room newly done over by Mrs. Reagan as a handsome museum of Californiana with early Spanish furniture, water-colours, Indian prints, Argonaut memoirs. Beyond this bastion of nostalgia and flanked by the American flag on one side and the flag of the Golden State on the other, sits in his small study the 56-year-old Governor, a slim dark-haired man with the figure of a ranch-hand, a college boy's grin, and an engaging manner quite his own. If you are a liberal or New Leftist spy expecting Everett Dirksen's senatorial piety, you are in for a disappointment. Equally, if you are a Birchite or other dino-saur hoping for the patriotic bellow and the double-armed all-American embrace, the man is a letdown.

Contrary to the campus rebel's view of him as an executive smoothie, there is no gloss to his rather craggy complexion, no whiff of pine needle after-shave lotion. His clothes do not give off the static electric charge of Madison Avenue vice-presidents grounded on ankle-deep carpets. He looks rather like a peregrinating secretary of a large union whose blue shirt and dapper suit have spent many a day squashed in the hold of a jet plane. He could be a *Guardian* correspondent!

This first impression is well taken, since for many years he was the president of S.A.G. (the Screen Actors' Guild) and travelled the country on the chicken, pea, and mashed-potato circuit organising and contracting for thirty-one affiliate unions of the American Federation of Labor. There was a lot of wrangling and all-night negotiations and general bitchery and betrayal there, enough experience of the political grind, anyway, to discredit the rather tedious ribaldry about a B-film actor turned Governor.

The truth is that an actor is a labourer, too, and in the depression, through the war, and afterwards, he bowed to what the studios decided was his worthy hire. So Reagan was 'Ronnie,' the crackling young New Dealer, resisting goon squads, fighting the industry for livable contracts, an Americans for Democratic Action man, and later the keen helper of Helen Gahagan Douglas, the liberals' goddess, in her campaigns for Congress.

How come, you feel compelled to ask him, that an A.D.A. liberal, a big Roosevelt man, and union organiser on the Clifford Odets model, turned Republican, and what's more a conservative Republican? Was there, over a time, some well-remembered trauma perhaps that profoundly changed his views? He knotted and unknotted his knuckles.

'Well, after the war there was a motion picture jurisdictional dispute between two unions. As president of S.A.G., I asked both unions to sit down with us. We met for seven months twice a day, we had our own Panmunjom, and once you thought you'd got an equitable settlement, one side would come in with seventeen new lawyers and seventeen new deals. You couldn't believe it, then friends of mine would say, "Come on, Ronnie, don't be so naïve, we're simply following orders. You want us to show you the card?" I didn't even believe then there were such things as Communists, but they had the whole deal tied up. If we dug in, pickets were provided, homes were wrecked, and so on.

'Once I went to Washington on behalf of thirty-odd unions to expound our tax policy to the House Ways and Means Committee. When I got there I was handed a booklet – "This is the A.F. of L.'s tax policy, this is what you read." Of course, it had the Government's support. When I got home I said to my wife: the tone of the speech is going to have to change, it's happening to other people. I'd been against trading our individual rights away to the industry. There came a time when I wasn't going to trade my rights away to the Government.'

His old friends mentioned, too, his shocked discovery that once you decide to build a home, you can suffer union slow-downs, inflated contracts, feather-bedding, and somehow fail to own the house you've saved for without an albatross of a mortgage. Of course, there is no Republican, as there is no

Catholic, like a convert. He reacted all right, but he reacted back to Jefferson, reading him in his own context and not in the chosen bits the New Dealers used for special purposes. It explains, I think, his strong tie to Goldwater, who remains a fervent Jeffersonian, the twentieth century notwithstanding. Unfortunately, the twentieth century has been unloosed on Reagan in the shape of an avalanche, which is to say the modern California that spawns and compounds all the technological vitality and the social ills that will one day afflict us all.

Harvesting the Grapes of Wrath

Sacramento, California, January 4, 1968

Ronald Reagan, who went at a bound from a television serial star, General Electric promotion man, and Goldwater helper to the Governorship of California, has been sitting in Sacramento, amid the cypresses and gingko trees, under the great white dome of the State Capitol, for over a year now. In the contrived intervals of a working schedule as tight as an invasion plan, he is off and around the country at rallies, college debates, and banquets, raising packets for the Republican campaign fund, a service that is either done in an orgy of altruism or on the off-chance, about which he is not quite able to convey the incredulity he mimics, that he might hold the trumping ace over the next Republican Convention, and panic it into nominating him for President.

For the time being, there's no doubt that he has his home-grown troubles. His handling of them is more significant than it would be in Vermont or, for that matter, in Ohio, because in twenty-five years California has developed from a lush fruit bowl, film studio, and sunny haven for retired farmers and playboys into the first State of the Union in more things than numbers. All the chronic social, industrial, and rural problems of America today are here in acute form. A man who can administer California with imagination and good order is one who, unlike anyone else, except perhaps a mayor of New York City, would hold powerful credentials to preside over the United States.

Once you have boasted about the power, the population, and the resources of the first State of the Union, you have to do something about the jungle growth of the cities; the turmoil on the campuses; the conflict about compulsory unionism between organised labour and the free-wheeling labour force; the unceasing inflow of 1,200 new settlers a day, loading the relief rolls and straining the welfare budget; not to mention the bewildering mobility of hundreds of thousands of part-time workers, deadbeats, runaway hippies, 'suitcase' farmers, and the shuttling agents of the Mafia.

All this is producing ruinous invasions of the treasury and subjecting a Governor who campaigned on economy to the embarrassment of a record five-billion-dollar budget, which by State law he is bound to balance. 'In the last eight years,' he says, 'the budget has had a twelve per cent annual increase. Last year it was sixteen per cent.' He puts this down partly, of course, to the open-handed fiscal extravagance of his predecessor, the Democrat 'Pat' Brown. But after a few months of a new Administration the voters are indifferent to the sins of the absent: they ask the immemorial question of the incumbent, 'What are you doing for me right now?'

Committed to a show of economy, he maintains that inflation and the State's growth would justify an annual budget increase of just over seven per cent. He has doggedly instituted a study of the tax system to try to achieve this miracle. But the demands of welfare, Medi-Cal, and free higher education for everybody 'are increasing at a rate so fantastic that to satisfy them we'd have to have a State tax increase every two years. Illinois, for instance, has reduced the number of people on welfare by eight per cent. Ours goes up by 54.6 per cent a year! And Medi-Cal by something between thirty and sixty per cent.' Medi-Cal is California's name for the State medical care programme which the Federal Medicare law allows each State to adopt. Reagan believes that in this, as in other forms of bounty, the theory of social welfare has gone way beyond the capacity of the State to afford.

'Look at this,' he snaps as he slides open a drawer and seizes a handbill, a promotion item for a free State convalescent hospital: 'fully carpeted rooms, modern automated beds, the best of modern treatment, television, three succulent entrees on every menu; the atmosphere of a resort hotel.' This, he says, 'is a delusion – that you can give everybody free the same level of care as the richest man can afford. The medically indigent are something else – and they should come first. But we've given a credit card to 1,300,000 people.'

In his big hassle with the Regents of the University of California about 'the traditional right of free education,' he tried, and failed, to institute a small tuition fee. He believes that somebody, the Federal Government or the State, is going to have to charge a fifty-cent fee for a doctor's visit, something for drugs, and some check on the general assumption 'that you can dash off to a brain surgeon with a headache.' 'I think you will find,' he says without producing the documents, 'that in the countries where they've introduced a national health service, they have underestimated their health budget by as much as five times.' California, at any rate, seems to be having its own grim experience of subsidising hypochondria on a mammoth scale.

What about the cities? He heaves a sigh and pops a cough tablet in his mouth against what he grinningly describes as 'a slight case of instant pneumonia.' He has deep doubts about the President's Commission study, or about encouraging the surplus farm population to come into the cities. 'My God, the O.E.E. [Office of Emergency Employment] brought the Indians in. It was a disaster – they learned to be delinquent, or alcoholic. I think we have to take a new look at the whole idea of great cities. I doubt that stacking them higher and higher is the answer; we should explore decentralisation and I don't

mean the fringe suburb. If the jobs stay in the city the sub-
urbanites are chained to the old cities, and the traffic and
maintenance programmes will become unbearable. I'm talking
about settling new towns in the open spaces. We might see how
far the people would move if the job moved with them.'

This is the long run. How about the short and frightful run of
riots and racism, burn, baby, burn? He is suddenly quite calm.
'Once we have violence, we've got to have enforcement –
prompt and certain. We've been lacking in enforcement. The
criminal must know he'll be punished at once.' He is so clear
and unspeculative about this that we don't pursue the toughen-
ing procedures of the Oakland police or the questionable
threats of Mayor Yorty of Los Angeles to crack down with
force on all malefactors or apparent malefactors when the
trouble starts.

And supposing he had to declare himself on the election
issues for 1968? 'Vietnam may not be there, but if it is it'll be
issue number one. Either way the great issue is an umbrella
issue, what I call the Morality Gap: crime, obscenity, delinquency, the abandonment of law. Demonstrations must be
within the limits of civil disobedience. Labour and student
disputes should start with negotiations, not, my God, with a
strike. Now, they all take to the streets at once.'

You leave him having gained an impression of an engaging
kind of energy. He is precise and thoughtful on finance and the
mechanics of welfare, quietly dogmatic about the social ferment. He talks no jargon, which is a rare relief. He chants few
slogans. He does not preach or intone. He sounds like a decent,
deadly serious, baffled middle-class professional man. This, as
an executive geared for social rebellion and reform, may be his
weakness. But it is his strength among the voters that, in a
country with a huge middle class, he so faithfully reflects
their bewilderment at the collapse of the old, middle-class
standards, protections, and, perhaps, shibboleths.

A Mule Cortège
for the Apostle of the Poor

Atlanta, Georgia, April 9, 1968

Once before, the ninth of April was memorial day throughout the South. One hundred and three years ago today Robert E. Lee tendered his sword to General Grant and was granted in return the release of 'your men and their mules to assist in the spring ploughing.' Today, on a flaming spring day, with the magnolias blooming and the white dogwood and the red sprinkling the land, they brought a farm wagon and its mules to stand outside the church on the street where Martin Luther King was born and, after the funeral service to carry his body four miles to his college and lay it to rest. The 'mule train' is the oldest and still most dependable form of transport of the rural poor in the Southland. And somebody had the graceful idea that a mule train would be the aptest cortège for the man who was the apostle of the poor.

From the warm dawn into the blazing noon, the black bodies wearing more suits and ties than they would put on for a coronation, moved through the Negro sections of the town towards the street of comfortable, two-storey frame houses where the coloured business and professional men live and where, across from Cox's Funeral Home, the Rev. Martin Luther King lived and preached, in the Ebenezer Baptist Church, a redbricked nondescript tabernacle.

Thousands of college students had volunteered to act as marshals to hold the crowds; but though there was a tremendous push and jostle of people before the service began, there were enough police on hand to stem the crush and hand the visiting celebrities through like very pregnant women.

The bell tolled out the tune of 'We Shall Overcome' and big cars slid up to the entrance, and out of them climbed the Attorney General, Ramsey Clark, and Mrs. John F. Kennedy, and Richard Nixon and Senator Eugene McCarthy, Governor and Mrs. Romney of Michigan, and Governor Rockefeller and John Lindsay of New York, the new Roman Catholic Archbishop Terence Cooke, Sidney Poitier, the Metropolitan Opera's Leontyne Price, Eartha Kitt, Sammy Davis, Jr., Bobby and Ethel Kennedy and brother Edward, and Dr. Ralph Bunche, U Thant's man and Dr. King's friend.

Over the breaking waves of street noise and the tolling bell, the strong baritone of the Rev. Ralph Abernathy, Dr. King's heir, chanted from time to time: 'We will please be orderly now . . . let us have dignity . . . please . . . there are no more seats in the church.' Somebody lifted a squalling baby and passed it out over the tossing heads to safety.

It is a small church, and shortly after 10:30 the last cars and the last mourners were slotted in their places. First, Mrs. King and her four children and the dead man's brother, and Harry Belafonte. Then at last an alert squad of aides and Secret Service men surrounding Vice-President Humphrey. The conspicuous absentee was Lester Maddox, the Governor of Georgia, a segregationist whose presence could upset a coloured funeral any place North or South.

The inside of the church impressively belies its outside. It is a pleasantly modern room with a single oriel window, above a white cross over the choir and the pulpit. The flanking walls have two simple Gothic windows decorated alike with a single shield bearing a cross and surmounted with the crown of Christ. Tiny spotlights embedded in the ceiling threw little pools of light on the famous and the obscure equally. The warm shadows these shafts encouraged gave an extraordinary chiaroscuro to the congregation, making Bobby Kennedy at one point look like the captain of Rembrandt's 'Night Guard' amid his lieutenants slumbering in the shade.

It was a normal Baptist service with Southern overtones of gospel singing and solos, by black girls in white surplices, of Dr. King's favourite hymns sung with impassioned locking of the hands and closed eyes. Through it all, Mrs. King sat back at a sideways angle with the carved, sad fixity of an African idol. Dr. King's brother covered his face with a handkerchief once and others dabbed at their eyes; and the youngest King daughter sagged over in deep sleep like a rag doll. But Mrs. King was as impassive as Buddha behind her thin veil while the prayers were given, the hymns, the eulogy by a New York dean as white as Siegfried, who had taught theology to Dr. King. Once there was a suspicion of a glitter in her eyes when the Rev. Abernathy told of the last meal he had with Dr. King, an anecdote as simple as a parable.

'On that Thursday noon in the Lorraine Motel, in Memphis, Tennessee, the maid served up only one salad, and Martin took a small portion of it and left the rest. Then someone reminded the girl that she had brought up one order of fish instead of two. And Martin said, "Don't worry about it, Ralph and I can eat from the same plate," and I ate my last meal that Thursday noon. And I will not eat bread or meat or anything until I am thoroughly satisfied that I am ready for the task at hand.'

There was one innovation that was nearly forgotten at the end. Both the casket and the family were ready to go, but there was a quick whisper in the Rev. Abernathy's ear and he announced that Mrs. King had requested a playback of one of Dr. King's last sermons. It was that premonitory vision of his inevitable end, and his voice resounded through the hushed church:

'I think about my own death, and I think about my own funeral . . . and every now and then I ask myself what it is that I would want said and I leave the word to this morning . . . I don't want a long funeral, and if you get somebody to deliver the eulogy, tell him not to talk too long . . . tell him not to mention that I have a Nobel peace prize — that isn't important. Tell him not to mention that I have 300 or 400 other awards — that's not important . . . I'd like somebody to mention that day that Martin Luther King tried to give his life serving others. I want you to say that day that I tried to be right and to walk with them. I want you to be able to say that day that I did try to feed the hungry. I want you to be able to say that day that I did

try in my life to clothe the naked . . . I want you to say that I
tried to love and serve humanity.'

Then the doors were opened and the family went out and all
the parsons, and the mule team bore its flowered casket and
moved towards the many, many thousands that had gone on
before to Morehouse College.

Out of the Boudoir,
into the Laboratory

April 21, 1968

Out of Boston, which forty years ago arrested H. L. Mencken
for selling a rather prim story about a prostitute, appeared
to-day the most detailed and exhaustive and humourless
treatise ever printed, not perhaps on the art of love but on its
mechanism, technique, physiology, biochemistry, neurology,
and erotic topography.

It is a clinical record of 382 women and 312 men (a seeming
misappropriation of partners that will be instantly explained)
in 12,000 acts of passion, observed, photographed, recorded,
measured, taped, and filtered under 'strict laboratory conditions.' It may be wondered if the last phrase is not a contradiction in terms. How strict is a laboratory that not only allows
such goings-on but invites participants and pays them,
sometimes to lie with their mates, or to meet and woo a
stranger, or simply to enter the laboratory alone and mas-
turbate for the glory of science and the illumination of
'problems of sexual inadequacy'? That is the avowed aim of
the eleven years of dedicated labour that has been given to this
high-minded experiment by Dr. William H. Masters, a
gynaecologist, and Mrs. Virginia E. Johnson, otherwise un-
identified. Their opus, *Human Sexual Response*, is 366 pages
long and is published today by Little, Brown and Co.

The pioneering couple were inspired by the late Dr. Alfred Kinsey, but didn't feel he had gone far enough. He simply wrote down what people told him about their sex life. Dr. Masters and Mrs. Johnson wanted to see them at it, just to be sure. Their findings are interesting, to say the least, and the publishers, figuring that the United States is well populated by people with a similar devotion to medical science, are preparing for a Masters and Johnson bonanza.

The experiment started in 1954, with the blessing and under the auspices of the Washington University Medical School of St. Louis, one of the half-dozen most eminent medical schools in the country. In 1964, the Reproductive Biology Research Foundation got in on the act, and other small foundations and philanthropists have come along to enable the good work to be classified as tax-exempt under the laws of the Federal Government. In brief, once the partners, or the volunteer masturbators, were installed in the lab, they were clamped, plugged in, clocked, and observed by various devices to record their blood pressure, respiration, and the chemical content of their sweat glands and vaginal and seminal juices. Under these heroic conditions, 694 men and women, mostly between 18 and 50 (but one or two warriors touching 80), were able to achieve orgasm, a feat that is a testimony to the clinical neutrality of the attending doctors or the deceptive cosiness of the surroundings.

Dr. Masters has been quick to say that he has 'made every attempt to avoid prurience and pornography,' as well he might, because the U.S. Supreme Court has thrown the booksellers into a tizzy by its recent judgment that the measure of a book's salaciousness lies not in its content alone but also in the motives of those who write, sell, or advertise it. The Supreme Court is on the lookout, in its own phrase, for 'the leer of the sensualist.' It won't find it in the Savonarola expression of Dr. Masters or in his text, which abounds in such items as: 'Two small muscles, the ischiacavernosus muscles, inset into the crura of the clitoris, have their origin bilaterally from the ischial rami.' However, the layman who would honestly like to know more about the processes which brought him on this planet will from time to time find words and phrases that strike a chord.

Out of it all has come the discovery that the vagina itself, and not the cervix, produces its own lubricant; that this liquid is death on spermatozoa; and that if it can be isolated, it may, in the thundering prediction of the *New York Times*, offer 'the most effective population control agent' ever found. That alone would justify and reward the weary eleven years of unflagging industry that Dr. Masters and Mrs. Johnson have given to measuring and photographing people in coitus.

Otherwise, the dedicated couple tell us (and 'tell' is the word, for they are talking, so to speak, *ex cathedra*) that women respond quicker, longer, and faster than men to sexual stimulation; that a large penis is no measure of potency; that the vagina and not the clitoris is the seat of orgasm; that sexual intensity varies from man to man and woman to woman (and also from man to woman); and that impotence in the ageing male can be quickly 'reversed' with a new, 'willing and responsive' partner – findings that have been suspected for centuries by honest husbands and enterprising travelling salesmen.

Bedlam in Chicago

Chicago, Illinois, September 5, 1968

Vice-President Hubert Humphrey overwhelmingly won the Democrats' Presidential nomination last night but he, the Convention, and most likely the Democratic party itself, were wounded beyond recognition by the spectacle, seen by stupefied millions, of a Chicago police force gone berserk in front of the biggest hotel in the world. In thirty years of attending presidential conventions, I have seen nothing to match the fury and despair of the delegations inside this

Chicago amphitheatre, or on the outside, anything like the jumping-jack ferocity of the police corps around the Hilton Hotel. They began by clubbing and taming peace demonstrators and jeering hippies and ended by roaming the hotel lobby like SS men and roughing up astonished guests, marooned families, and other innocents sitting or walking through the hotel lounges.

By mid-evening, while nominating orators were extolling the saintliness of five candidates (Humphrey, McCarthy, McGovern, a Southern Governor, and a Negro parson), the night air along Michigan Avenue was dense with tear gas, roaring multitudes of youngsters, the smart crack of billy clubs, and the clatter of running feet.

Senator Eugene McCarthy opened up his headquarters in the hotel as an emergency hospital, and he and his daughter moved among the injured comforting them and bathing their wounds. Senator McGovern, the other dove candidate, stood at the window of his fourth-floor suite reeling with disbelief and nausea. He turned back from the thing itself to the wider view of it being shown on television. He telephoned his floor manager, Senator Abe Ribicoff of Connecticut, on the Convention floor. When Ribicoff came to the rostrum to put McGovern's name in nomination, he abandoned his smooth text, stared coolly at Mayor Daley and the entire Illinois delegation no more than 50 feet away and cried, 'With George McGovern as President we would not have Gestapo tactics in the streets of Chicago.'

Through a tidal wave of boos and derisive cheers, the Illinois delegation stood and lunged their fists at him. Ribicoff, an elegant and handsome man, slowly said: 'How hard it is to accept the truth.' This was too much for the Mayor of Chicago. Dropping his calculated Edward G. Robinson smile, he rose and shouted inaudible horrors at the first man to confess to this Convention that the Democratic party had been mocked, in the name of security, to make a gangsters' holiday.

Thereafter, scores of young men employed by a private

detective agency locked arms around the Illinois delegation and denied any access to them by other delegates, the press, the television floor reporters, or Convention officials. These same 'security' boys, wearing nondescript armbands or flagrant Humphrey buttons or even no badges at all, have enraged the press and the television reporters all week by their dogging presence, their systematic jamming of the aisles, their blocking of the necessary contact between heads of delegations. Last night they outdid themselves, in their mulish way, and this morning the three television networks and a host of newspapers filed protests with the City of Chicago, the Governor of Illinois, and the National Committee of the Democratic Party.

Even in the clearing haze of the morning after, another crystalline day of late summer, it is almost impossible to describe the progress of the Convention plot; for every parliamentary move on the floor was baffled by the street battles thundering from the television screens in the corridors and soon after by the rage of the delegates who had watched them. Let it be said, then, for the sober record that the Convention was gavelled into a rough approximation of order at 7:15 by the midget chairman from Oklahoma, Congressman Carl Albert, the House majority leader. The actors Ralph Bellamy and Paul Newman, the national heart-throb, recited a memorial tribute to Adlai Stevenson of Illinois which very few people bothered to hear. But for thirty seconds or so, the Convention rose and bowed its head. It was the first and last moment of silence or serenity in the whirlwind of the night.

The nominators came in turn and praised their man, but as the word of the battle of Chicago came in, even the orators began to salt their bland stuff with acid asides. The television reporters were complaining, in full view of the nation, about these 'thugs' and 'faceless men' at their elbows. Paul O'Dwyer, the Democratic choice for Senator in New York, walked out and held a caucus of New York, California, and Wisconsin delegates and urged them 'to decline to participate in this mockery.' The purpose of this rebel caucus was declared to be 'to bring to a grinding halt this Convention unless these atrocities are stopped.' Don Peterson, a liberal of Wisconsin, was the man chosen to attempt this enormity, which has happened only once, 108 years ago. His first chance to be heard by the Convention came when Wisconsin was called, in the roll of the States, to put a name in nomination or to pass. Peterson, ignoring the niceties of protocol, shouted in a measured way, 'Mr. Chairman, is there no rule that will compel Mayor Daley to suspend these police state tactics on the streets of Chicago?' In the following bedlam, little Carl Albert gavelled him down and went on with the roll.

The next and last challenge came when Peterson, in the middle of the actual balloting roll call, shouted into an ocean of sound a motion to 'adjourn this Convention forthwith for two weeks, three weeks, until we can meet in another city.' Justifiable or not, this was an irrelevance. When Wisconsin was called to register its Presidential vote, Peterson asked 'in all courtesy' what had happened to his motion. The chairman, hoarse as a frog by now, shouted that the rules permitted no motion or other business to interfere with a roll call. 'Reluctantly,' Wisconsin cast its vote.

At the end Hubert Humphrey had run up the commanding total of 1,761-3/4 against McCarthy's 601, McGovern's 146-1/2, with 67-1/2 votes for the Negro parson, 12-1/2 for Senator Kennedy, and a sprinkling of oddities, including three votes for the football coach of Alabama State university.

The band blared in with Roosevelt's victory song, 'Happy Days Are Here Again.' But it was a funeral march. There were almost as many boos as cheers. The euphoria of the winners was, I suppose, genuine enough at the moment. But the sight of it on television revealed a gruesome irony. The only unreal place to be last night was in the Convention itself. Fenced in with barbed wire, ringed around with Mayor Daley's tough guys, cut off from the living world of television, the amphitheatre was a circus in the middle of a plague. Most of the delegates, it was obvious, had no idea what the grim

Ribicoffs and Petersons were talking about. Some personal grudge, no doubt, against Mayor Daley. It was a terrifying demonstration of McLuhanism: the only people who got the whole message were the millions frozen with terror in front of their television screens. To-day, delegates from New York and California and several other states lodged formal complaints with the Justice Department; and Attorney General Ramsey Clark has promised a full investigation of the Chicago disorders and the behaviour of the police.

If there is any consolation in all this for the ordinary agonised citizen it is that Mayor Daley was revealed as an arch bullyboy, the manager of this Convention inside and out, the last of the city bosses in his dreadful and final hour of glory. The Chicago newspapers are the first to say so. From pundits to gossip columnists this morning, the local press is seething at the dictatorship of the man who only a few months ago roared into power for the fourth time with a seventy-five per cent majority of the votes. 'Hubert in a Shambles' was the Chicago *Daily News* headline over a piece that began: 'Hubert H. Humphrey could have gotten a better deal in bankruptcy court.' And its national correspondent wrote: 'The biggest name on the casualty list from the battle of Michigan Avenue last night was Richard J. Daley.' 'How long will it be,' moaned a woman social columnist, 'before Chicago's name stands for anything but horror in the minds of the world?'

'At least,' said a Chicago police official this morning, 'no one was killed.' No one, that is, except the Democratic party. Now that the smoke and clatter and weeping have died down, there is only a faint rhythmical sound ruffling the horizon on this beautiful day. It is the sound, North, South, East, and West, of the Republicans counting votes.

Where Now Is the New World?

Chicago, Illinois, October 24, 1968

In the 1930s the better clubs of the richer cities rumbled with the threats of business men to leave the country if 'that man in the White House' was re-elected. Roosevelt was re-elected again and again and yet again, but the agony of his enemies was never severe enough to drive them into remote exile.

In the 1940s and 1950s, the migration fever passed over to New Deal liberals, who swore that if Dewey — or, later, Eisenhower — went to the White House, they too would take off for New Zealand. Through the surprising good offices of Harry Truman, Dewey kindly provided a stay of deportation, but through the eight Eisenhower years there was no evidence that New Zealand ever saw them.

Now, the same itchy types are shuddering at the thought of President Nixon and vowing to settle instead in the new Utopia of the American liberal: England. There is no cause for Mr. Enoch Powell to spring to the barricades of the immigration shed. All these restless people are white, most of them W.A.S.P.s, who cannot bear the prospect of a President less literate than Stevenson, less remote than Eugene McCarthy. It is a safe bet, anyway, that after November 5 they will still be here viewing with little pride and pointing with much alarm to the student rebellions, the school strikes, the police slow-downs, the truculence of the Wallaceites, the stews of the cities.

Here in Chicago, though, there is a man who is neither a W.A.S.P. nor a liberal nor a Wallaceite who is leaving the country no matter who is elected. A carpenter, a Catholic, second-generation American, with a Polish immigrant grand-father, he is what Mr. Nixon calls 'the new forgotten man': a decent, industrious working man with middle-class habits and a tidy, roomy bungalow (two bathrooms, two-car garage) little different in style or social milieu from the house that Mr. Daley, the Mayor of Chicago, bought thirty years ago and has lived in ever since. This man has shared the aspirations of his grandfather's kind: a life in a new and better world unalarmed by pogroms or secret police, comfort beyond the dream of a sweating peasant, education for his children, pride in an egalitarian country. Like very many of the victims of the depression, who were once the liberal's favourite charity object, Ed Koralski is more conservative than his patrons. He is nervous at the influx of Negroes into his district. He is angry at the waste of schooling entailed in school teachers' strikes. He was shaken by the riots in Detroit, Cleveland, and Chicago. He is shamed by the slow decay of his neighbourhood, the uncollected garbage, the junkie kids, the nightly despair of some of his friends on the police force who are assailed as 'pigs' on the streets and who go in twos now against the Black Power tactics of ambush and false alarms.

A year ago Ed Koralski went to the savings bank and withdrew nearly $3,000 and he and his wife flew to Australia at the urging of a second cousin. He looked it over and he liked what he saw. He is moving, election or no election, come Humphrey, Nixon, or Wallace. In Australia he will earn a little less than a third of his wages here. But he feels he is doing the right thing for his family. They will grow up, he believes, in health and safety in the sort of land to which his grandfather emigrated. He is not alone in this prejudice. There are even scholars at the University of Chicago who see Australia as Roosevelt's America, a wide-open land moving with confidence out of its pioneer past into industrial democracy.

Ed Koralski may not start a trend. But he leaves behind, here and in dozens of comfortable working-class districts from Boston to Kansas City and on to Los Angeles, a troubled population that yearns for a peaceful land, preferably here. He shares the sentiments of a factory order clerk in Bridgeport, Connecticut, who spoke from the heart to a reporter: 'The radicalism, the war, the taxes — everything is getting worse instead of better. None of the politicians seem to have any answers for people like me. No one does.'

Take a random poll among such people and the voting habits of a lifetime are seen to be in dissolution. Seventy per cent of them have always voted Democratic. Less than twenty-five per cent now mean to stay with Humphrey, forty per cent are going for Nixon, and twenty per cent for Wallace. They are articulate about their reasons. If the war in Vietnam is to go on, they incline to a tougher military effort. They see their own standards, of what it is to be decent, dependable, and 'respectable,' flouted by the next-door hippies and the high school rebels. They are afraid of the next stage in the black rebellion. They are full of anecdotes about people on relief, avoiding jobs, and milking the welfare funds.

These are not red-necks or white trash, and most of them believe the Negro has had a bad break and must have equal rights. But they see around them violence, brazen codes of rudeness, children high on pot or worse, flagrant absenteeism at the factory, and no one in sight to bring a new sort of order to the Negroes' rage to live. 'Ed Koralski,' says a neighbour, 'has the right idea, and if I were twenty years younger I'd be up and away. As things are, we mean to stay and hold on to what we have, and hope the kids will grow up right.'

The Most Beautiful Woman I Know . . .*

February 27, 1969

In writing any piece that has to do with taste and appetite (my favourite casserole dish, great actors of yesteryear, Is Jazz Dead?) you do well to stop and ask who you think you are writing for. A lot of space and time could be saved at the start if we all attached warning labels, as they do on bottles of medicine: 'Not to be taken by children under 12, or by

---

* This was one of a series in which the editor of the *Guardian* invited each of the paper's feature writers to choose his own 'most beautiful woman.'

diabetics.' Why explain how to cook ravioli to people who loathe pasta? How possibly to interest people in the development of jazz piano, from Jelly Roll Morton to Thelonius Monk, who are stuck with sheet music? Journalism whines with the burden of old men's nostalgia, disguised in the form of protests against the decline of lieder singing, sensible poetry, political honesty, good food.

How, then, to begin to be persuasive about something so ticklish, so idiosyncratic, as a taste in females? Long ago, when I used to be a regular customer of the late lamented Billy Minsky, the great impresario of burlesque, I noticed that the strippers who provoked the most clamant applause were not, by any standard, the prettiest or the lushest girls. Bodies come in every shape and size, and men in search of their fundamental satisfactions don't look for the Miss America contest's crusading measurements: they don't want a standard, more often they want a substandard, of the bizarre, the odd, and the ripe. Francis Bacon expressed his own peculiar preference with impressive solemnity: 'There is no beauty that hath not some strangeness in proportion.' Or, Mark Twain's words: 'A difference of opinion is what makes horse races.'

So I am aware, like the intellectual uncomfortably stopping to discover folk art in the business of striptease, that it is a personal sexual whim which makes the immediate choice and the subsequent rationalising that goes to justify it.

On a higher plane, if that's what we're aiming at, I'm afraid the problem is much the same. As college students, we used to thrash unnecessarily, in fear, over a famous puzzle of the time. Is it Looks or Character you should be searching for? William Empson said somewhere that this was much like the Victorian squabble about Sound versus Sense in poetry. The Victorians believed very much in 'pure beauty' and 'pure sound,' whether or not the stuff made much sense; just as they mooned over those frail giraffes who lean out of the paintings of Rossetti and G. F. Watts. These were the all-time Victorian beauties. In my generation they produced a giggle, but I'm told that the fashion is reverting to them again and that art students flock into the Chapel of Jesus College, Cambridge, not any longer to marvel at the medieval windows but to kneel before the dreadful ladies in the Burne-Jones window. What matters, concluded Empson, is 'what the Looks mean to you and the possible relations of the Character with your own.'

So anybody choosing 'the most beautiful woman,' while pretending to show that he's been around a good deal more than you and is picking out something as indisputable as the tallest building in the world or the champion long-jumper, is really involved in defending a very personal view of beauty and then boosting the most conspicuous example of it he can recall.

So be it. I will state my sexual and aesthetic preferences and then move on to something more scientifically verifiable. During the nineteen-twenties we were brainwashed, by Anita Loos and a spate of popular songs, into believing that 'Gentlemen Prefer Blondes.' Since we were all desperate at the time to be thought the last surviving examples of the dying cult of the gentleman, we obediently preferred blondes. And there was a time when my idea of a wonderful Christmas vacation was dancing with a girl from Preston who looked like Laura La Plante. I discovered only about ten years later that my own preference ran to brunettes, and that I was as invulnerable as Saint Paul against any redhead ever spawned.

Also, I came to recognise that I could resist to the death any dame whose figure resembled an ironing board. This left me a lot of time for study in the nineteen-twenties and, more recently, has meant that confronted by the present generation of air hostesses I can concentrate on almost anything else. I am absolute proof against the present fashion of lean, plain Jane models and the present mode in college girls. In other words, I am treading water till women come back. Without embracing the extremity of emigrating to Istanbul, I yearn for the return of the 9-stone-plus female with dark hair, full lips, dark eyes, long thighs, recognisably female hips, and a fetching *décolletage*. I am ravished beyond reason by the innumerable beauties who inhabit the Hawaiian Islands. As a group or race, I should pick the best-looking young women of Ethiopia as the most beautiful prime females I have ever seen.

Coming closer to home, I have to admit that the accident of my moonlighting trade (for nine years as a television M.C.) brought me into respectable contact with most of the current movie and theatrical crop. They were and are not more beautiful than the current crop of secretaries. They simply have more verve and more ego. I have sat on a love seat and lit, through a long evening, the cigarette chain of Greta Garbo. She was magnificent but so extrasexual, so much the chiselled goddess above and beyond the likes of you and me, that I was untouched.

However, there is one who moved in beauty like a brilliant Manhattan night. Throughout the late 1940s and the early 1950s she could be photographed from any angle, in any posture, and everything about her – her brow, eyes, ears, neck, lips, cheek bones, jaw, clavicle – was a continuous enchantment. In my time, and for me, there has never been anyone like her. She is Ava Gardner.

Eisenhower

April 3, 1969

It is, I think, a decent custom which prescribes that we shall say nothing but good about the dead. I found it binding enough some years ago to excuse me from writing an obituary piece about the late Senator Joseph McCarthy. It seemed to me, while he was alive and when he died also, that he had done irreparable harm to the reputation of the United States. And the moment of his going was not the time to say so. But this custom is, I take it, an injunction of good manners to be observed while the grief of the family is still sharp. It's not meant to last for ever and a year or two after a man's death – as, for instance, now with John F. Kennedy – it is possible to weigh his strengths and weaknesses without running the risk of tastelessness.

But the journalist is in a specially difficult position from the moment the breath gives out in a public man. A journalist is, by literal definition, a man who writes from day to day. And no newspaper or broadcasting station that I ever heard of recognises the journalist's obligation, as a citizen and a man, to say nothing for a while. The easy way out is to canonise the dead man in the moment of his dying. It may be insincere but it's tactful. And at such a moment insincerity is thought to be better than the truth. I discovered this most painfully when Adlai Stevenson dropped dead in London. Of all the politicians I have known, he was the one I knew best. The one who came closest to producing the embarrassment which a political journalist ought to be most careful to avoid: never to know a public man well enough that he inhibits you from writing about him frankly and fully while he's living his public life. When Stevenson died I wrote a piece about him which never saw the light of day because, I take it, people who knew him not at all might have been outraged by the discovery that he was a human being, with frailties like you and me. For a week or more it was necessary to pretend that he was a saint: a wicked saint, but a saint.

Now what, after a quarter of a century, have we left for Dwight David Eisenhower? What are we to say about a man who was the most popular hero of his time and who was above all else likeable? Stevenson made a wry remark when he was asked just after the 1952 elections why he'd lost: 'Who did I think I was, running against George Washington?' Four years later, Stevenson was seduced into running again, if only because in September 1955 he was as sure as the next man that Ike would never recover from the first massive heart attack he suffered in Denver.

The last time I saw Eisenhower was on his farm down in

Gettysburg. He was by then very much an old country squire, sitting on his terrace with his back to the light and the book held rather high in his hands because, like many more of us whose eyesight does weird things from week to week, he was just then in between glasses, so to speak. His glasses were perched on the end of his nose, and by holding the book high and looking through the top of the lenses, he could get things in focus until the new bifocals arrived. From time to time he put the book down and squinted out across his fields to the pasture. And he would watch the cattle going in, or scrutinise a blighted elm, or remark that a particular feed grass he was using burnt out too quickly in the drenching summer heat of that very hot valley.

We all, they say, revert to our origins in old age, and if you did not know who Ike was you would have guessed, and rightly, that he was a lifelong farmer – and by now, a prosperous one. They were having a fierce drought that summer in Pennsylvania, as everywhere else in the East, and as the sun declined and the evening became bearable, we strolled out onto the grass and towards a small circular lawn which was a precious thing to Ike. It was a putting green and it had only one hole, with a flag stuck in it whose pennant was stamped with the five stars of a General of the Army. Strangely, this one hole was invisible because it was so grown over with weeds that I doubt you could have sunk a cannon-ball in it. I asked about this and he said with that almost strenuous earnestness he brought to all questions of morals: 'Well, you see, the Governor of Pennsylvania put out a proclamation over a month ago, I guess, asking people to save water and do no watering of lawns, golf courses, and so on. Looks pretty sad, doesn't it?'

In retrospect, it was a pretty sad occasion. In his old age there were two things Ike lived for: his farm and his golf. At that time he was beginning to be plagued by innumerable ailments. And I remember on that particular morning he was a little querulous because he had had some tests made on an affliction of his diaphragm and the results were not in. But what worried him more was arthritis in his hands. And the next day I remember his rubbing the joints and looking at them and wondering if he would ever play golf again. I hinted in subsequent conversation that he had the golf bug pretty badly. 'In the worst way,' he said. 'I didn't take it up until after the war when I was in my mid-fifties, when I was at SHAPE. And, as you know, it takes two years to learn to hit the ball. And sometimes, during briefing sessions, I'd let my mind wander from the disposition of the Russian armies and so on, and just fret about my game. There was a time when I used to dash out of Paris to St. Cloud and say: never mind the Russian threat to Europe – if only I can straighten out this terrible duck hook that I've developed.'

Well, it will be a relief to us all to remember that Ike had, at all times, an overwhelming sense of mission – whether you agreed or not with the mission didn't matter. And that while he was in Paris, and while he was in the Presidency, there were certain priorities in his mind that had the force of moral absolutes. One was the security of Western Europe, and we ought not to forget, now that Europe is repaired and going its own way, that it was Ike's authority and the certainty of the attitude he conveyed to the Russians which kept Europe untouched in the dangerous days, when the Russians were able and sorely tempted to overrun the Continent. It is a curious psychological fact, never satisfactorily explained, that the Russians seemed to respect the peaceful intentions of a professional soldier more than they did those of Ike's predecessor or his successors. I doubt there ever would have been that meeting in Vienna between Khrushchev and the President of the United States during Ike's regime. But the Russians, looking at Kennedy, were fooled – as we all were – by his extreme appearance of youth, and assumed that he was an amateur and highly vulnerable to warlike threats. We never came so close to a showdown with Ike. And the Russians, still unconvinced about Kennedy, had to try the bold bluff of the Cuban missiles before they learnt that Kennedy, in spite of all his campaign rhetoric about the declining reputation of the U.S. under Ike, shared Eisenhower's same inflexible view that Western Europe was an essential outpost of the United States.

This, and much else in American foreign policy, has been constant, though the ferocity and length of American Presidential election campaigns cause the parties to contrive an absurd drama out of their differences and pretend they're offering the people drastically opposite policies. In time, it may seem that American foreign policy — towards Europe, anyway — was all of a piece since Harry Truman warned the Russians about Greece, to the day that Johnson warned them again about Berlin. But the man who secured this policy and gave it stamina was Eisenhower. And for that, perhaps more than anything, I believe, we are all in his debt. Whether he was a great President, or even a very good one, is something that I don't think it possible to decide to-day. Arnold Toynbee, for example, has the rather alarming conviction that the man responsible for our present ills and for the coming of Doomsday is Harry Truman. And that John Foster Dulles's brinkmanship was only a way of saying what Truman had long ago been doing. Eisenhower, it seems to me, had two golden periods, of which the second was his first term as President. The first, of course, began with his appointment as Supreme Commander of the Allied Forces.

Many harsh and even ribald things have been said about him as a soldier. The sheer luck of being promoted above many superiors and picked by General Marshall for the Supreme Command when Marshall himself was begged to take it three times by Roosevelt, and the fact that Ike had never had a field command. He may not have been, as Montgomery was, a soldier's soldier, but he was, for the war years, the ideal choice for an essential task: that of uniting by his own likeable and fair personality the warring elements of many allied nations and many diverse temperaments and some very rum characters. The one touch of genius he had was that of a peacemaker among Americans, Englishmen, Frenchmen, Poles, bristling with national pride and driven by ambition. It may be, in fact, that such immortality as Eisenhower achieves will be guaranteed by two qualities that do not usually, in a worldly world, guarantee a man much more than the affection of his friends: by the force of them, Eisenhower was able to make trusting friends of about 250 million people fighting for their lives. They are candour and decency.

The Lost Hours of Edward Kennedy

July 24, 1969

In the moonless early hours of Saturday morning, the 19th, a car tumbled off a bridge on a tiny island off the coast of Massachusetts. A girl was drowned. The driver escaped. It is, on the face of it, a routine holiday misfortune. But the driver was Senator Edward M. Kennedy, the leading contender for the Democratic Presidential nomination three years from now, and he did not show up on the main island of Martha's Vineyard, where he was staying, for another eight hours to report to the police. So, this morning at Edgartown, on Martha's Vineyard, the authorities applied for a complaint to be filed against Senator Kennedy accusing him of the statutory offence of leaving the scene of an accident and failing to report it 'within a reasonable time.' A court will decide on Monday whether to prosecute. The outline of the story is fairly clear, but there is a dark gap of eight hours which Senator Kennedy will have to illumine to the jury's satisfaction.

Senator Kennedy had flown down to Martha's Vineyard from his summer home on Cape Cod for a weekend of boat races and parties. Among the guests were several friends and former campaign workers of both Senator Kennedy and his dead brother Robert. One of them was Mary Jo Kopechne, a 28-year-old former secretary to Robert Kennedy. Sometime late on Friday evening, Senator Kennedy left his hotel on Martha's Vineyard and drove his car on to the ferry that runs the few hundred yards between the Vineyard and the small island of Chappaquiddick, lying to the east. He went to a party given by an old friend of his brother, and later left with Miss Kopechne to ferry back to Edgartown.

He took the wrong turn, came upon a narrow bridge, failed to stop in time, and the car fell into the water and turned over. According to his later statement to the police, he had no idea how he managed to free himself from the car, though he did remember 'repeatedly diving down' to see if the girl was there. At last he was out on the bridge and the bank and recalls walking back 'exhausted and in a state of shock to where my friends were eating.' This was presumably the cottage where the party was still going on. 'There was a car parked in front of the cottage and I climbed into the back seat. I then asked someone to bring me back to Edgartown.'

The puzzles accumulate in these last sentences. The police figure, from the Senator's own story, that the car fell into the water sometime between midnight and 1 a.m. The ferry across the channel does not run between midnight and 7:30 in the morning.

Where was the Senator between, say, 1:30 in the morning and 7:30 when the ferry service resumed? Could he have stayed mum in the parked car all those hours without arousing at least the curiosity of the remaining partygoers? Who was the 'someone' who took him back to the Vineyard and when?

The papers today rehearsed yet again the record of doom that has dogged the Kennedy family: the retarded sister, the brother killed in the Second World War, the sister dead in an airplane crash, the famous victims of Lee Harvey Oswald and Sirhan Sirhan. Before or since all these disasters, the youngest and last male of the line has had few ordeals to face that might so crucially affect his political future as that of unravelling the eight blank hours between his abandoning his sunken car and his appearance at the Edgartown police station.

The Ghastly Sixties

January 3, 1970

In time the Sixties, like the Gay Nineties and the Roaring Twenties, will no doubt acquire their distinguishing epithet. As a beginning, we might quite simply suggest the word ghastly.

This is not said lightly or cynically. In thirty-seven years' experience of the United States, from the pit of the depression to the apotheosis of Richard M. Nixon, I have known no stretch of American life so continuously disheartening as the six lean years that were so dreadfully announced by the shots in Dallas and were echoed in Watts and Detroit and Newark, that re-echoed on the motel balcony in Memphis and the hotel pantry in Los Angeles, and rumbled obscenely on the streets of Chicago and through the stadiums of the 1968 Presidential election campaign. That, to be fussy, leaves four preceding years of what may now be seen as the fool's paradise of the Kennedy era, which is what I truly believe it to have been.

Vietnam was practically heralded by the ringing, and ringingly hollow, boast of the Inaugural: 'Let every nation know, whether it wishes us well or ill, that we shall pay any price, bear any burden, meet any hardship, support any friend, oppose any foe to assure the survival and the success of liberty.' After six years of opposing their Roman might to a foe that, like Gibbon's earlier 'barbarians . . . were inured to encounters in the bogs,' even the most belligerent hawks in the Pentagon admit to America's capacity to fight no more than 'two and a half wars,' not by any remote possibility the forty-three wars which the United States is by treaty bound to undertake.

In 1960 the United Nations announced the Development Decade as an urgent mission whereby the rich nations would start to close the gap with the poor. At the end of the decade U Thant had nothing better to report than that the gap had widened alarmingly, and that what lies ahead for many of the poor nations is a reign of famine and revolution.

In 1961 John Kennedy announced, to universal applause, the Alliance for Progress, the high-minded disbursement of billions of dollars to Latin America. To-day, with no sign of a Latin American economic union and with the population growth-rate as headlong as ever, the sour prediction of an eminent Colombian economist has been fulfilled: 'Twenty billion dollars in ten years will help us to stand still.'

In 1963, only a month or two before his assassination, John Kennedy looked back numbly on nearly a hundred bills – for public housing, civil rights, Medicare, public health, land conservation, model cities, tax reform, etc., etc. – that were petrified in the appropriate committees of Congress. A notable political scientist and an admirer of Kennedy wrote a book called *The Democratic Deadlock*. It might well be that the Congressional system is too torpid, too unresponsive to the pace of essential reform, to be able much longer to steer the country towards a governable United States. But in 1963 much of this deadlock had to be attributed to Kennedy's fatal incapacity to respect the sincerity of his Congressional opponents, to trade one conviction for another, and to retain the friendship of the vital committee chairmen who had once opposed him.

Probably the best thing that happened in the political life of the nation during the decade was Lyndon Johnson's healing gift with friend and foe and his consequent ability to put through the eighty-ninth Congress between January and October of 1964 a volume of domestic reforms which, in a period of easy affluence and Congressional complacency, far surpassed that given to Franklin Roosevelt in the depth of the Depression by a frightened and submissive Congress. And this was done on top of huge appropriations for defence, which took up about half ($46.9 billions) of the total budget ($119.3 billions).

It is conceivable that, if there had been no Vietnam, Johnson would have moved, with his rogue-elephant's strides, into the transformation of urban life, the purifying of air and water, and the lifting up of the Negroes into the equality which he came to, first reluctantly and then with the vigour and passion of a convert. It has to be remembered that the Civil Rights Bills, from Eisenhower first to Johnson last, were his doing; and, in the most wasteful episodes of rioting and violence, it should not be forgotten that more was done in Johnson's five years to liberate the Negro than in the previous 350 years, exactly, of his subjection. It is, plainly and tragically, not enough. But it is, in an historical view, a great deal.

But whenever we begin to take comfort, to hope for a new era of radical reconstruction (of the cities, of the State legislatures, of the protection of what we now call 'the environment') we stumble into Vietnam. The continuing curse of it is that it has almost ceased to be an issue in itself, it is like some technological monster in a horror movie that terrifies and befouls all the life around. Until it is over, we shall not know whether the will, as well as the money, is available to bind up the cities' wounds, to advance the Negro with a 'deliberate speed' that he will accept as the best that can be done.

It is possible that the Negro, and the radical youth, black and white, are already too cynicised – by Vietnam, by widespread corruption in state and in municipal government, by the respectable inroads of the Mafia, by the climate of violence – to accept any longer the habit of creative compromise that is essential to effective government of the people by the people and which, in truth, has been the genius of the American system since its founding. Perhaps by now there are not enough believers left to rescue and reform the system. If this is so, what seems to be the most fearful possibility is a dogged reaction by the middle-class mass, and the arrival of fascism by popular democratic vote.

Other nations have their hippies and their rock culture, their drugged youth and their 'alienated' students, the Babylonian heritage of the Sixties, plunging its unhandleable populations into headier and headier materialism. Only America has suffered the traumatic disillusion, in ten short years, of losing its status as the beneficent leader of the world and turning into a giant, writhing in its own coils, suspect, frightened, and leaderless.

There has never been a time when so many Americans despaired of their own past and present and renounced their old cocky boast to roll up their sleeves and face the toughest job. The one consolation must be that in the Sixties, after two decades of enjoying a self-deception that is common to all the 'developed' nations, the Americans at last began to grapple with the real problems of their society, horrendous though they may be.

'Put Not Your Trust in Princes . . .'

November 6, 1971

It has always been cited as an irrepressible symptom of America's vitality that her people, in fair times and foul, believe in themselves and their institutions. Indeed one of the national characteristics that has most constantly outraged visiting critics, from John Wesley to Simone de Beauvoir, is a blithe indifference to chastisers obviously shipped over from Europe for nothing but the good of the natives. The frustration of these high-toned critics is compounded further by the irritating fact that Americans pay them handsomely to hear what's wrong with the New World.

The natives can afford this largesse because the visiting critic, while often touching on odd and interesting complaints, rarely gets to the heart of the matter and never unravels the fine mesh of corruption, the knotty grain of politics, so expertly as the domestic muckrakers. Witness, as late examples merely, Mike Royko's clinical analysis of the running of a city machine in his book on Mayor Daley's Chicago, *Boss*. Or Gay Talese's *Honor Thy Father*: an account, written from under the carpet, of the comings and goings of the Mafia.

In the past, then, and more so in the present, it was the local boy who stripped bare the local scoundrel. Arnold Bennett and Israel Zangwill might notice and deplore the sweatshop pallor of immigrant seamstresses, but it was Lincoln Steffens and Jacob Riis who set the bomb under the city fathers and fired Theodore Roosevelt to bellow for reform.

Something new and alarming is happening to the American conscience. It is pricked, but not to great action. The two books I have mentioned would have started a political movement had they been written in the 1890s. New York City's Knapp Commission, it must be said, has unmasked and documented the most frightening degree of bribery and corruption in every department of the police; but the believing citizen retreats into the shrug of saying it only confirms what he has always suspected. Because, it appears, his confidence in the leaders of most American institutions is at the ebb.

Louis Harris has just put out the findings of an opinion poll that was first tried out in 1966. At its first appearance, it was not much more than a social curiosity, and its results panicked nobody. The lead, and possibly leading, question was, 'As far as the people running these institutions are concerned [what the pollster meant was 'As far as you are concerned'], would you say you have a great deal of confidence, only some confidence, or hardly any confidence at all, in them?' Granted that the 'only' in the second phrase, and the 'hardly at all' in the last one, are practically invitations to the response 'You're darn tootin',' the question was first put at a time – after the Kennedy assassination, Watts, the Detroit bonfires, the beginning of the uproar on the campuses – when distrust of political leadership and of the Establishment branches in education, banking, advertising, etc., was militant. The real question was: How far did distrust go beyond the militants?

The answers, five years ago, were both instructive and disturbing. Only forty-one per cent of Americans had 'great' confidence in organised religion; twenty-five per cent in what they saw on television; only thirty-one per cent in the Warren

Supreme Court; twenty-one per cent in the moguls of advertising; forty-one per cent in the 'executive branch of the Federal Government' (meaning President Johnson and his Administration); and a wretched twenty-two per cent only in organised labour – a thunderous decline since the John L. Lewises and Walter Reuthers were the heroes of the first and second New Deals. But, way back there in 1966, fifty-five per cent 'greatly' trusted the main business corporations, sixty-one per cent the educators, sixty-seven per cent the banks, sixty-two per cent the military, seventy-two per cent the doctors, and a modest forty-two per cent the Congress.

Today, the movement of public disrespect for the hierarchy of American leadership is that of a landslide. Now, only twenty-one per cent have great trust in the President and the Administration; fourteen per cent in organised labour; twenty-three per cent in the Burger Supreme Court (which was supposed by its conservative bent to rally the vast majority of the silent); only nineteen per cent in Congress; thirty-six per cent in the banks; twenty-seven per cent in the military, and thirteen per cent in advertising. Only the doctors retain the reverential mystique of their profession, though even there the universal trust has declined from seventy-two per cent to sixty-one per cent.

So roughly two-thirds of the American people can muster 'only some' confidence in the men who govern their lives. And for the Congress, the President, the Supreme Court, and the military the seal of approval is willingly given by only one American in five.

In his comments on these figures, Harris reports 'a universal scepticism.' And while as a symptom of national morale it may well be dire, some of the reasons for it reveal not so much a shrug as an awakening to the facts of late-twentieth-century life that is surely no bad thing. Vietnam has sapped the prestige of the military. The stock market decline has blasted the general confidence in the know-how of Wall Street. The disclosure of universal pollution has stilled the once universal 'gee-whiz' response to the wonders of science. The educators are distrusted, it seems, not for their numbing jargon and general pomp (which their more violent detractors abundantly share), but for failing to put down the campus riots. As for the advertisers, who still presume in their chic clarion voices that they dictate our discriminating choices, they have sunk to a heartening all-time low in public esteem.

Americans are generally thought to be the world's prize sucker for the smart sell, whether raucous or velvety. It could be, on the contrary, that from long exposure they are the prize sceptics about anything offered as 'better' or 'best.' Forty-two per cent of them have 'only some' confidence in advertising, and another forty per cent have 'hardly any.' So, even on the darkest days, with Vietnam going on and on, and the Great Lakes turning into sewers, eighty-two Americans in every 100 continue to disbelieve what they are told. In the rude and violent days of Jefferson's campaign for the presidency, the percentage was, from all accounts, about the same.

J. Edgar Hoover

May 11, 1972

By the time he was 26 Hoover had become Assistant Director of the F.B.I., an institution which like several others under the benign blind eye of President Harding was a shambles of indirection, carrying an actual odour of corruption. The F.B.I. was and is the investigating arm of the Department of Justice; you would expect its agents to have professional probity, if nothing else. Yet at the time Hoover moved in, the head of the Department of Justice itself, the Attorney General, was a highly dubious character later brought to trial for conspiracy, and lucky to get off. The Attorney General's hand-picked F.B.I. Director was another oddity who picked as his assistant – Hoover's predecessor – a man who had survived a trial for murder and had served during the war, if 'served' is the word, as a German spy. This man, Gaston Means, was openly called by Hoover 'the greatest faker of all time.' Well, he at least did die in a Federal prison. Who, Hoover may well have asked himself, will police the policemen?

In 1924 he was appointed F.B.I. Director by a new Attorney General, a wholly different cast of man, Harlan Stone, who was later to become a distinguished ornament of the Supreme Court. I ought to stress that the F.B.I. is not a national police force. And it cannot interfere in crimes, however large or gruesome, committed inside a State unless a Federal crime is involved. The chaotic scene in the Dallas hospital in November 1963 was caused by the question of who was to be in charge of the dying President. It was not then a Federal crime to kill the President of the United States: the first responsibility rested with the Dallas police.

It took Hoover ten years – it took him until the rash of kidnapping and racketeering in the Thirties – to get Congressional approval for having the F.B.I. armed, and to have its own fleet of motor-cars. In the ten years between his taking over and his sudden emergence as the all-American gang-buster, Hoover made his great contribution to law enforcement. And it remains, whatever excesses of zeal and egotism made him later tramp over the hallowed ground of civil liberties by wire-tapping and compiling private files on suspected radicals and leftists. What he did first was to recruit the F.B.I. staff entirely from lawyers and accountants. He brought in filing experts, he refined and organised the best fingerprint file in the world. He invented an Identification Bureau that went far beyond finger-printing: spectro-chemistry, for instance, for spotting the authors of anonymous letters. He was, I suppose, the first – certainly the best – adaptor of science and electronics to police work. Today there are 4,000 local crime centres, affiliates of the F.B.I., that have immediate access to thirty-odd computer systems based on the Washington headquarters. Kidnapping was a plague when he came in, and his network of information was created to track criminals down as they whizzed across State borders and became automatically immune from arrest for a crime committed under the laws of another State. In the gangland days of the Thirties Hoover had his finest decade. And he had another quick run of fame when his Bureau descended all across the country on German and Italian agents within days of the attack on Pearl Harbor.

Hoover's notoriety, as distinct from his merited fame, was due to the vanity and sense of untouchability that afflicts powerful men who stay too long in absolute authority over any job; forty-eight years is a long time for a man to be a headmaster, let alone to be the chief criminal investigator of a great nation. His personal habits maintained the dogged respectability his mother instilled in him, and which he then instilled into his agents. No long hair, no fancy shirts, no coffee breaks, nothing so unseemly as a woman seen smoking in the office, no reading of *Playboy*. A hint of extramarital shenanigans and the man was out. Hoover himself arrived at the office in his car with his assistant, a Mr. Tolson, at precisely nine o'clock. At precisely 11:30 they left for lunch. These two, bachelors both, had lunch and dinner together six days a week for over thirty years. Hoover personally supervised the huge daily file of confidential reports on everything from espionage to petty theft in a government office. He was generally regarded by the liberal press and some conservatives as a monster Big Brother. He was regarded in a recent poll by eighty per cent of Americans as a national asset. Three Presidents waived the retirement age and eight Presidents of every political stripe trusted him, depended on him, and looked on him as a permanent fixture of the Republic like the Washington Monument. That has never been explained. One day it will have to be.

M*A*S*H: One of a Kind

February 12, 1983

It is one of the unsolved mysteries of American television that *M*A*S*H*, a tragi-comedy about an unpopular war almost as dire in its effects as Vietnam, should have retained for more than a decade a popular rating way up there in a catalogue of trash of many varieties. Night after night, week after week, year after year, its siren song of 'Incoming wounded!' beckoned thirty-three million or so away from teary soaps, drug sagas, frantic sitcoms, and marshmallow porn. It is not the intention of this piece to unravel this knotty problem, except to identify some of the elements that made *M*A*S*H* — as the song says — 'an isle of joy' in an ocean of junk.

War movies of two sorts — the knockabout farce and the grimly sentimental 'pity-of-it-all' epic — have been standard products of the American film industry from *Shoulder Arms* to *Apocalypse Now*. Their usual elements were predictable enough to guarantee for each kind an audience that knew exactly what it was going to get. In most of the epics, against a background of artillery fire and ruined woods (World War I), or mopped-up villages and Pacific jungles (World War II), we had half a dozen or so familiar types: the solemn colonel, the hip-hup sergeant, the rough diamond, the goldbrick, the gentle weakling, the company comic, the plucky kid and his mentor — our hero — the clean-limbed star played by John Gilbert, Gary Cooper, Kirk Douglas, Burt Lancaster, *et al.* In the farces, the blood-and-guts action had to be indicated as an unpleasantness far in the future, while Wheeler and Woolsey or Bob Hope made adorable asses of themselves in basic training.

Apart from a glut of shameless morale-builders made during World War II — in which the Nazis were always bullies, the Japanese always shifty, and our chaps decent and heroic, if in cantankerous ways — most war movies were made in retrospect, when the real thing was comfortably over. The fact that

Chaplin's *Shoulder Arms* came out while World War I was still on can now be seen as one freakish consequence of a frontline censorship so ironclad that the chuckling audiences had only the faintest notion of the scale and hideousness of the enormous slaughter. Offhand, I don't recall any uproarious comedies about Vietnam.

So, all right, *M*A*S*H* started, also, when the Korean War was all over. Even so, Ring Lardner Jr.'s original movie script, filmed and shown seventeen years after the fighting ended, was enough of a shocker (joking surgeons whose hands, just below the frame, were fiddling with intestines) to cause the British film historian Leslie Halliwell to call it 'the great anti-everything film, certainly very funny for those who can take it'; and Judith Crist to write: 'The laughter is blood-soaked and the comedy cloaks a bitter and terrible truth.' Not, you would say, the sort of thing likely to spawn a television series that would last eleven years.

But we have come to take its 'blood-soaked' scene for granted and to adopt a whole family of characters who were novel and astonishing in many ways. Let me count the ways.

First, instead of a commanding officer who looks like a grey-flecked 'man of distinction' in a whisky ad we had, first, Henry Blake, half dolt, half locker-room buddy; and then Sherman Potter, a sentimental, bandy-legged holdover from World War I. Both of them, however, were soldiers of much horse sense who knew — as C.O.s came to know in any war later than World War II — that parade-ground discipline is impossible to maintain in conscripts bogged down in a jungle clearing. The colonels' tolerance of Klinger's idiotic trans-vestism was a big shock to early viewers. But it provided a constant reminder of how much eccentricity had to be put up with in a small group of often over-worked human beings pushed to the limit of sanity by nothing but boredom. One veteran doctor of a Mobile Army Surgical Hospital unit re-called to me that above everything else boredom was the pitiless enemy, so that childish entertainment, dressing up, lotteries, cartoon movies, casual sex, petty racketeering, and practical jokes became essential therapy.

(The actual boredom came to include hideous routines – having to do with the disposal of human wastes and the daily examination of the Korean 'service' girls on the line – that even *M*A*S*H* chose to sidestep.)

This basic condition of life in 4077 must have been grasped by the writers early in the series, and it made us accept a wildly varied cast of characters and impossibly unmilitary behaviour that the training manuals and all previous army scripts had never imagined. Thus, the C.O.'s ranking subordinates offered the startling novelties of a woman major and her light-of-love, the asinine chauvinist and reluctant husband, Maj. Frank Burns – both, I should guess, impossible bits of casting in any previous war movie. And, just to ram home the lesson that excessive devotion to 'loyalty' and 'security' was an almost obscene nuisance, we had the paranoid C.I.A. snooper.

Offsetting these weirdos was a group of comparative inno-cents such as every soldier has encountered, though perhaps not in the movies: Father Mulcahy, no heroic priest he, in the mould of Bing Crosby or Pat O'Brien, but a limited, slow-witted nice man; Radar, befogged, unsure even of his virginity; Dr. Freedman, the sensible, believable psychiatrist, a million miles away from the Hollywood fusspot with the Viennese accent; the absurd Winchester, to remind us of another world – ours – and other values, preposterous maybe, but the values we all pretend to aspire to. Finally, Trapper and B.J. – two amiable variations on the smart ass's sidekick, the smart ass being no one but Hawkeye.

Hawkeye was the hinge. Played less well, by an actor less high-strung, less deeply forlorn, the whole series could have expired in its infancy. Somebody had the wit to spot him at the beginning as Hamlet and Horatio rolled into one: the brilliant neurotic and the normal hero. He was the one who kept the place in a happy ferment: the enviable expert surgeon and also the mischief-maker all pent-up soldiers yearn to be.

And yet, Hawkeye represented, more than most, the one quality that held together the whole family: the quality of fundamental decency. This was the sheet-anchor of a crew awash in exhaustion, emergencies, bad temper, physical peril. The patient came first, the patient of either side and any colour. And the only golden rule that everybody recognised was that no big brass, no visiting congressman, no C.I.A. inquisitor, or other busybody must be allowed to forget it. It was here that every viewer, according to personal taste and judgment, had to decide how often the series ignored the messiness of life and spilled over into the neatness of sentimentality.

All in all, the series was remarkable, a marvel, in staying so close to ordinary life and peopling a formula with what in television is something of a curiosity: a company of complex, recognisable human beings. Let us stifle a starting tear and bid farewell to M*A*S*H 4077, and pray that no Hollywood smarties are licking their chops and drafting some carbon-copy series. M*A*S*H, like *The Honeymooners* and *Upstairs, Downstairs*, was one of a kind. Let it stay that way.

The Best of His Kind

September 6, 1984

The brief intermission before the last act of the presidential election and the high summer pause in the public bustle of life allows me to do something I had meant to do three weeks ago — an intention which was, unfortunately, overwhelmed first by the Ferraro finances and then by the Republican circus in Dallas. A great man died but since he was neither a movie or a rock star, nor a famous author, anarchist, footballer, or Central American dictator, you are unlikely to have heard about him.

Let me introduce him by recalling a cocktail party held many years ago for a posse of visiting English book publishers. The host was himself a publisher and he had invited the opposite numbers of the British guests. That was the problem for one young Englishman, who nudged his way through the babble to an old and artful publicity man who had set up the party: an old roly-poly man who looked like a Chinese Buddha but was actually once a penniless Russian immigrant and now the very Richelieu of American public relations. Asked what was troubling him, the Englishman said: 'Well, it's all very exciting, but my problem is I don't know who's who, I mean, who is the American equivalent of Faber and Faber, say? Who is the Cassell's man? Who might I avoid? Who should I defer to? D'you see what I mean?' The old Russian always saw what you meant, even before you meant it. He dusted the cigar-ash from his Légion d'Honneur boutonnière and said: 'You don't need to spot every identity. All you need to know is the two ends of the gamut. Now, if you'll look discreetly over in that corner, you see the tall, laughing fella with the glasses. He is "in the book business." In the opposite corner, the man who looks like the Archduke Franz Josef. He is Alfred Knopf. He is a *publisher*. In fact, he is *the publisher*.'

This distinction, between the old-time publisher (wholly devoted to books) and the new breed, who have gone into 'the book business' as they might have gone into banking or real estate, is growing so blurred that for some people that anecdote needs an explanation.

Authors are now marketed like promising movie starlets and must rattle around the nation's television stations to try to assert a saleable identity different from that of the other starlets. If they are marked down, remaindered, the publisher writes it off as a tax loss, putting it down to amortisation of his product. The American humourist Calvin Trillin once said that 'the shelf-life of a hardback book is somewhere between milk and yoghurt.' And the fittest – publishers who survive – are those who can collar the highest price for the paperback rights.

If they are notably successful at this, they are sooner or later bound to be bought up as subsidiaries of computer firms, movie companies, or conglomerates which see no reason to look on a book as a marketable product different from vacuum-cleaners or a soft drink. Even the firm of Alfred A. Knopf, which for seventy years or so was a good and private concern, was absorbed – as a business – into a larger book firm which in turn became owned by an electronics corporation and then by a newspaper chain. But so long as Alfred Knopf lived – and let us pray, long after he is gone – the imprimatur of the house of Knopf, its discerning and scholarly editors, its standards of choice, even its beloved typefaces, will remain sacrosanct.

Alfred Knopf was the son of a father (a German grandfather) who was a prosperous New York financial consultant, a man who, from all accounts, set an example or, in the current jargon, provided the role model, for his son: a mustachioed, imperious man who must have earned the jocular title, which passed on to his son, of 'the last of the Habsburgs.' The son, Alfred, graduated from Columbia University in 1912 and was treated by his father to a postgraduate tour of Europe. Alfred was already steeped in books and meant to be not just a reader but a maker of them. He was only twenty but he made it his business to seek out Galsworthy and Katherine Mansfield, and he listened to the gabby Frank Harris and decided at once to be a publisher. He came home, was an accountant with a publishing firm for three years, and, at the age of 24, decided to go it on his own. His father set him up, but only to the extent of a telephone and a desk, not yet a room. He bought an English translation of four plays by Emile Augier. Emile Augier? Alfred was not under the delusion that he was floating the *Pickwick Papers*. He liked this Frenchman's work and thought it ought to be published. For the next sixty-odd years that was his guiding motive.

Ten of his first dozen books were translations of what he decided were promising unknowns or the unjustly neglected.

Of course, he knew well that somebody had to pay for the French poet or the young Argentine novelist, or the history of the American fur-trapping trade that would sell no more than 2,000 copies. As necessary ballast to the high-flying unknowns he published one or two popular romantic novelists, and in the early Twenties had a windfall in the cryptic thoughts of a Lebanese mystic, Kahlil Gibran, who for the past fifty years or more has been the Chairman Mao of successive generations of many undergraduates, aesthetic scribblers, flower people, and other mooching brooders. At last count, I believe, Gibran's *The Prophet* had sold thirty million copies.

But from the 1920s through the 1980s the Knopf list – over 5,000 titles – is staggering in its majesty, intelligence, comprehensiveness, and daring. No writer of any prime or suspected distinction – of any country or colour – no poet, scholar, jurist, historian, music critic, essayist, ever went unread or unconsidered. What set Alfred apart from all other equally catholic and enterprising publishers was his assumption that a serious publisher owes it to the role of readers to introduce them to the best that is being written anywhere around the world.

Sixteen of his discoveries, or writers he banked on when they were either unknown or favourites of a minority, turned into winners of the Nobel Prize for Literature, including Knut Hamsun, Thomas Mann, Yasunari Kawabata, Sigrid Undset. Twenty-six others – most unknown when he first published them – won the Pulitzer Prize. Never was there a publisher less chauvinist, less insular – through a time when nationalism was taking a new and ferocious lease on life. He published, early on, people who came to be classics in their native England, America, Germany, Spain, France, Portugal, Russia, Greece, Chile, Argentina, Brazil, Korea (Kim Young Ik), Egypt (Waguih Ghali) and Finland (Aino Kallas). Without exception, the latter exotics were introduced to the English-speaking world by Knopf, not to mention the more familiar eminences that he either introduced us to or impressed on us early in their careers: such as Eliot, Pound, André Gide, Albert Camus, Ilya

Ehrenburg, Sholokhov, Wallace Stevens, H. L. Mencken, and on and on.

Towards the end, Alfred's great frame seldom pattered into the office but he still chose his editors with great care; he regularly let out a blast at the bestseller list (which he forever regarded as a species of fraud); and he could, until the last few months, look up and contemplate with justifiable pride his own compound in a Third Avenue skyscraper, the private international zone which was the House that Knopf built. Remember the name: Alfred A. Knopf, dead at 91. Simply, the best publisher of the twentieth century.

Golf: The American Conquest

March 31, 1985

The first time I played the old course, at St. Andrews, I had one of those inimitable Scottish caddies who – if Dickens had played golf – would have been immortalized in a character with some such name as Sloppy MacSod. A frayed cap. A rumpled topcoat, green with age. Pants that drooped like an expiring concertina over his wrinkled shoes. His left shoulder was permanently depressed from all the bags he'd carried. He re-lighted the stub of a cigarette that was already disappearing between his lips and tramped off at a crippled angle. A straight drive produced the tribute: 'We're rait doon the meddle.' The first slice evoked: 'You're way awf in the gorrse.' (Scottish caddies, like nurses, alternate between the first person plural and the second person singular as a handy method of distributing praise and blame.) From then on, he said very little, rarely nodding in approval, more often wiping his nose with the back of his hand by way of noting, without comment, my general ineptness. The fact is, all questions of skill aside, the wind had risen to a blasting thirty-odd miles an hour. 'I hate wind,' I said.

He squinnied his bloodshot eyes and sniffed: 'If there's nae wind, it's nae gowf.'

Such a remark is inconceivable anywhere in the United States, though it is an idiom as hackneyed in Scotland as 'biting the bullet' in America. Not that Scotland is unique as a wind-blown country. Throughout the Southwest, in Texas as much as anywhere, the wind rides free, but golfers must learn to cope with it; they do not consider it – like the fences in show-jumping – an essential element of the game. The simplest explanation, and it is quite possibly a true one, of why the Scots look with disdain on such things as calm sunny days, winter rules, cleaning the ball on the green, and – God save us! – electric carts is that these devices are thought of as comfortable evasions of a game handed down by the Old Testament God as a penance for original sin.

Certainly, it is well established that the earliest courses were designed by nobody but God, and the most unquestioned authority on their history, Sir Guy Campbell, maintains that 'almost all [the courses] created after the advent of the gutta [percha] ball, around 1848, outrage nature in every respect, and they are best forgotten.' This veto would dispose of every championship course we know anywhere on earth, excepting only the Old Course and – just in time – the incomparable Dornoch, to the north, which this year will receive its first British Amateur championship.

Nature, then, according to the Scots, and to many Britons and some Americans still extant, is the only true golf course architect. In other words, the game, which originated on the coastal shelf of eastern Scotland, was seen from the start as a challenge, on stretches of terrain that to most other humans were plainly not meant for a game at all. The attested origin of golf might well have come from Genesis; it is at once fascinating and ridiculous.

The tides, receding from cliffs and bluffs down the millennia, left long fingers of headlands that in time were thus separated by wastes of sand; no doubt, way back there in the Palaeolithic period, some Scots tried lofting a ball from one link to another. In time, they found life easier, but not much, banging a ball along the coastal flats. By then, rabbits and foxes had messed up the smooth grasses, and swales burrowed by sheep huddling against the wind made what came to be called bunkers. At some unrecorded date, when the game had retreated to the meadows far beyond the headlands, sand was deposited in these swales as a sentimental reminder of the sand wastes between the links. Little holes were now scooped out by knives, for by now (we are already in the fourteenth century) an idea had dawned on the Scots that had never occurred to the Dutch during their national pastime of banging a ball across a frozen pond at an adjoining post. The Scottish brainwave? That the ball might be hit into a hole.

So a golf course was never planned. It emerged. And considered as the proper setting for a game, a golf course — compared with a tennis court, a pool table, a chess board – is an absurdity. Considered as a move in the Ascent of Man, it is hard to conceive of a smaller, more laboured, step. For by the time the game really took hold, in the fifteenth century, the land it was played on was thoroughly beaten up by the nibbling rabbits, the darting foxes, the burrowing sheep, not to mention the ploughmen, tramping farmers, and the ruts left by their cartwheels. It struck the Scots, as it would not have struck any other race, that here was the Calvinists' ideal testing ground. The bunkers, the scrubby gorse, the heather and broom, the hillocks and innumerable undulations of the land itself, were all seen not as nuisances but as natural obstacles, as reminders to all original sinners that in competition with the Almighty, they surely would not overcome.

But the grim Scots went on trying, using first the old Roman ball stuffed with feathers and then inventing one made of gutta-percha, which bore into the wind straighter and farther. It was left to an American, at the turn of our century, to come up with the modern rubber-cored ball, which the British with surprising promptness allowed as the 'accepted missile.' But from then on, the American influence, in this as in many other departments of British life (cocktails, bobbed hair, paper napkins, frozen foods, supermarkets, parking meters, etc., etc.), has been looked on at first with horror, then with suspicion, then with curiosity, then with compliance, eventually with pride by later generations that assume the invention was home-grown.

Until the end of World War I, the Americans appeared to have had little influence on the game. They had been playing it for a bare quarter-century, beginning by obediently fashioning links courses on the coasts of Rhode Island and Long Island. However, two of the five clubs that set up what was soon to be known as the United States Golf Association were incorporated on inland courses: at Brookline, Mass., and, a thousand miles from the sea, near Chicago. The best American professional players went to Britain rarely; in fact, the best of them were immigrant Scots. If they made the trip, it was to pay tribute to the ancestral home, as a parish priest might want sometime to visit the Vatican. But, in the 1920s, the Americans – in the persons of Walter Hagen and Bobby Jones – went to Britain not as acolytes but as conquerors. It was an appalling shock to the generation that pictured the regular visits to the United States of Harry Vardon and other established British pros as missionary expeditions to teach the Colonials. Evidently, there was something about American golf that had escaped the British.

There were many things. The Scots assumed that since it was their game, they must be the natural masters of it. The English, south of the border, had come to look on it as an agreeable, if sometimes an infuriating, pastime. The Americans, it was learned, prepared for it as if for a tour of duty with the Marines. The British were taught to acquire a graceful swing; the Americans learned to bang the ball 250 yards and pick up the niceties of the short game later on.

The British retained their loving prejudice in favour of a links course, and to this day the British Open is played on nothing else. But since only a fraction of the American population lived by the sea, the Americans were forced to be less mystical about the creation of their inland courses. They initiated what Guy Campbell deplored as 'The Mechanical Age' by building in our time a great variety of splendid courses, in every sort of landscape, that owed very little to the Creation and everything to the bulldozer, rotary ploughs, mowers, sprinkler systems, and alarmingly generous wads of folding money. Also, long before Americans were regarded as a threat to the British dominance of the game, they had been busy in secret adapting the golf club itself to their damnably ingenious factory processes. The perforated steel shaft, the aluminium-headed putter with a centre-shaft, the pitching wedge with a slotted face, the sand wedge. In turn they were banned by the British, and in turn they were reluctantly allowed.

A typical progression, from hugging the characteristics of the primitive game to accepting the American century, is that of the size of the ball. For as long as any living golfer can remember – back to 1921, anyway – the British have played with a ball 1.62 inches in diameter, while the Americans came to standardize at 1.68 inches. When, in 1951, the world's ruling body of golf, the Royal and Ancient Golf Club of St. Andrews, publicly acknowledged that in the United States the ruling body (self-proclaimed as such in the 1890s) was something called the United States Golf Association, a period of *détente* was triumphantly initiated by the decision of the two bodies to standardize the rules of the game (in everything except the size of the ball).

It became slowly but painfully apparent that playing a different-sized ball in the championship matches of each country would present a problem, if not an ultimatum. The R. & A. followed the usual practice of British diplomacy. They thought a sensible compromise was possible, in the shape of a ball somewhere in between. They manufactured two experimental balls, 1.65 and 1.66 inches in diameter, respectively. They were offered to the Americans as a proud solution. The Americans, however, remembering Jefferson and the Louisiana Purchase (which was unconstitutional, and sneaky, but worked) had a better idea. Why not compromise, they suggested, by using *our* ball? And so it was. The bigger American ball is now compulsory in all R. & A. championships and in British professional tournaments.

The British manufacturers maintain, against alarming evidence to the contrary, that the ordinary club player in Britain prefers his little ball. Naturally, they want to believe that a monopoly they have held for so long is the consumer's preference. But their day – like that of the builders of the hansom cab – is done.

And so with many other traditions and practices of the heyday of British golf: 1457–1956 (1457 was the date when King James II of Scotland published his famous interdict against the game, which was running rampant throughout his kingdom, threatening the national security by seducing the young from their archery practice). I pick 1956 as a watershed, tilting the game once and for all toward the American shore, because it was the year when a Chicago advertising man, one Walter Schwimmer, being pressed by friends to polish up his escutcheon by getting into 'cultural' television, mortified them by dismissing ballet and drama as fringe benefits. He voiced the odd opinion that most people 'want to see somebody doing expertly what they do badly.' He thought bowling and/or golf would be just the thing. He set up a golf game between Sam Snead and Cary Middlecoff and sold it to A.B.C.

After Schwimmer, the deluge. A surge in the game's popularity, not least among non-players who didn't know a mid-iron from a midwife. A greatly expanded pro tour. The emergence of golf heroes as recognisable as film stars, dogged immediately by lawyers and ten-percenters able to coax a troop of sponsors into disbursing undreamed-of monetary rewards. In 1947, Jimmy Demaret topped the pros' money list at $28,000. In 1984, Tom Watson's take on the tour was $476,260, a useful supplement to the larger income to be derived from his television commercials. Inevitably, the potential pro, who once learned his game in the caddie shack, now learns it on a university golf scholarship. And the first-rate amateur, once he has picked up his degree (appropriately in Business Management), is determined to turn into a millionaire pro as soon as possible.

In the running, and financial exploitation, of their own pro tour, the British, in concert with the Europeans, are not far behind. But we are talking mainly about the changes in the amateur game, as it is played in Britain by something like 2.5 million, in this country by 13 million and still rising.

Well, much has changed but much remains. The most noticeable departure from the old British game has to do with its surrender to the watering of the putting greens. As long ago as the 1940s Bobby Jones lamented that the British adoption of what he called 'the soggy American green' would see the end of the necessary run-up shot, whereby the ball is punched to run almost as far along the ground and on the green as it had flown through the air. And it is true that today, except on the wind-skimmed greens of Scotland, the American 'target' golfer can hit a high long-iron approach on a British course with the near-certainty that the greens will receive the ball from any angle and hold it, if not quite like a horseshoe tossed into a marsh. (Still, the British Open has never been won by a high-flying American who has not mastered the run-up shot.)

There are, however, three immemorial characteristics of British golf that amaze Americans and pass unnoticed by Britons, since they are accepted as ordinary facts of life: the clubhouse; the Secretary; the foursome. The sturdiest of these relics is the British clubhouse, which nowhere remotely resembles the Intercontinental Hotel look of, say, the Westchester Country Club or the Spanish grandee's castle of Seminole. Except on Johnny-come-lately courses, the British clubhouse is a lumbering Edwardian structure, hallowed with wicker or worn, lumpy leather chairs, a rug installed before the

Boer War, and a locker room, with no lockers, that Americans are apt to confuse with a cell in a maximum-security prison.

The stone floors, the scuffed benches, the leaky faucet, the prewar nail brush (on a chain) so upset British golfers with much experience of America that the late Stephen Potter suggested, as a ploy of 'Transatlantic Guest Play,' that the British host, off-handedly apologizing for the simplicity of it all, should say: 'At least, no danger here of what happened to me at your club: getting lost between the sauna and the cinema.'

Lately, I am told, there has been a brisk increase in proposals to remedy these rude amenities, and in some places the stuffed leather and wicker furnishings have been replaced by airport plastic. But no American wishing to help in the modernization programme should dare to inquire the whereabouts of the 'Suggestion Box' unless he is ready to face the glowering eye of the Secretary and cower before the immortal line: '*I* am the Suggestion Box!' The Secretary, indeed, is a character quite unlike any official known to an American club. He is at once the manager, the senior starter, the rules administrator, the supervising treasurer, the *de facto* chairman of the board, and the Führer. His only counterpart in this country was the late Clifford Roberts, the unchallenged dictator of Augusta National.

Finally, there is the game itself. There are middle-aged Englishmen, and Scots of all ages, who contend that foursomes (called but rarely played in America, Scotch foursomes) is 'the only game of golf and nae other.' Four players, as two teams, use two balls only, driving alternately and then playing alternate shots. The dwindling number of its advocates say that foursomes is the best team game, and the most rousingly competitive, ever devised by a golfer. It does, of course, bypass any handicap system. And the British, aping Americans in their native competitive frenzy and their itch to flaunt an improbable low handicap, are succumbing in droves to the four-ball, five-hour match, and soon will be feeding their scores into the downtown computer that disgorges, once a month, a ream of handicap statistics on stock tickertape.

And, too, the British play golf everywhere on Sundays, a blasphemy long prohibited in Scotland. They have abandoned their old flannels and cricket shirts and, to the distress of the older members, the young now mimic the fine flower of the all-American dresser, even down – or up – to the baseball cap, or visor. They use fluffy or leather or polyester covers for their woods, where once they allowed them to clank and jangle in a canvas drainpipe bag slung over the left shoulder. They are losing caddies (to welfare) as rapidly as we are, and, except at the Old Course, pull their clubs along in what they call trolleys and we call handcarts. Electric carts are all but unknown. There are two at the oldest of British clubs, that of the Honourable Company of Edinburgh Golfers. But the vast majority of Britons have never seen one. The only one I ever saw in England was imported by the late Earl of Leicester from Germany, an armoured monster that looked as if it had been designed by a veteran of the Afrika Corps who had heard about a golf cart but had never seen one.

So the British, of all ages, still walk the course. On trips to Florida or the American desert, they still marvel, or shudder, at the fleets of electric carts going off in the morning like the first assault wave of the Battle of El Alamein. It is unlikely, for some time, that a Briton will come across in his native land such a scorecard as Henry Longhurst rescued from a California club and cherished till the day he died. The last on its list of local rules printed the firm warning: 'A Player on Foot Has No Standing on the Course.'

Notes

P. 1 INEVITABLE OR INIMITABLE: Richard Rose, 'America: Inevitable or Inimitable?' in Richard Rose (ed.), *Lessons from America* (New York: John Wiley, 1974; London: Macmillan, 1974), 1.

P. 2 EVANS: Martin Evans, *America: The View from Europe* (New York: W. W. Norton, 1977).

P. 3 LASKI'S WORDS: quoted in Albert Guerard, 'Tocqueville on Democracy,' *New Republic*, 112 (April 30, 1954), 594.

P. 3 IN THE MOST FAMOUS SECTION: Alexis de Tocqueville, *Democracy in America*.

P. 3 FEASIBLE AND TOLERABLE: H. G. Nicholas, 'The Relevance of Tocqueville,' in Rose, *Lessons from America* (New York: John Wiley, 1974; London: Macmillan, 1974), 44–6; see also Hugh Brogan, *Tocqueville* (London: Fontana, 1973).

P. 3 SAFIRE: William Safire, *I Stand Corrected: More on Language* (New York: Times Books, 1984).

P. 3 BREWSTER: quoted in *Current Biography*, 83.

P. 4 GELATT: 'Mid-Atlantic Man,' *Saturday Review* (October 1, 1977), 46–7.

P. 4 AMERICANIZED ENOUGH: *ibid.*

P. 4 INCORRIGIBLY DETERMINED THEN: *Alistair Cooke's America* (New York: Alfred A. Knopf, 1973; London: The Bodley Head, 1973), 9.

P. 6 A BETTER TRADE FOR ME: editor's conversation with Mr. Cooke.

P. 7 EDWARD VIII: this experience is recorded in the essay 'Golden Boy' in Cooke's *Six Men* (New York: Alfred A. Knopf, 1981; London: The Bodley Head, 1977).

P. 9 EMPLOY REUTERS: editor's conversation with Mr. Cooke.

P. 9 GO NEW YORK: *ibid.*

P. 9 SPRIGHTLINESS: T. S. Matthews, *The Sugar Pill: An Essay on Newspapers* (New York: Simon and Schuster, 1959), 140–41.

P. 10 THE MOST GENERALLY POPULAR: *ibid.*, 134.

P. 10 COOKE IS A NUISANCE: *Guardian*, March 25, 1968, 8.

P. 10 AMERICA'S EXPERIMENT: see especially 'Letter from America,' B.B.C., October 5, 1958 and December 17, 1967.

P. 11 TO RUN UP AND DOWN: *Talk About America* (New York: Alfred A. Knopf, 1969; London: The Bodley Head, 1968), 2.

P. 11 I HAVE SEEN THE PAST: this speech was printed in the *Congressional Record* and reprinted in Cooke's *The Patient Has the Floor* (New York: Alfred A. Knopf, 1986; London: The Bodley Head, 1986), 41–7.

P. 12 ITS DECADENCE AND ITS VITALITY: *Alistair Cooke's America* (New York: Alfred A. Knopf, 1973; London: The Bodley Head, 1973), 388.

FOR THE BEST IN PAPERBACKS, LOOK FOR THE

In every corner of the world, on every subject under the sun, Penguin represents quality and variety – the very best in publishing today.

For complete information about books available from Penguin – including Pelicans, Puffins, Peregrines and Penguin Classics – and how to order them, write to us at the appropriate address below. Please note that for copyright reasons the selection of books varies from country to country.

In the United Kingdom: Please write to *Dept E.P., Penguin Books Ltd, Harmondsworth, Middlesex, UB7 0DA*

If you have any difficulty in obtaining a title, please send your order with the correct money, plus ten per cent for postage and packaging, to *PO Box No 11, West Drayton, Middlesex*

In the United States: Please write to *Dept BA, Penguin, 299 Murray Hill Parkway, East Rutherford, New Jersey 07073*

In Canada: Please write to *Penguin Books Canada Ltd, 2801 John Street, Markham, Ontario L3R 1B4*

In Australia: Please write to the *Marketing Department, Penguin Books Australia Ltd, P.O. Box 257, Ringwood, Victoria 3134*

In New Zealand: Please write to the *Marketing Department, Penguin Books (NZ) Ltd, Private Bag, Takapuna, Auckland 9*

In India: Please write to *Penguin Overseas Ltd, 706 Eros Apartments, 56 Nehru Place, New Delhi, 110019*

In Holland: Please write to *Penguin Books Nederland B.V., Postbus 195, NL–1380AD Weesp, Netherlands*

In Germany: Please write to *Penguin Books Ltd, Friedrichstrasse 10–12, D–6000 Frankfurt Main 1, Federal Republic of Germany*

In Spain: Please write to *Longman Penguin España, Calle San Nicolas 15, E–28013 Madrid, Spain*

In France: Please write to *Penguin Books Ltd, 39 Rue de Montmorency, F-75003, Paris, France*

In Japan: Please write to *Longman Penguin Japan Co Ltd, Yamaguchi Building, 2–12–9 Kanda Jimbocho, Chiyoda-Ku, Tokyo 101, Japan*

The Patient has the Floor

For over twenty years Alistair Cooke has bearded experts in their dens and corridors of power from the Mayo Clinic to the US Military Academy and, not least, the House of Representatives. Covering many of the issues which engage us and spark our liveliest prejudices, these essays – originally delivered as lectures – stand as brilliant demonstration of what Cooke calls 'the journalist's main function: to be the link of communication between the expert and the layman'. And, as we have come to expect, they never fail to be controversial and stimulating, witty and gloriously readable.

Six Men

With these superbly realized portraits, Alistair Cooke brings to life six men he has known and admired during a lifetime of journalistic encounter: Charlie Chaplin, Edward VIII, H. L. Mencken, Humphrey Bogart, Adlai Stevenson and Bertrand Russell.

'Alistair Cooke is a great reporter, a great recounter of events' – Terry Coleman in the *Guardian*

'*Six Men* is the journalist's memoir *par excellence* . . . top of the class' – *Newsweek*

'Alistair Cooke, in addition to his many other gifts – his humour, his sense of proportion, his combination of a scholar's erudition with a journalist's sense of the present – is a master of prose ... genuinely supple, genuinely moving with the rhythms of the spoken voice' – John Wain in the *Listener*

'One of the most gifted and urbane essayists of the century, a supreme master' – Benny Green in the *Spectator*

'The best broadcaster on five continents' – Harold Nicholson

'He is always delightful and at his best a master' – *New Statesman*

Letters from America 1946–1951
Talk About America Letters from America 1951–1968
The Americans Letters from America 1969–1979
Six Men
The Patient has the Floor